Redirect

Redirect

THE SURPRISING NEW SCIENCE OF
PSYCHOLOGICAL CHANGE

Timothy D. Wilson

LITTLE, BROWN AND COMPANY
New York Boston London

Little, Brown and Company
Hachette Book Group
237 Park Avenue, New York, NY 10017
www.hachettebookgroup.com

First Edition: September 2011

Little, Brown and Company is a division of Hachette Book Group, Inc.
The Little, Brown name and logo are trademarks of Hachette Book Group, Inc.

The publisher is not responsible for websites (or their content) that are not owned by the publisher.

Library of Congress Cataloging-in-Publication Data
Wilson, Timothy D.
    Redirect : the surprising new science of psychological change /
by Timothy D. Wilson. — 1st ed.
        p. cm.
    Includes bibliographical references and index.
    ISBN 978-0-316-05188-0
    1. Psychological change.   2. Parenting.   3. Happiness.   4. Evaluation.   I. Title.
    BF632.W55 2011
    155.2'5 — dc22   2011002764

10   9   8   7   6   5   4   3   2   1

RRD-C

Printed in the United States of America

To my parents,

Elizabeth DeCamp Wilson and Geoffrey Wilson

Contents

Redirect

Redirect

Small Edits, Lasting Changes

Police officers Gary Felice and Prince Jones were the first to respond to a house fire on De Leon Street in Tampa, Florida. When they arrived, they heard what every emergency worker dreads—screams for help from inside a house engulfed in flames. Through a window, they could barely make out the silhouette of a man stumbling and falling, just short of escape. Felice and Jones frantically tried to break down the door, which was secured with burglar bars. It took five minutes of tugging, pulling, and smashing before the door finally gave way, but by then it was too late. The man was "curled up like a baby in his mother's womb," said Jones. "That's what someone burned to death looks like."[1]

The next day Gary Felice saw a picture of the victim in the paper and realized that, to his horror, he had known him—it was Tommy Schuppel, forty-two, a popular X-ray technician at a local hospital. The fact that Felice had seen his friend die haunted the officer, so much so that he had trouble eating and sleeping. His bosses sympathized and wanted to help, so they did what many police departments do: they scheduled a Critical Incident Stress Debriefing (CISD) session for Felice.

The premise of CISD is that when people have experienced a traumatic event they should air their feelings as soon as possible, so that they don't bottle up these feelings and develop post-traumatic stress disorder. In a typical CISD session, which lasts three to four hours, participants are asked to describe the traumatic event from their own perspective, express their thoughts and feelings about the event, and relate any physical or psychological symptoms they are experiencing. A facilitator emphasizes that it is normal to have stressful reactions to traumatic events, gives stress management advice, answers questions, and assesses whether participants need any additional services. Numerous fire and police departments have made CISD the treatment of choice for officers who, like Gary Felice, witness horrific events— indeed, some departments require it. It is also widely used with civilians who undergo traumatic experiences. Following the September 11, 2001, terrorist attacks, more than nine thousand counselors rushed to New York City to help survivors deal with the trauma and prevent post-traumatic stress disorder, and many of these counselors employed psychological debriefing techniques.[2]

Psychological debriefing sounds like an effective intervention, doesn't it? An ounce of prevention is worth a pound of cure, and surely getting people to talk about their feelings, instead of bottling them up, is a good thing. Or is it?

Let's put CISD aside for a moment and consider another approach. Instead of asking Officer Felice to relive the trauma of Tommy Schuppel's death, suppose we let a few weeks go by and see if he is still traumatized by the tragic event. If so, we could ask him to complete, on four consecutive nights, a simple exercise in which he writes down his deepest thoughts and emotions about the experience and how it relates to the rest of his life. That's it—no meetings with trained facilitators, no stress management advice—just a writing exercise that Felice does on his own four nights in a row.

Which approach do you think would be more effective—CISD, in which people express their thoughts and feelings right after a traumatic event with the help of a trained facilitator, or the writing technique, which people do in private weeks after the event? If you are like me (and the hundreds of police and fire departments that use it), you would put your money on CISD. Surely early interventions are better than later ones, and offering people the services of a trained professional is better than asking them to sit and write by themselves. But we would be wrong.

It took research psychologists a while to test CISD properly, in part because it seemed so obvious that it was beneficial. When they did, they found something unexpected: not only is CISD ineffective, it may *cause* psychological problems. In one study, people who had been severely burned in a fire were randomly assigned either to receive CISD or not. Over the next several months, participants completed a battery of measures of psychological adjustment and were interviewed at home by a researcher who was unaware whether they had received CISD. Thirteen months after the intervention, people in the CISD group had a significantly *higher* incidence of post-traumatic stress disorder, were *more* anxious and depressed, and were *less* content with their lives. Similar results have been found in studies testing the effectiveness of CISD among emergency workers. It turns out that making people undergo CISD right after a trauma impedes the natural healing process and might even "freeze" memories of the event. (This may have been the case with Gary Felice—according to a journalist who interviewed him four years after the fire, Felice seemed unable to get rid of the mental image of Tommy Schuppel lying dead on the floor.)

In 2003, after reviewing all tests of the effectiveness of psychological debriefing techniques, Harvard psychologist Richard McNally and his colleagues recommended that "for scientific and ethical reasons, professionals should cease compulsory debriefing of trauma-exposed people." Unfortunately, this message has not been widely disseminated or heeded. In 2007, after a disturbed student at Virginia Tech University killed thirty-two students and faculty, students and emergency workers underwent stress-debriefing techniques similar to CISD.[3]

What about the writing exercise? This technique, pioneered by social psychologist James Pennebaker, has been tested in dozens of experiments in which people were randomly assigned to write about personal traumas or mundane topics such as what they did that day. In the short run, people typically find it painful to express their feelings about traumatic experiences. But as time goes by, those who do so are better off in a number of respects. They show improvements in immune-system functioning, are less likely to visit physicians, get better grades in college, and miss fewer days of work.[4]

THROUGH YOUR EYES ONLY

Why does CISD fail to work, and why is the writing exercise so powerful? It has to do with people's interpretations of what happens to them—as we will see shortly, the writing exercise helps people redirect those interpretations in healthier ways than CISD does. But first, some words about the importance of personal interpretations.

For centuries, philosophers have recognized that it is not the objective world that influences us but how we represent and interpret the world. Social psychologists have added the important proviso that these subjective interpretations are formed quickly and unconsciously. When something happens to us, our brains kick into gear and try to make sense of it as best we can—so rapidly that we don't even know that we are *interpreting* rather than *observing* the world. For example, take a look at the picture opposite. What do you see? A duck looking to the right? Or is it a bunny looking to the left? Which is it, anyway? It is not objectively either one; it depends on how your mind interprets it. What's more, we often don't know that we are interpreting as we observe. When you first looked at the picture, it probably just appeared to you as either a duck or a bunny—you didn't realize that you were making sense of the drawing in a particular way.

How do our minds know how to interpret something? One way is by relying on past experience. If you have a pet rabbit, you probably saw a bunny in the picture. Another way is by using the context in which we experience something. When people were shown a picture similar to the one above on Easter Sunday, 82 percent of them identified it as a bunny. When people were shown the same picture on a Sunday in October, 90 percent identified it as a duck or similar bird.[5]

As another example, look at the two words printed below in large type. Did you have any trouble reading them? "Duh," you think, "the first word is obviously 'THE' and the second word is obviously 'MAT.'" But look closely at the second letter in each word. That letter is actually a drawing of something that looks like a football goalpost with the tops bent inward. When you saw this drawing between the letters *T* and *E*, your mind instantly interpreted it as the letter *H*. But

THE
MAT

when you saw that same drawing flanked by the letters *M* and *T*, your mind instantly interpreted it as the letter *A*.

Such instant interpretation happens not only with pictures but also with our understanding of what other people do and say. When your boss says in a grave voice that times are tough for the company and that she is going to have to give you a pink slip, you know to start packing up your office and not to thank her for her thoughtful gift of lingerie.

But events are often more ambiguous than in that example. Suppose that, after a staff meeting, your boss tells Jack, a longtime employee, to take the rest of the afternoon off. What do you make of this? Maybe your boss is rewarding Jack for his hard work; he has been putting in long hours of late. Or maybe she has decided to fire him and is interviewing his replacement that afternoon. The reasons why people do what they do are often mysterious, and we have to fill in the blanks. The interpretation we come up with matters, because it dictates how we feel and act (e.g., whether we are envious of Jack or feel sorry for him).

Nowhere is this truer than in interpreting what happens to us. Suppose you are a student in your first semester of college, sitting in a calculus class waiting for the professor to hand back the first test. You are a little nervous, because the test was difficult, but you got good grades in high-school math and you're confident that you did okay. When the professor hands back your test, you are thus shocked to see that you got a D.

Your personal interpreter will immediately kick into action, trying to make sense of why you did so poorly—and the answer you come up with will be a crucial determinant of what happens next. Maybe you conclude that you didn't study hard enough for the test and view this setback as a wake-up call to try harder. Or maybe you interpret the D as a sign that you aren't college material after all, a confirmation of your worst fears about your abilities (or lack thereof). You start skipping class and missing homework assignments; after all, why knock your head against the wall when you clearly don't have what it takes?

Many of us would adopt the first interpretation, viewing the bad grade in a way that motivates us to try harder. Research shows that most people have an optimistic outlook on life, believing that they have good prospects in the future and that they are masters of their fates—even if this involves some exaggeration and "spin." Seeing the world through rose-colored glasses makes people happier and motivates them to try harder when they encounter obstacles in their way. This doesn't mean that we are blind to reality—convincing ourselves that we have what it takes to be a famous opera singer when we can't carry a tune will lead to failure and heartache. But putting as positive a spin as we can on events—such as viewing one bad grade as an indication that we need to work harder, rather than as a sign that we should give up—serves us well.[6]

Unfortunately, we don't always succeed in adopting such rosy views. As much as we might try to make sense of things in ways that assuage our feelings and motivate us to do better, sometimes we get bogged down in a pessimistic frame of mind. Our interpretations are rooted in personal narratives about ourselves, and these narratives aren't always so positive, as is the case with teenagers who feel like rebels without a cause, college students who are convinced they were admissions errors, and adults who always seem to assume the worst about their relationships. As we will see in chapter 4, people have *core narratives* about relationships that are rooted in their early interactions with their primary caregivers, and these narratives act as filters, influencing interpretations of their adult relationships—sometimes in unhealthy ways.

In short, the way in which we interpret the world is extremely important. Our interpretations are rooted in the narratives we construct about ourselves and the social world, and sometimes, like the pessimistic calculus student, we interpret things in unhealthy ways that have negative consequences. We could solve a lot of problems if we could get people to redirect their interpretations in healthier directions.

Well, this all sounds good, you might think, but it's hardly news. Of course some people have maladaptive ways of thinking about themselves and the social world, and of course it would help to get them to construct better stories. Further, there is a well-known form of psychotherapy designed to do just that, namely, cognitive-behavioral therapy (CBT). CBT assumes that maladaptive interpretations — negative thought patterns — are responsible for many mental health problems, and that the best way to treat those problems is to make people aware of their thought patterns and learn how to change them. The student who immediately assumes the worst about one bad grade, for example, is at risk for depression and might benefit from cognitive-behavioral therapy, in which he would learn to recognize and change his negative assumptions about himself.[7]

Psychotherapy is great for people who need it, especially those with serious problems such as depression or debilitating anxiety. But there is a new way to redirect people's personal interpretations that is quick, does not require one-on-one sessions, and can address a wide array of personal and social problems. It can help people like Gary Felice, who have witnessed traumatic events; people like our hypothetical student, who assume the worst about their abilities; teenagers experiencing problems of adolescence; and people like you and me who want to find ways to be a little happier. It sounds like magic, but in this book we will see how and why it works.

STORY EDITING

The new approach began with the theorizing of Kurt Lewin, who helped found the field of social psychology in the 1930s and 1940s. Lewin championed the subjectivist view we have already articulated, namely, that in order to understand why people do what they do, we have to view the world through their eyes and understand how they make sense of things. But he had a more radical insight: not only do we need to view a problem through other people's eyes, we can also change the way they view it with relatively simple interventions. True, people's self-views are often embedded in years of family dynamics, personal relationships, and cultural forces, and we can't always expect people to revise these views overnight. If a teenager is a rebel without a cause, it doesn't do much good for his parents to implore, "Please change your view of yourself" any more than it would to say, "I would appreciate it if you would lay off the crystal meth, lose the lip piercing, and take flute lessons." Narratives are often like an oil painting to which we add a little daub each day. Revising that narrative would mean scraping away layers of paint and starting over again with a fresh canvas — a daunting task, to say the least.

But, as Lewin noted, sometimes it is possible to change people's interpretations fairly easily if we find just the right approach. During World War II, Lewin demonstrated this by getting people to change what seemed like an intractable food preference — namely, an aversion to organ meats (e.g., kidneys and hearts), which were in greater supply at the time than traditional cuts of meat. Simply lecturing people about the importance of this alternative food source didn't work. Instead, Lewin convened groups of homemakers to discuss the issue. During the meetings, a trained leader skillfully steered the conversation to the ways in which obstacles to serving organ meats could be overcome (e.g., how to deal with complaints from one's family). Women who took part in these groups were much more likely to serve organ meats, in the following week, than were those who simply listened to the lecture.[8]

Since then, new generations of social psychologists have refined Lewin's idea into an approach that I call *story editing*, which is a set of techniques designed to redirect people's narratives about themselves and the social world in a way that leads to lasting changes in behavior.

In this chapter, I introduce the basics of the approach; then we will see how it has been used to advantage in specific areas. In later chapters, for example, we will see how story editing has been used to make people happier, improve parenting, solve adolescent behavior problems, and reduce the racial achievement gap in schools.

Let's first be clear about what it is we are trying to change. The term "story editing" implies that we are targeting long-standing personal narratives that people have constructed about themselves and the social world, and, indeed, we often are. In chapter 3, for example, we will discuss core narratives that help people understand some of the most basic questions in life. But at other times, we are targeting people's quick, initial spin on events, such as the student's explanation for his poor grade on the calculus test. Editing people's initial interpretations of events is an important way of redirecting their narratives, just as altering a few key details at the beginning of a novel changes the story yet to come.

How does story editing work? One way is to get people to redirect their own narratives, as they do in the Pennebaker writing exercise. This approach is most useful for people who have failed to come up with a coherent interpretation of an important event in their lives. Something has happened that doesn't make sense and is unpleasant to think about. They try to put it out of their minds, which makes it even less likely that they will succeed in explaining or coming to terms with it. The writing exercise, it turns out, is an effective way to get people to reinterpret such episodes. The traumas that cause prolonged stress are usually the ones that we can't make sense of; they are profoundly troubling because they seem like meaningless, random acts that don't fit into our view of the world as a predictable, safe place. Furthermore, we often spend a lot of psychic energy trying to banish the events from our minds, rather than taking the time to dissect the events and find some meaning in them. This is exactly what the writing exercise does—it allows us to take a step back and reframe what happened. In fact, the people who benefit the most from the exercise are those who begin by writing a jumbled, incoherent account of the traumatic event, but in the end tell a coherent story that explains the event and gives it meaning. At this point, the event is less likely to intrude into people's thoughts, and they don't have to spend psychic energy trying to suppress it.[9]

This is story editing in its simplest form: inducing people to make sense of an event that has gotten under their skin. As Susan Sontag said in her journal, "I write to define myself—an act of self-creation— part of [the] process of becoming." To be sure, the writing technique is not a magic cure for all psychological problems. Sometimes we can't construct a coherent narrative on our own, and in such cases psychotherapy can be a big help. As we saw, cognitive-behavioral therapy is specifically designed to teach people how to turn negative thinking patterns into healthier ones. But the writing technique has proved to be remarkably beneficial for people with a wide range of traumatic experiences.[10]

Why doesn't CISD accomplish the same thing? One reason is the timing. As anyone who has ever been unexpectedly left by a lover knows, the worst moment to work through the loss is right after we find the Dear John note taped to the bathroom mirror. Time does indeed heal at least some wounds; once we are done throwing furniture or sobbing into our pillows, we can take a step back and put as good a spin as we can on what happened. ("We were never really suited for each other, and besides, it's great to have more closet space.") If time goes by and we are still bothered by a traumatic event, we probably haven't succeeded in making sense of it and we might need the extra boost the writing exercise can give us. In short, one reason CISD fails is that it makes it harder for people to take that step back and gain some perspective on what happened. Forcing people to talk about the traumatic event right after it happened can even solidify memories of it, which makes it harder for people to reinterpret the event as time goes by.

Sometimes, though, people need more of a nudge than simply writing about their problems. They may be barreling down a particularly destructive narrative track, as was the case with the calculus student who got the bad grade. Like a railroad worker operating a switch, we need to redirect him onto a healthier track. One way to do this is to spoon-feed people a better interpretation of their behavior. As we will see in chapter 4, this works particularly well with children. Labeling kids as "helpful people," for example, encourages them to internalize this view of themselves. We have to be more subtle with adults; rather than simply giving them a label for their behavior, we need to get them to reach that conclusion themselves. I call this approach *story prompting*, because it involves redirecting people down a particular narrative path with subtle prompts.

To understand story prompting, let's take a closer look at our hypothetical college students, whom I will call Bob and Sarah. "I guess I'm just not smart enough to make it here," Bob thinks after getting the D on the calculus test. "I probably should have gone to the local community college instead." As we saw, Bob skips several classes and studies only halfheartedly for the next test. "Why try," he thinks, "when I clearly don't have what it takes?" Bob does even worse on the next test, which comes as no surprise to him—after all, he already knows that he's not college material. Bob is caught in a self-defeating cycle. His assumption that he has low ability causes him to give up on studying, which of course guarantees that he will do poorly on the next test, thereby confirming his low opinion of himself, leading to even less effort.

Sarah reacts quite differently after getting a D. "I guess the kind of studying I did in high school won't work for this class," she concludes. "I'll need to get in gear for the next test." She attends every class, sits

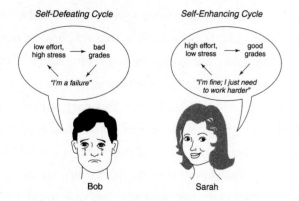

in the first row, and raises her hand to ask questions when she doesn't understand something. She reads and rereads every chapter in the text and pores over her notes. Her hard work pays off with an A on the next test. This gives her new confidence in her ability to make it at college, which increases her efforts in her other classes. She develops a self-enhancing cycle of thinking, which makes her study harder, improves her grades, and reinforces her belief in the value of hard work, leading to further academic successes.

How might we redirect Bob's thinking to mimic Sarah's? Again, this might seem like a daunting task. Bob's negative thinking could be rooted in chronic low self-esteem, parents who conveyed the wrong message about his academic successes, or even some sort of genetic predisposition toward self-defeating patterns of thinking. Wouldn't it take years to undo such a long-standing pattern of thought? Is it even possible? Not only is it possible, according to the story-editing approach, it might not be that hard, if we catch people at the right time. Students who get a bad grade early in college are at a key fork in the road in terms of how they explain academic setbacks, and it might be possible to redirect them down Sarah's path. After all, most college students did well in high school, and it shouldn't take much to convince them that lots of people struggle at first but do better when they learn the ropes and figure out how to study for college courses.

To find out, a colleague and I conducted the following experiment. We targeted first-year college students who seemed to be caught in a self-defeating cycle (like Bob)—namely, those who were not doing as well as they wanted and were worried about their grades. The students came in for what they thought was a survey of first-year students' attitudes toward college life. We told them that they would see some of the results from our previous surveys of upper-class students, so that they could get an idea of the kinds of questions we would be asking. We then showed them survey results indicating that many students have academic problems in their first year but that these problems get better as time goes by; for example, participants read that "67 percent [of the upper-class students] said their freshman grades were lower than they had anticipated; 62 percent of the students said their GPA had improved significantly from the first semester of their freshman year to their upper-class years." (These data were from an actual survey we had conducted earlier.) To make this message more concrete, we showed participants videotaped interviews of four upper-class students who conveyed the same message about grade improvement. These students answered questions about their major, career plans, hometown, and leisure-time activities, and then conveyed some key information: their GPAs for the first semester of their freshman year, the second semester of their freshman year, and the semester they had just completed. All students reported a steady increase; for example, one student reported getting a 2.0, a 2.6, and then a 3.2.

That was all there was to it—a thirty-minute session in which students learned that lots of people struggle academically at first but then improve their grades. We made no attempt to delve into participants' academic history, inquire about their study habits, or counsel them on how to manage stress. In fact, participants didn't even know that the purpose of the study was to help them improve their academic performance. We figured that the simple message that lots of people struggle at first but do better later might make a lightbulb go off in the students' heads, triggering the thought, "Maybe I'm *not* an admissions error who should have gone to community college—I just need to learn the ropes and try harder, like those students I heard about." In other words, it might have prompted students to think more like Sarah than Bob.

The results indicated that the story prompt worked. Compared to a randomly assigned control group of students who didn't get any information about grade improvement, those who got the story prompt achieved better grades in the following year and were less likely to drop out of college. These results are particularly dramatic considering how small and seemingly inconsequential the intervention was—the students took part in a thirty-minute psychology experiment in which they were shown some statistics and saw some brief videotapes about other people's grades.[11]

Thus far we have seen two forms of the story-editing approach: the writing exercise, in which people reinterpret a problem by writing about it, and story prompting, in which people are directed down a particular narrative path with the hope that it will bump them out of a self-defeating thinking pattern. A third technique, called the *do good, be good* approach, involves changing people's behavior first. This idea goes back as far as Aristotle, who suggested that people acquire virtues "by first having them put into action…we become just by the practice of just actions, self-controlling by exercising self-control, and courageous by performing acts of courage." In other words, people's behavior shapes the personal narratives they develop. If they act kindly toward others, they begin to see themselves as having kind dispositions, and the more they view themselves as kind, the more likely they are to help others—thereby strengthening their new narrative. We will see some fascinating examples of how this do good, be good principle has been used to change people's narratives in ways that helped solve some seemingly intractable social problems.[12]

SUSTAINED CHANGE

A major advantage of the story-editing approach is that small edits can lead to lasting change. The Pennebaker writing exercise would not be very impressive if it led to only a temporary shift in the way people interpret their problems; instead, it has been found to lead to sustained change over a period of weeks and months. My intervention with first-year college students would not be very useful if it caused students to alter their explanation of their problems only in the moment, or if they reverted to their self-defeating thoughts as soon as they got back to their dorms. Instead, it led to a long-term improvement in grades and to lower dropout rates.

How could such a small intervention have long-lasting effects? It did so because it was self-sustaining. Initially, the intervention may have led students to entertain the idea that effort might pay off, causing them to study harder for their next test. When this worked, it probably strengthened their belief that they were not admissions errors but in fact could do well, which made them try even harder the next time. In short, we seem to have triggered a positive cycle of self-reinforcing thinking.

The same thing happens with the do good, be good approach. People adopt a new behavior, such as doing volunteer work, which triggers a tentative revision in their self-views. "I guess I'm the kind of person who really cares about my community," thinks a new volunteer at the homeless shelter. This makes it more likely that he will continue to volunteer or help in other ways, until sure enough, he has a new self-concept: community volunteer, helpful neighbor, someone you can count on. We will see lots of examples where initial edits in people's stories lead to lasting changes of this sort.

To summarize, the story-editing approach tries to change people's personal interpretations of themselves and the social world in ways that make them happier and lead to more desirable behaviors. It is a family of approaches developed by social psychologists that includes writing exercises, such as the one developed by James Pennebaker; the story-prompting approach, in which people are directed toward new ways of explaining and understanding their behavior to replace self-defeating thinking patterns; and the do good, be good strategy, in which people are encouraged to create new interpretations by first changing their behavior. The key to each approach is that people end up with a more desirable way of viewing themselves that builds on and reinforces itself, leading to sustained change.

To be sure, this approach is not the cure for all societal problems. No one would argue that the cure for homelessness is to get homeless people to interpret their problem differently. Sometimes big structural changes are needed to attack deep-seated problems. But story editing can help solve many vexing problems, even some seemingly deep-seated ones.

TESTING IT

Well, you might ask, how do we know that the story-editing approach works where other approaches, like CISD, fail? A theme of this book is that we can only answer this question by conducting carefully controlled scientific studies. Without such rigorous research, we would never have found out that CISD doesn't work, whereas the Pennebaker writing technique does. Sadly, such research is rare, and there are countless interventions in use today that have never been adequately tested.

To illustrate how unusual it is for social and psychological interventions to be tested scientifically, let's draw an analogy from the history of medicine. Suppose that the year is 1850 and you fall ill with a respiratory infection. Your local doctor comes to see you, and because you are lucky, he decides to administer a relatively harmless treatment called blistering. He presses a red-hot glass on your chest, creating a ring of blisters that will supposedly draw phlegm out of your lungs. If it's not your lucky day, the doctor opens a vein in your arm and drains a liter or two of your blood. It would make perfect sense to a nineteenth-century physician to administer bloodletting in order to restore the balance of the four bodily humors (blood, yellow bile, black bile, and phlegm). This was the treatment George Washington received when he came down with a respiratory infection at age sixty-seven; his doctors drained more than half his blood over the course of a day, thereby hastening (or maybe even causing) his demise.

Fortunately, most medical treatments are now tested scientifically before being widely implemented. But the same cannot be said of attempts to solve the major social and behavioral problems of our day, such as racial prejudice, adolescent behavior problems, drug use, and post-traumatic stress disorder. The same goes for advice given in countless self-help books about how to live a happier and more fulfilling life, and for parenting books that tell us how to raise our children. Many "solutions" are like nineteenth-century medicine—treatments that seem to make sense but are ineffective or even do more harm than good. Some diversity-training programs, for example, are like blistering—they are somewhat painful to endure and have no beneficial effects. Some well-known programs to prevent drug use and delinquency are like bloodletting—they actually do harm, increasing the likelihood that teens will experiment with cigarettes and alcohol and commit crimes. In the chapters to come I will confer a "blistering" or "bloodletting" award on many current programs in order to identify the ones that don't work or do harm.

Even when effective approaches are discovered, often they are not widely disseminated, in part because they violate common sense. Again, a medical analogy is apt: who would have thought, until research showed it to be so, that giving people mold from bread would be an effective way to treat infections? I hope to show that, unlike the many ineffective behavioral interventions that are in use today, the story-editing approach is like penicillin: it may violate common sense, but it works.

In the next chapter, I describe how interventions can and should be tested using scientific techniques. This chapter provides the basic knowledge needed to understand the experiments that we will encounter in the book, and will allow readers to make discerning judgments about interventions that they might be asked to undergo. Armed with this basic knowledge, Gary Felice could have questioned whether CISD had been tested properly. Parents could question school administrators about the effectiveness of the particular anti-drug and bullying-prevention programs used in their schools, and all of us, when reading a popular self-help book, could question how well its claims have been tested.

Beginning with chapter 3, we will see how the story-editing approach has been used to address personal issues—including how to be happier and become better parents—and societal issues, including how to reduce teenage pregnancies, lower teen violence, reduce alcohol and drug use, lower prejudice against minority groups, and close the achievement gap in education. What these diverse issues have in common is that they are rooted in people's self-narratives, narratives that can be redirected with the story-editing approach. Further, the story-editing solutions can be applied by people in their everyday lives, as described at the end of each chapter in sections called Using It.

CHAPTER 2

Testing, Testing

Does It Work?

Hoa Young, an Asian American woman who works for the St. Paul, Minnesota, office of Planning and Economic Development, is no stranger to ethnic insensitivity. Although she has lived in the United States for nearly forty years, people sometimes treat her as a foreigner. One woman came up to her at a bus stop and asked her in a loud voice whether she spoke English—and then gave her literature about how she could be saved by embracing Jesus. Young was thus in favor of a mandatory diversity-training program for all employees of the city of St. Paul. The employees watched six actors from a company called Theatre at Work enact sensitive workplace scenarios that involved issues of race, gender, religion, and xenophobia. An employment-law attorney moderated the sessions, which included a question-and-answer period.

The diversity program was clearly a well-intentioned attempt to increase tolerance, reduce conflict, and make sure people followed the law. Mayor Randy Kelly endorsed it, noting that "it is sure to raise awareness and sensitivity to issues we as public servants encounter on a daily basis." Shoua Lee, another Asian American city employee, seemed to agree. "I have been in so many of those situations," she said.

"Then I kick myself for not saying anything." But not everyone was so sanguine about the program. "I reject the message they are sending about diversity," argued one middle-aged white man. "We should have a common culture and a common language. And it should be American culture, which is the greatest in the world."[1]

How could we tell whether the skits performed by Theatre at Work were effective? It probably never occurred to the creators of the program, or the city that adopted it, that the program should be vetted scientifically before it was implemented so widely—just as it didn't occur to hundreds of police and fire departments to vet Critical Incident Stress Debriefing (CISD), which, as we saw in chapter 1, turned out not to work. When similar fiascos occur in the medical establishment, such as the rushing of drugs to market before they are adequately tested, there is justifiable outrage and a call for more stringent testing procedures. Why aren't there similar outcries about behavioral interventions?

THE FAILURE OF COMMON SENSE

Policy makers, self-help authors, and nonpsychologists of all stripes often rely on common sense to tell them how to solve problems—more so, certainly, than medical researchers do when considering whether a new chemical compound will relieve pain from migraines. Common sense tells us, for example, that showing people skits depicting workplace scenarios will raise their consciousness about diversity issues, and that getting people to talk through their feelings about a recent traumatic event is helpful. But common sense can lead us astray by not taking into account how the human mind really works—specifically, by failing to consider how small changes in people's narratives can have a lasting impact on their behavior.

We will encounter many examples of the failure of common sense throughout this book. Know some teens headed for trouble? Scare the heck out of them by taking them to prisons and funeral homes. Want kids to avoid drugs? Bring police officers into their classrooms to explain the dangers of drugs and give lessons on how to resist peer pressure. These approaches make perfect sense but, it turns out, they are perfectly wrong, doing more harm than good. It is no exaggeration to say that commonsense interventions have prolonged stress, raised the crime rate, increased drug use, made people unhappy, and even hastened their deaths. The problem is that these interventions failed to take into account a basic premise of the story-editing approach, namely, that in order to solve a problem, we have to view it through the eyes of the people involved and get them to redirect their narratives about it. But how do we know that story editing works any better than commonsense approaches? In the remainder of this chapter we will see how.

WHAT ARE WE TRYING TO CHANGE?
The first question to ask with any intervention is, what is it that we want to change? And how can we measure that change? Diversity education programs such as Theatre at Work, for example, typically have several objectives, namely, (a) to instill awareness of the law and company policies, (b) to increase sensitivity to members of different groups, (c) to reduce prejudice, (d) to reduce discriminatory behavior, (e) to increase diversity in hiring and promotions, (f) to increase productivity in the workplace, and (g) to reduce lawsuits (or liability in the event of a lawsuit).

Measuring some of these outcomes is relatively straightforward: if we want to know whether employees are aware of the law and a company's policies, we could give them a simple knowledge test, such as asking whether it is legal to ask a job candidate whether he or she is married. Measuring other outcomes, such as how prejudiced people are, is more challenging. Social psychologists have conducted a lot of research on this question, developing a number of ways of measuring people's attitudes, including both questionnaire measures and indirect tests that are typically administered on a computer. Another approach is to measure not what people say but what they do. After a diversity-training program is implemented, for example, are fewer complaints filed about discriminatory behavior? Is there an increase in productivity in the workplace?[2]

Questions about how to measure people's beliefs, attitudes, and behaviors are not trivial, but we can usually agree on what we want an intervention to change and how to measure that change. A more difficult question is whether the intervention is *causing* the desired change. It would be simple if there were a machine that displayed people's thoughts on a computer screen, so that we could track those thoughts and see how they were influenced by our interventions. But fortunately (for those of us who would prefer to keep our thoughts to ourselves) no such mind-reading machine exists. We can put people in a magnetic resonance imaging (MRI) scanner and measure the flow of blood to different areas of their brains, or place electrodes on their scalps and measure the electronic activity of their neurons with electroencephalography (EEG). Although these techniques yield useful information, they are not "mind-reading" devices that reveal people's specific thoughts, such as whether they are attributing a bad grade to low intelligence (as Bob did in chapter 1) or to the need to try harder (as Sarah did in chapter 1).

DON'T ASK, CAN'T TELL

Why not just ask people whether they have benefited from a program? This was the approach adopted by the Theatre at Work company (who performed the diversity-training skits in St. Paul). On their website, they report a study in which a researcher interviewed eight people who had attended a Theatre at Work performance and asked them to assess the impact the performance had on them. The results were encouraging: the attendees said that the workshop "had a noticeable impact on their interactions with coworkers as well as family members." Similarly, researchers have asked people who took part in Critical Incident Stress Debriefing (CISD) sessions how helpful the intervention was, with encouraging results. In one study, 98 percent of police officers who witnessed traumatic events and underwent psychological debriefing reported that they were satisfied with the procedure.[3]

Unfortunately, such testimonials can be misleading. Sometimes people are less than truthful; perhaps they knew that the debriefing didn't help much but they did not want to rain on the researchers' parade. Although such disingenuousness can be an issue, there is a more fundamental problem with asking people about the effectiveness of interventions: they often don't know the answer. True enough, we are the only species (as far as we know) endowed with consciousness, that navel-gazing, contemplative, sometimes angst-ridden ability to introspect about ourselves and our place in the world. But it turns out that consciousness is a small part of the human mental repertoire. We are strangers to ourselves, the owners of highly sophisticated unconscious minds that hum along parallel to our conscious minds, interpreting the world and constructing narratives about our place in it. It is these unconscious narratives that social psychologists target.[4]

This doesn't mean that we are clueless about ourselves. We usually don't have any trouble knowing how we feel, such as how happy, sad, angry, or elated we are at any given point in time. We are not very good, however, at knowing *why* we feel the way we do. Our minds don't provide us with pie charts that we can examine and say, "Why am I feeling sad right now? Let's see, 37 percent of the reason is that my spouse has been ignoring me, 28 percent is because I learned that my aunt is seriously ill, 13 percent is because of the state of the economy, and the rest is because my serotonin levels are a little low right now." Instead, we develop theories about the causes of our feelings, just as we develop theories about the causes of other people's feelings. These theories are often correct—most of us are good observers of ourselves, and we may have noticed that when our spouses ignore us we do feel sad and resentful. But few of us are perfect at knowing exactly why we feel the way we do because life is not a controlled experiment in which only one thing varies at a time, making it easy to see what effect it has on us. Instead, there are usually lots of plausible influences on our feelings and it can be difficult to tease apart which ones really are responsible for our current moods or attitudes.[5]

This is especially true when we encounter a novel situation—such as an intervention designed to influence our feelings and behavior—and have nothing to compare it to. When people have taken part in a diversity-training program, for example, how are they supposed to know to what extent, if at all, their current feelings and attitudes were influenced by the program? To answer this question they would have to know how they would be feeling if they had *not* participated in the program. This was the problem faced by many of the participants in the CISD studies. Let's say that after undergoing the debriefing procedure they were still upset by the traumatic event they had witnessed. "Well," they might think to themselves, "I would probably be feeling even worse if it weren't for the CISD intervention. The facilitator seemed nice and everyone seems to believe in it, so I guess it helped me." Unlike George Bailey in the movie *It's a Wonderful Life*, we don't have angels who can show us what our lives would be like under different circumstances.

Actually, it's even worse than that. Once people have gone through a program designed to help them in some way, there is a tendency for them to misremember how well off they were before the program began, thereby overestimating the effects of the intervention. One experiment, for example, found that a study-skills program had no effect on college students—after the program their study skills were no better than those of students who hadn't taken part in the program.

But the participants *believed* that the program had been effective, because they mistakenly recalled that their skills had been much worse before the program began.[6]

In short, when it comes to evaluating the effectiveness of an intervention, I advocate a "don't ask, can't tell" policy—researchers should not assess the impact of a program by asking people how much they benefited from it. Human beings simply are not very accurate at assessing the causes of their own feelings, attitudes, and behavior. To be clear, I am not arguing that researchers should throw away their questionnaires and stop interviewing the recipients of interventions or those who implement them. The don't ask, can't tell policy should apply only to questions about how people were *influenced* by an intervention, because they can't be expected to answer this question accurately. Asking people about their feelings, attitudes, opinions, and knowledge can be quite valuable—if we know what to compare their answers to.

VIVA THE EXPERIMENTAL METHOD

What should that point of comparison be? One common approach is called a pre-post design, in which researchers compare people's beliefs, attitudes, or behavior before an intervention to their beliefs, attitudes, or behavior after the intervention to see if any changes have occurred. Suppose, for example, that before participating in a diversity-training program, only 30 percent of employees knew that in their state it is illegal to ask a job candidate whether he or she is married. Right after the program, 90 percent answer this question correctly. This would be pretty good evidence that the employees learned something useful from the program. Usually, however, the goal is to bring about long-term change, not just a fleeting blip in people's knowledge. Here, things get dicier for the pre-post design, because the more time that passes, the less sure we can be that it was the intervention rather than something else in a person's life that caused the change. Instead of administering our questionnaire right after the program, what if we waited a few weeks to see if it had lasting effects? The results are encouraging—85 percent of the respondents answer correctly that in their state it is illegal to ask about a job candidate's marital status. But who knows what happened in the weeks following the intervention? Perhaps people forgot what they heard in our program, but picked up the information from a new company manual that just came out, or talked with coworkers, or read an article in the newspaper.

In other words, pre-post designs are imperfect because they do not control for things that might have influenced people other than the intervention. As seen in our example, this is especially problematic when we are measuring long-term change, because the longer we wait to measure our variables of interest, the more other things occur in people's lives that could contaminate our results.

A better approach is to compare the people who received the intervention with a control group. Say we compared the employees who took part in our diversity-training program with a control group of employees who did not, and the ones who took part were more likely to know that it is illegal to ask job candidates about their marital status. For the sake of the argument, say that they also did better on other important measures—they showed more tolerance toward members of other races and were less likely to have complaints filed against them. Sounds like very good news for our intervention, doesn't it?

But ah—there is still a critical ingredient missing from this evaluation of our program: *random assignment to condition*. If we didn't randomly assign people to a control group, our results would be hard to interpret, because we could not rule out the possibility that the control participants differ in key respects from the people who received the intervention. This is the classic "correlation does not equal causation" problem: just because one variable (whether people took part in our program) is correlated with another (their tolerance toward their coworkers several weeks later) does not mean that the first variable *caused* the second one to occur.

Let's say that participation in our program was voluntary and we compared those who chose to take part to a control group of participants who chose not to. This would be a flawed experiment because tolerant, knowledgeable people might be more inclined to volunteer to undergo diversity training and thus would show more tolerance down the road — not because the program worked but because of who they were at the outset. One study did in fact find that people who showed intercultural sensitivity and competence to begin with were more likely to volunteer for a diversity-training program. So scratch the idea of letting people choose which group to participate in.[7]

Instead, we could get a little more sophisticated and administer our intervention to people in one unit of a company and compare their beliefs and attitudes to people in a different unit who did not receive the intervention. This would be a better experiment because it avoids the "self-selection" problem, whereby people decide for themselves whether to receive the intervention. It is still possible, however, that employees in the two units differ in important ways. Maybe the people in one unit are younger, work in a part of the company that is more racially integrated, have more interracial friends, more tolerant bosses, or differ from the other group in any number of other ways that could influence the results of the experiment.

Random assignment is the Great Equalizer. If we divide people into two groups on the basis of a coin flip (and if the groups are reasonably large), we can be confident that the groups do not differ in their backgrounds, tolerance for members of other groups, personalities, political leanings, hobbies, or in any other way that might influence their behavior. It would be extremely unlikely that one group would have significantly more cat lovers, vegetarians, hockey fans, or marathon runners than the other, just as it would be extremely unlikely for a fair coin to turn up heads forty times on fifty flips. Thus, if the group that received the diversity training showed more tolerance than the group that did not, we could be confident that the training, and not some unrelated difference in people's backgrounds, was responsible for the change.

STATISTICAL MAGIC?

Some researchers claim that there is a good alternative to the experimental method: if we can't randomly assign people to conditions, then we can statistically adjust for variables that might bias our results. Say we did a study in which we found that the more people exercise, the longer they live. Because we did not randomly assign people to exercise a lot or a little, we can't be sure whether it was the exercise that prolonged people's lives or whether it was some third variable (e.g., maybe the exercisers smoked less than the nonexercisers). No problem, some researchers say. Just measure how much people smoke, use a statistical procedure called multiple regression that adjusts for the influence of third variables such as smoking, and presto, we have our answer. Essentially, this procedure looks at whether exercisers live longer at a given rate of smoking; for example, whether nonsmoking exercisers have longer lives than nonsmoking couch potatoes. If they do, we can be pretty sure that exercise has beneficial effects. The problem is, we can never measure all the "third variables" that might cloud our results. Suppose, for example, that exercisers are more likely to use sunscreen and wear their seat belts than couch potatoes are, but the researchers didn't ask people about those habits. We cannot statistically control for things we don't measure.

There are several well-known studies that fell into this trap and yielded misleading results, sometimes with life-and-death consequences. One was a survey that asked thousands of women questions about their health and whether they were taking hormone replacement therapy at menopause. The researchers found that the women who used hormone replacement therapy had fewer heart attacks than those who did not, after statistically controlling for a host of potential confounding variables. Many physicians relied on this study to recommend hormone therapy for their patients. But a later clinical trial, in which women were randomly assigned to receive hormone therapy or not, yielded the exact opposite results: hormone therapy *increased* the risk of heart attacks. It now appears that women in the first study who chose to undergo hormone replacement therapy were healthier at the outset in ways that the researchers did not measure, which led to the misleading results. Only by randomly assigning people to conditions can researchers be confident that they have controlled for all possible confounding variables and have identified a true causal effect.[8]

What if a statistical analysis finds no association between two variables? Doesn't that prove that one is not causing the other? Not necessarily. A recent study surveyed human resources managers at more than seven hundred organizations in the United States to find out the kinds of strategies the companies were using to increase diversity. They also examined the percentages of women and minority managers the companies actually hired, as gleaned from reports the companies had filed with the Equal Employment Opportunity Commission. It turned out that whether companies had diversity-training programs for their employees was unrelated to the number of women and minorities they had hired as managers. This appears to be pretty damning evidence against the effectiveness of these programs, and, in fact, that is just what the authors concluded: the diversity-training programs were ineffective at "increasing the share of white women, black women, and black men in management."[9]

But again, not so fast! In this study, unmeasured third variables might have masked an actual causal effect of diversity programs. It is possible, for example, that the companies that implemented diversity programs differed in key respects from the ones that did not. Perhaps companies with unfair hiring practices were under pressure to do better, and rather than changing their actual hiring policies, they implemented diversity-training programs to take the heat off and make it look like they were doing something constructive. If so, any causal effect of these programs would be hard to detect, because it was the companies that were unwilling to change their hiring practices that were most likely to be implement the programs.

In short, it takes a true experiment to settle the question of what causes what. If we were able to randomly assign companies to either implement or not implement diversity programs, for example, we could control for all possible confounding variables. The companies resistant to change, and those committed to it, would be divided evenly between our two groups. As simple as this sounds, it is not a lesson that is widely heeded—multiple regression is the tool of the trade for many economists, sociologists, and psychologists.

In these researchers' defense, sometimes it is impossible, for practical or ethical reasons, to perform an experiment using random assignment to condition. To find out whether capital punishment influences the murder rate, for example, we could not randomly assign some cities or states to implement the death penalty and others to ban it. But I think that researchers are often too quick to throw in the experimental towel, deciding that random assignment to condition is impractical. It often seems difficult to test a new intervention that is designed to help people in some way, for example, when in fact it *is* possible to randomly assign people to a condition in which they receive the intervention or to a control condition in which they do not. If people in the intervention condition show more desirable responses to a statistically significant degree, we can be much more confident that the program is working. This is how I knew that my academic intervention with college students worked (see chapter 1): the students who received it got better grades, and were more likely to stay in college, than the students randomly assigned to the control group. If no differences are

found between the intervention condition and the control condition—
and we did our experiment well, with a large sample size—then we
need to worry. This is in fact how we know that CISD does not work
to reduce post-traumatic stress: a number of studies randomly assigned
people to either undergo the procedure or not undergo it (the control
group) and found no difference between the two groups (in some cases
they found that the control group was better off).[10]

START SMALL

I certainly don't mean to imply that it is easy to conduct experiments.
Designing the appropriate control condition, for example, can be a
tricky business. Even more vexing, some interventions may not be so
easily packaged into a few sessions and delivered only to people in a
treatment condition. Instead of evaluating a diversity-training exercise
such as Theatre at Work, for example, suppose we wanted to test the
effectiveness of a new way of teaching children to read. It might take
six months or a year to tell whether the program is working, and meanwhile, the children randomly assigned to our control group don't get
the benefit of the new program. Though this is indeed a difficult trade-
off, it is no different from the one faced by medical researchers when
they test the effectiveness of a new treatment. People are randomly
assigned to control conditions until the researchers and the medical
community at large are convinced that the treatment works. Why
should we have different standards for social, psychological, and educational interventions?

One solution is to conduct experimental tests of small-scale interventions, rather than beginning with massive efforts to bring about
large-scale change. Before instituting a mandatory diversity-training
program throughout the federal government, we might want to test it
experimentally in one or two offices. Before requiring that all police
officers and firefighters undergo CISD, we might test its effectiveness

in a few small, well-controlled studies. Some of the reasons for starting small are obvious: it limits risk (unintended negative effects of an intervention) and saves money. Another reason is that it is difficult to predict how a scaled-up version of an intervention will work in the real world. Social scientists have many powerful theories about how things work, many of them based on small studies done in research laboratories on college campuses. Although these theories are excellent starting points, we can't be sure how they will play out in real-world settings, so it is best to start small and see what happens.[11]

This lesson applies to the story-editing approach as much as it does to any other intervention. It can be difficult to predict whether a particular intervention will succeed in getting people to adopt healthy, self-sustaining narratives; thus it is advisable to begin with small trials. James Pennebaker's first test of his writing technique, for example, was conducted with forty-six college students who were randomly assigned to different writing conditions, and my initial test of the academic improvement intervention involved forty college students randomly assigned to conditions. One problem with such small studies, of course, is that they are, well, small, involving a limited number of people rather than large, representative samples. But if promising results are found in small-scale experiments such as these, researchers can follow them up with replications and extensions to other groups of people, and eventually to large-scale implementations. Both the Pennebaker writing technique and my academic improvement intervention, for example, have been replicated numerous times with people of different backgrounds and nationalities.[12]

PEERING INTO THE BLACK BOX

There are additional difficulties with conducting experimental tests of the story-editing approach. The premise is that people's behavior emanates from their interpretations of the world and that these interpretations can often be redirected with relatively simple interventions. But these interpretations are often hard to verbalize, which means that we can't rely on people to tell us whether our interventions worked in the way we think they have. The don't ask, can't tell principle applies as much to studies of story editing as to any other, making it difficult to directly test our hypothesis that we have changed people's interpretations in the specified way.

In my intervention with first-year college students, for example, the participants who received the message that many students struggle at first but do better as time goes by improved their grades and were less likely to drop out of college, relative to the participants randomly assigned to a control group. But exactly how did this happen? We hypothesized that our message interrupted a self-defeating cycle of thinking in which the students blamed themselves for their academic problems, and prompted them to switch to a self-enhancing cycle of thinking in which they decided they could do better if they tried. But the astute reader will have noticed that I didn't discuss any evidence showing that people changed their thinking in this manner. And that's because there wasn't any. Well, not much—we did find that people who got the intervention raised their expectations about their future academic performance more than people in the control group did, which is consistent with the predicted change in their thinking style. But that was the only shred of evidence consistent with our notion that people's interpretations had changed in the way we expected them to.

This example reveals the limits of the research psychologist's tools and measures. The mind is largely a black box that is inaccessible to its owner, and researchers don't have mind-reading machines that reveal what's in the black box. There is thus a lot of guesswork about how our interventions are working. We try to deduce what is happening inside the black box by seeing how different inputs change the outputs. Note that this approach is the same in any other science in which researchers cannot directly observe the processes they hypothesize to be occurring. The idea that diseases can be caused and spread by microorganisms, for example, was developed before scientists had the ability to directly observe the microorganisms. Dr. Ignaz Semmelweis, a Hungarian obstetrician working in Vienna in 1847, noticed that up to 30 percent of women who delivered babies at Vienna General Hospital died of puerperal fever, whereas very few women who delivered at home died of puerperal fever. He further observed that the women who died in the hospital were likely to have been examined by doctors who had just conducted autopsies. He formed the hypothesis, quite radical at the time, that puerperal fever was caused by a contagious organism that the doctors were unknowingly transmitting from the cadavers to the women. To test this hypothesis he had the doctors wash their hands in water and lime before examining the women. Deaths by puerperal fever dropped to about 2 percent, thereby confirming his hypothesis. Did Semmelweis's bold experiment prove the germ theory of disease? It did not, because he had no way of directly measuring the presence of microorganisms. His results were certainly consistent with the theory, however, and—even better—he found a simple, inexpensive way of solving a deadly problem.

Research on story editing is at very much the same point. Simple interventions have been found to solve big problems. We don't always know exactly why, because we cannot directly measure the thoughts inside the black box that we believe we have changed. Social psychologists are clever methodologists, however, and have prodded and probed the black box in ways that have produced some provocative results. In the rest of the book we will see what they have found, beginning with research on how to become happier.

CHAPTER 3

Shaping Our Narratives
Increasing Personal Well-Being

G us Godsey is the happiest person in America, according to an article *USA Weekend* magazine published in 2003. Now, I wouldn't
take this claim too seriously, because the *USA Weekend* editors eliminated half the population right off the bat, namely, women. "We knew it
had to be a guy," they wrote. "Even though women have been shown to
have higher emotional highs, they also have lower lows. Men maintain a
more consistent blend of happiness." This is an odd statement, because
research has shown that women are actually happier than men on average (though the gap has narrowed in recent years).[1]

For another thing, the magazine limited its search to people in the
city of Virginia Beach, Virginia, because this city had placed first in
lists of the best places to live in America. Although that made the
search a lot easier—the editors didn't have to look beyond the borders
of that resort city—I wouldn't be so quick to eliminate people living
in Cleveland, Dubuque, Spokane, or any other part of America,
because research shows that where we live does not influence our happiness as much as we think it does.

But even though Gus may not be *the* happiest person in America, there is no doubt that he is a very happy guy. The *USA Weekend* editors sent him to a website to take four standardized tests designed to measure happiness and life satisfaction, and Gus aced them all. As the author of the *USA Weekend* article put it, "He comes off as 10 gallons of happiness in a 5-gallon bag." What makes Gus so happy? What are the ingredients of happiness, anyway, and how did Gus get so many of them?[2]

Well, you might think, Gus must be fabulously wealthy and able to get whatever he wants without lifting a finger (other than to retrieve his credit card from his wallet). He probably owns houses all over the world, zips around in a private Learjet, orders whatever he wants from a four-star private chef, and gets front-row seats at all the best concerts and plays. Who wouldn't be happy with all these riches?

Lots of people, it turns out. As we will see, money is not the primary cause of happiness, as long as we have enough to meet our basic needs. Indeed, Gus Godsey is not some Bill Gates–like billionaire, but rather a stockbroker who lives a pretty ordinary life, by the standards of middle-class America. At the time he won the "happiest person" title, he didn't own a McMansion but lived in a twenty-three-hundred-square-foot home. He was a forty-five-year-old married guy with two kids who went to work every day, rooted for the Green Bay Packers, and was fond of Sears Craftsman tools. No Learjet, no private chef. So what makes him so happy? Does he know some secret that you and I could learn, which would move us closer to him on the happiness scale?

Although we do not have complete control over the things that make us happy, our well-being is intimately tied up with the way in which we think about ourselves and our place in the world—the personal interpretations that are the very subject of this book. In this chapter, we will see that, using the story-editing approach, we can change our views in ways that will make us happier—but not necessarily in the ways that we might think. In fact, there is an awful lot of misinformation out there about how to live a happier and more fulfilling life, much of it propagated by the self-help industry. Let's begin by dispelling some of those myths.

HOPE FOR SALE: THE SELF-HELP INDUSTRY

Visit the self-help section in your local bookstore and you will see shelves of books that promise to improve your life in any number of ways. You can read about a breakthrough program to end negative behavior and feel great again, the secrets to daily joy and lasting fulfillment, five simple steps to emotional healing, ways of overcoming self-defeating behaviors, how to break the emotional bad habits that make you miserable, and how to stop worry and anxiety from ruining your relationships. And let's not forget the bestselling books by Dr. Phil and Tony Robbins, as well as Louise Hay's *You Can Heal Your Life*, Stephen Covey's *The 7 Habits of Highly Effective People*, and Rhonda Byrne's *The Secret*.

These books sell and sell fast, to the tune of more than $700 million in sales in 2005. When other forms of self-help are added to the mix, such as infomercials, seminars, and personal coaches, the total amount spent on self-improvement in the United States reached a staggering $9.6 billion in 2006.[3]

The speed with which self-help books fly off the shelves would seem to suggest that they really do improve our lives. But I have a wise friend who points out that whenever there are multiple solutions to one problem we can be pretty sure that none of them works. (She developed this theory when her dog kept getting sprayed by skunks: each person she consulted offered a different remedy for getting rid of the odor, none of which worked.) Similarly, the very fact that there are so many self-help books on the market might be a sign that none of them is effective. After all, if one of them really did unlock the secret to everlasting happiness, it would corner the market and crowd out all the others. But instead, there is what is known in the self-help industry as the eighteen-month rule, which is that the person most likely to buy a self-help book is someone who bought one eighteen months earlier.[4]

Steve Salerno, in his book *Sham: How the Self-Help Movement Made America Helpless*, argues that there are huge costs associated with the public acceptance of what he calls SHAM, which stands for the Self-Help and Actualization Movement. Buying into the claims self-help books make, he argues, can lead to blaming oneself for failure and avoiding treatments that actually do work. Further, very little of the advice offered in self-help books has been tested scientifically, despite the fact that there are ways to do so—and, indeed, there have been many good scientific studies on how to become happier. But most self-help authors are either unaware of this research or opt not to discuss it. Instead, they offer mantras that are like the twenty-first-century version of patent medicines. Similar to their nineteenth-century counterparts, whose main ingredient was often alcohol or cocaine, these "remedies" make people feel good but don't cure what ails them.

What's the harm in that, you might ask, as long as people know what they are getting? Maybe a better analogy is that reading a self-help book is like buying a lottery ticket: for a small investment, we get hope in return; the dream that all our problems will soon be solved without any real expectation that they will be. But there may be real harm in self-help books. As an example, let's take a look at one of the most popular self-help publications of all time, Rhonda Byrne's *The Secret*. *The Secret* was distributed as both a film and a companion book, released in 2006. Both have been phenomenally successful. The DVD has sold more than two million copies and the book more than four million copies.

What *is* the secret, anyway? It turns out that it's pretty simple: it's the "law of attraction," which says that thinking about something makes it more likely to happen to you. Once you understand this basic "law of the universe," there are three simple steps to getting whatever you want: first, think about it—focus on the positive and not the negative. If you are trying to shed a few pounds, for example, don't think about the fact that you are too heavy; those negative thoughts will make you heavier. Think instead about slipping on a pair of your favorite jeans and buttoning them over a perfectly flat stomach—that's a positive thought that will make you thinner. The second step is to *believe* in what you want and have faith that it will soon be yours. Again, no negative thoughts allowed—those jeans will fit perfectly very soon. The third step is to *receive* the idea of having what you want, feeling as you will once you get it. Imagine what it will be like to wear those jeans and adopt those feelings now.

All these steps can be boiled down to the power of positive thinking, which has been touted in various forms for many years, most famously (pre-*Secret*, anyway) by Norman Vincent Peale in his 1952 book, *The Power of Positive Thinking*, which was on the *New York Times* bestseller list for more than three years and has sold more than five million copies. Peale offered ten lessons for building one's confidence, many of which sound a lot like those found in *The Secret*, such as "Formulate and stamp indelibly on your mind a mental picture of yourself as succeeding...Your mind will seek to develop this picture," and "Whenever a negative thought concerning your personal powers comes to mind, deliberately voice a positive thought to cancel it out."[5]

As we will see shortly, scientific research shows that some forms of positive thinking are indeed beneficial. But again, self-help books typically ignore this research and embed their messages in questionable ideologies. In Rhonda Byrne's case, the belief system is a New Age philosophy that is unabashedly evocative of *The Da Vinci Code*. The "secret" has been known by a select few throughout history, Byrne informs us, including the Babylonians, Plato, Shakespeare, Beethoven, Abraham Lincoln, and Albert Einstein, but has been hidden from the rest of us until she uncovered it by searching the Internet.

How can positive thoughts have such power? *The Secret* doesn't disappoint—it provides an explanation to back up its amazing claims. It turns out that thoughts have frequencies that are magnetic, attracting things that are on the same frequency. What's more, human beings have incredible transmitting power: "The frequency you transmit reaches beyond cities, beyond countries, beyond the world. It reverberates throughout the entire universe." Once the object of our desire receives these thought frequencies, it moves closer to us, because these thoughts are magnetic.

I don't mean to nitpick, but there are a few questions that come to mind about this scientific explanation of the law of attraction. How, exactly, does sending out thought frequencies make something materialize in our lives? Let's say I have my heart set on a new wide-screen TV that is sitting in the showroom of my local electronics dealer. I ask the universe for the TV, believe that I will get it, and receive positive thoughts and feelings about it. My positive thought frequencies zoom out of my head and into the showroom, and because they are magnetic, the TV moves closer to me. But wait a minute—does it actually inch closer each day? Won't the store personnel be a little suspicious when they arrive in the morning and find that the TV has moved to the loading dock? And how exactly does the TV get into my living room? Does it swoop in through the chimney like Santa delivering presents on Christmas Eve? Aren't there a few unresolved questions here?

I know, I know, I'm being too literal about thought frequencies. They're not magnetic in a physical sense, I gather, but rather in some mysterious, cosmic way that makes things come true, much like rubbing Aladdin's lamp makes a genie come out and grant our wishes. If I focus my positive thoughts on the TV, maybe I'll wake up to find that I won it in a raffle or got a windfall of cash that would allow me to buy it. Exactly how this happens isn't clear, but that's why it's a *secret*, you numbskull—the ways of the universe are mysterious.

But what if I'm not the only one who wants that particular television? Suppose that Joe across town has his heart set on the very same model—which happens to be the last one in stock. Joe, too, has read *The Secret* and starts thinking positive thoughts. Do our thought frequencies compete with each other? If Joe thinks more positive thoughts than I, does the TV inch closer to his house, only to creep back when I turn up the volume on my positive thoughts? Here I go getting too literal again—though one does wonder, with the phenomenal success of *The Secret*, how we are *all* going to get what we want. Only one of us can have that particular TV or the last brownie on the plate, and I can only imagine how cluttered the cosmic airwaves are getting with all those positive thoughts colliding with one another.

But there are other problems with *The Secret* besides its questionable science. One is the blame it confers on people who don't succeed in attracting what they want. If you don't get the TV or that last brownie, if you are poor, or if, God forbid, you contract a serious illness—well, it's your own damn fault. The book makes no bones about this. Dr. Joe Vitale, one of the experts quoted in *The Secret*, says, "Now I know at first blush that's going to be something that you hate to hear. You're going to immediately say, 'I didn't attract the car accident. I didn't attract this particular client who gives me a hard time. I didn't particularly attract the debt.' And I'm here to be a little bit in your face and to say, yes you did attract it." You did so, you see, because you were thinking negative thoughts.

In March of 2007, *Saturday Night Live* broadcasted a biting parody of the atrocious finger-pointing inherent in *The Secret*. Rhonda Byrne (played by Amy Poehler) and Oprah Winfrey (played by Maya Rudolph) visit Darfur, the site of some of the worst poverty and violence in the world. (The real Oprah was a fan of *The Secret*; she had Byrne on her show twice, after which sales of the book skyrocketed.) On the *SNL* skit, Oprah and Byrne pooh-pooh a Darfurian man's lament about starvation in his country, chastising him for having negative thoughts. As scathing as this skit was, it was satire: *The Secret* doesn't really mean to blame children for their own poverty and star-vation, does it? Well, apparently, it does. In March of 2007, Bob Proc-tor, one of the "experts" most quoted by Rhonda Byrne, was interviewed by Cynthia McFadden on the TV show *Nightline:*

MCFADDEN: Children in Darfur are starving to death.
PROCTOR: Yeah.
MCFADDEN: Ha...have they attracted that starvation to themselves?
PROCTOR: I...I...I think the country probably has.

Another problem with *The Secret* is that it can steer people away from effective solutions to their problems by suggesting that good health, love, and riches are theirs for the asking if they just think about them. Rhonda Byrne reports that she cured herself of farsightedness in three days by imagining that she had perfect eyesight—to the point where she no longer needs reading glasses. Even more startlingly, in the book, a woman claims that she cured herself of breast cancer in three months, without medical treatment, by believing that she was healed. "Illness cannot exist in a body that has harmonious thoughts," Byrne explains, and "nothing is incurable."[6]

Do people really take *The Secret* that seriously? Unfortunately, some do. A friend of mine who teaches at a highly regarded liberal arts college reports that one of her students arrived at her office, gave her a DVD of *The Secret*, and told her that she needed to watch it to improve her life. (One suspects that simply thinking positively hadn't resulted in good grades for the student, and that he figured he might still get an A if he could turn his professor on to *The Secret* so that their thought frequencies would be aligned.)

There have been reports of people seeking therapy after failing in the dream world of *The Secret* and of people who go on spending sprees for things they can't afford in the belief that thinking positive thoughts will lead to windfalls of cash. And lest you think these are fanatics who have misunderstood the message, make a quick visit to *The Secret*'s website (http://thesecret.tv/). Click on "Gifts for You" and scroll down to "The Bank of the Universe," where you can download a "universal check" by following these instructions: "Print out the check, then fill in your name and the amount you wish to receive, in the currency of your choice." Doing so, it seems, will attract that amount of money to you. Go ahead and fill it out! If a Brink's truck arrives at your door tomorrow with a bag full of cash (in the currency of your choice), you can thank me for the tip.[7]

But unfortunately the Brink's truck isn't likely to show up, no matter how many checks you fill out from the Universal Bank (Un)Limited. Don't waste your money on self-help books such as *The Secret*, I suggest, unless they are based on actual scientific research of the sort described in the remainder of this chapter. Let's begin with a look at research on what it is that makes us happy in the first place.

WHAT REALLY MAKES PEOPLE HAPPY?

Earlier we considered the question of whether Gus Godsey, the "happiest person in America," may have gotten that way by accumulating wealth. Indeed, the idea that material riches make us happy has been around for a long time. In fact, the original definition of the word "happiness," traced back to 1530 by *The Oxford English Dictionary*, was "good fortune or luck in life," which reflected the belief that happiness comes from external circumstances largely outside of a person's control. Psychologist Shigehiro Oishi, who has examined the historical definitions of happiness, notes that it was not until the 1961 *Webster's Third New International Dictionary* that the definition of happiness as "good fortune; good luck; prosperity" was deemed archaic. Rather than uncontrollable things that happen to people, happiness came to mean a pleasant internal state or the satisfaction of one's desires. Oishi suggests that because life became more controllable over time, happiness was no longer viewed as the result of whims of fortune but something that people could strive for and achieve.[8]

This isn't to say that happiness is completely under our control. In fact, a sizable portion of our happiness is determined by our genetic makeup, which is good news for those of us who inherited lots of "happy" genes and bad news for those of us who did not. I'm sure this doesn't come as a big surprise; we all know people who have a naturally sunny disposition and others who are so grumpy that they can barely crack a smile even under the happiest of circumstances. Another thing that is obviously hard to change is the economic and political environment in which we live, such as whether we happen to be born into an impoverished family in a country plagued by human rights abuses, poverty, violence, and political instability (think of Zimbabwe) or into a comfortable family in a politically stable country such as the United States. Research shows that people living in Zimbabwe, for example, are among the unhappiest in the world. Similarly, people in several of the former Soviet-bloc countries report low levels of happiness. An American journalist, during a visit to Prague in 2009, gave this explanation of why Czech citizens seem so dour:

> On the tram and the metro no one was listening to music, or reading, or smiling. Almost everyone was staring, downcast, at a spot on the floor. Richard [the tour director] explained that this was a hangover from decades of Soviet rule. When tourists started flocking to the city in the '90s, they noticed that no one in Prague laughed. It was the result of decades of conditioning. "If you stood out, if you drew attention to yourself, you were suspect. And you never knew who was looking, so people just retreated."[9]

To be fair, Czech citizens report greater levels of happiness on international surveys than do the citizens of several other former

Soviet-controlled countries, such as Armenia, Moldova, Belarus, and Ukraine. But they report a much lower level of happiness than do the residents of countries such as Denmark, Canada, Ireland, New Zealand, and the United States.[10]

In addition to political and economic conditions, there are other life circumstances that are not completely under our control but exert a major influence on our happiness. Good health and enough money to meet our basic needs are obvious examples. Another is being blessed with loving family and friends. In fact, happiness researchers will tell you that the number one predictor of how happy people are is the quality of their social relationships. We are an incredibly social species, and frequent contact with friends and family is vital to our well-being. Health, money, and love are controllable to some degree, of course, but if they were completely under our control no one would die of cancer, poverty would disappear, and there would be no more lonely-hearts clubs.

Happiness, then, is due in part to the hand we are dealt, in terms of our genes and life circumstances. Some happiness researchers have tried to estimate the extent to which human happiness is due to these uncontrollable factors, arguing, for example, that 50 percent of happiness is genetic and 10 percent is due to life circumstances. I don't think that such numbers mean very much, because the effects of our genes are not independent of the effects of our environment—the two interact in complex ways. As the emerging field of epigenetics shows, environmental conditions can influence the activation and expression of certain genes and not others. Maybe, for example, "curmudgeon" genes are especially likely to be activated when people are under severe stress, but lay dormant otherwise. Further, the nature of our life circumstances—whether extreme or moderate—surely influences how much impact those circumstances have. I doubt that people living in Zimbabwe would agree that their life circumstances account for only 10 percent of their happiness.

ROOM TO MANEUVER

But surely we need more than good genes and comfortable living conditions in order to be happy. If that were all there was to it, we wouldn't be much different from our mammalian cousins, including pigs, who are content when they have room to forage, ample food, and a nice mud bath to wallow in when the weather turns warm. Well, one could argue, maybe we *aren't* that different from pigs; it's just that we have more sophisticated needs than a good mud bath (unless it's the kind found at an expensive spa). Give me the human version of comfortable living conditions, this argument goes, such as a McMansion, fancy cars to fill its three-car garage, and a wide-screen TV, and I'll be as happy as that pig. But, as we saw with Gus Godsey, this argument is flawed. As long as we have enough resources to meet our basic needs, adding Lexuses and McMansions to the mix won't make us all that much happier in the long run. In the final analysis, it is not material goods that make people happy.

That's because of a big difference between us and pigs: we have a huge brain, with a well-developed prefrontal cortex, with which we can ponder our life circumstances and our place in the world. We need to find meaning in our lives—to acquire what Aristotle called *eudaimonia*, a life well-lived with a sense of purpose and virtue. How do we define "a life well-lived" and "virtue"? This question has occupied philosophers for centuries and I certainly won't answer it here. My point is simply that happiness is at least in part a function of how we think about ourselves and our place in the world. It's not just about things; it's about our personal take on our lives.

But let me be very clear about what I *don't* mean. Happiness doesn't exist solely inside of our heads, disconnected from reality. I would never argue that a resident of Zimbabwe should just develop a better interpretation of his or her lot in order to be happy (sounds like another *Saturday Night Live* skit in the making). Nor would I argue that we should focus only on our personal viewpoints at the expense of changing our behavior. If I were to give one piece of advice for how to be happier, it would be to carve out more time to spend with friends and loved ones, because, as we've seen, the best predictor of happiness is the quality of our social relationships.

But happiness is partly in our heads—some ways of viewing the world make us happier than others, even if our objective circumstances remain the same. There are plenty of middle-aged stockbrokers in America but only one Gus Godsey—his outlook on life makes him happier than others. And further, some kinds of perspectives make people act in ways that bring them happiness—by drawing them closer to other people, for example.

What kinds of perspectives make us happy? Research reveals three key ingredients: *meaning*, *hope*, and *purpose*. First, it helps to have answers to the most basic questions about human existence and our place in the world, in a way that allows us to make sense of why bad things sometimes occur. Second, it helps to be optimistic—not because positive thoughts magically attract things to us, but because optimistic people cope better with adversity. Third, it helps to view ourselves as strong protagonists who set our own goals and make progress toward them; in other words, to have a sense of purpose. The good news is that there are relatively simple story-editing exercises any of us can do to shape our views in these directions.

FINDING MEANING

As we've seen, one of the main differences between us and the rest of the animal kingdom is that we have a large brain with which we can construct elaborate theories and explanations about what is happening in the world and why. This gives us a huge advantage—after all, we are the ones who domesticated pigs and now use them as a food source, rather than the other way around. But our ability to think and ponder and reflect comes with a heavy price tag, namely, awareness of our own mortality. We are the only species (as far as we know) aware of what is ultimately in store for us. We can gaze into the dark sky on a clear night and think about how small and insignificant we are, how fleeting is our time on earth, and how we are nothing more than tiny temporary specks in an endless universe. Getting a little nervous? It is so unsettling to think such thoughts that we have developed narratives that provide comforting answers. These are *core narratives*—worldviews that explain creation, the purpose of life, and what happens after we die, thereby helping us deal with the terror of gazing into the sky and seeing ourselves as insignificant specks.[11]

Organized religions are important sources of core narratives. Virtually all faiths explain how we came to be, how we ought to live, and what happens to us after we die. Many studies show that religious people are happier than nonreligious people. To get these benefits, though, you can't just go down to your local church, synagogue, or mosque and fill out a membership card. Religious people are happier only if they truly believe and those beliefs are shared by their loved ones. If people have fragmented religious beliefs that are not well integrated into their overall lives, and if these beliefs are not supported by their loved ones, they are no happier than anyone else. Research also shows that people who believe in the devil and hell are less happy than people who do not. Apparently, worrying that we might end up at Satan's side in everlasting flames confers less happiness than believing that—no worries!—we are guaranteed a spot in the eternal Eden.[12]

Core narratives don't have to be religious in nature. "Whatever gets you through the night," as John Lennon sang, can reduce existential terror, as long as it is a coherent set of beliefs that explains life's mysteries. Being a cat person might even work, as in the Sam Gross cartoon opposite.[13] The guru in that cartoon is surely happier than the one in a cartoon by Lee Lorenz that depicts a guru sitting on a mountaintop wearing a T-shirt that says, "Life is a bitch, then you die." We all need core narratives to make sense of life's most basic questions.

"The meaning of life is cats."

To a large extent, we acquire core narratives from our culture and parents and religions. We are provided with a ready-made belief system about the major questions in life, and for many of us, this is perfectly fine. Perhaps we went to church with our parents, have continued with that religion, and are happy with the spiritual guidance it provides. Other people, however, question their core narratives at some point in their lives, coming to believe that the religion they were brought up with does not provide all the answers or that the prevailing cultural view about "the good life" is not for them. If they are lucky, they are able to find a new set of core beliefs that answer life's most basic questions.

What about those of us who struggle with our basic beliefs? Some of us have lost faith in the core beliefs of our childhoods and haven't found a compelling new narrative. I'm afraid that there is no easy fix here; we can't wave a magic wand and suddenly believe in Christianity or Judaism or, for that matter, the wonder of cats. Most of us have at least some core beliefs, however, whether they are our political views, our desire for social change, or a passion for sports (in the words of Annie Savoy, from the movie *Bull Durham*, "I believe in the Church of Baseball"). In order to develop and validate those beliefs, one thing we can do is to hang out with like-minded individuals. I say this with some reluctance, because seeking out only people who share our beliefs, and avoiding those who do not, is not a good way to stretch one's mind and is likely to contribute to the polarization of viewpoints that is so endemic today. But the fact is that interacting with people who share our core beliefs is a way to strengthen and validate those beliefs.

Further, other people are a source of comfort when our most basic core beliefs are challenged, such as when we are reminded of our own mortality. When Americans first heard about the terrorist attacks on September 11, 2001, their first impulse, in many cases, was to seek out loved ones. Even strangers can reduce our anxiety. A friend told me a story about a time when she was on a commercial airplane that developed engine trouble. The pilot announced that he would have to make an emergency landing and it was far from certain that the plane could land safely. As the plane lurched and yawed on its approach, an older man seated next to my friend asked if she would mind if they held hands. She had not spoken previously with the man, but readily agreed to his request, and they squeezed their hands tightly together as the plane bounced on the runway and finally skidded safely to a stop. My friend reports that she received great comfort from that small gesture; it was reassuring to face the abyss hand in hand with someone—even a complete stranger—rather than alone.[14]

Understanding Life's Setbacks

It is thus critical to have core narratives about the basic questions of life. But let's say that we have that covered—we have a coherent narrative that keeps existential terror at bay and loved ones who share those views. That's great, but we are still going to experience the spills and tumbles, hassles and setbacks that plague everyone from time to time. The better we can understand and explain negative events such as relationship breakups, business failures, or medical problems, the faster we will recover from them. Obviously, some kinds of explanations make us feel better than others; as we will see shortly, optimists put more of a positive spin on negative outcomes than do pessimists, enabling them to cope better and bounce back more quickly. But achieving *some* understanding of a negative event is preferable to having no understanding at all. In fact, we feel worst when we are in a state of uncertainty, either about why something terrible has happened to us or about the likelihood that a negative event will occur.

Suppose, for example, that you are in your twenties and that one of your parents died of Huntington's disease, which causes nerve degeneration in the brain and slowly kills people in middle age (it is the disease that killed the singer Woody Guthrie). The disease is genetically transmitted, and if one of your parents had it, you have a 50 percent chance of getting it yourself. But because the symptoms of the disease generally don't appear until people are in their thirties or forties, you must endure many years of living in uncertainty. Recently, however, a genetic test was developed that can, in most cases, identify whether you have inherited the gene that will trigger the disease. You can take the test and find out the good news—you didn't inherit the gene—or the really bad news—you have the gene and, because there is no cure for Huntington's, you will die of the disease in middle age. Would you take the test? Maybe it would be best to leave well enough alone and let nature take its course.

According to at least one study, that would be the wrong decision. Researchers followed a sample of young adults who had a 50 percent chance of getting Huntington's disease and who agreed to take the genetic test. The participants completed measures of depression and psychological well-being before they knew the results of the genetic test, right after they got the results, six months later, and one year later. Those who got the bad news were, of course, initially devastated, reporting considerably more distress and depression than did those who got the good news. At the six-month and one-year points, however, the two groups were indistinguishable—those who knew that they would die at a relatively young age were no more depressed, and expressed just as much well-being, as did those who knew that they were disease-free. The participants who learned they had the gene received the worst news one can get, and yet within six months they were as happy as anyone else.

Even more striking were the results of a third group—those for whom the test was inconclusive or who had chosen not to take the test. At the beginning of the study, before any genetic testing had begun, this group was as happy and well-adjusted as the others. But as time went by, this group did the worst: at the one-year mark, they exhibited significantly more depression, and lower well-being, than those in the other two groups—including the ones who had found out that they had inherited the Huntington gene. In other words, people who were 100 percent sure that they would get the disease and die prematurely were happier and less depressed than people who were 50 percent sure that they were healthy and disease-free.

This study illustrates, I think, how adept people are at making sense of even the worst news. Those who learned that they had inherited the Huntington's gene found a way to come to terms with it, by incorporating this news into their narratives and finding some meaning in it. Perhaps they relied on their religious beliefs about God's will, or maybe they developed a view of themselves as people whose time would be short but who would live life to the fullest. Those who remained uncertain about their health status could not undergo this restorative process of narrative change, because there was always the possibility that they didn't have the gene. In other words, the uncertain person doesn't know what to make sense of, whereas the certain one can begin the process of meaning-making and understanding and explanation for even the bleakest of outcomes. And by so doing, that person adapts and recovers—because once we reach an understanding of what something means and why it occurred, we dwell on it less and its impact wanes.[15]

Thus, making sense of negative outcomes is the first step to recovering from them, a principle that has been demonstrated in many areas of life. Studies of bereavement, for example, find that people who recover the quickest from the death of a loved one are those who can find some meaning in their loss (religious beliefs can be of help here). Many forms of psychotherapy involve giving clients a framework within which to understand their problems and experiences, such as childhood traumas. And by understanding them, they dwell on them less, as noted by a character in Ian McEwan's novel *Enduring Love:* "People often remark on how quickly the extraordinary becomes commonplace... We are highly adaptive creatures. The predictable becomes, by definition, background, leaving the attention uncluttered, the better to deal with the random or unexpected."[16]

What if we haven't succeeded in making a traumatic event seem understandable and predictable? Are there story-editing approaches that we can use in our everyday lives to hasten this process? Indeed there are, and we have already encountered one of them in chapter 1: the Pennebaker writing technique, in which people wait until they have some distance from a problem, then write about it for at least fifteen minutes on each of three or four consecutive days. As we saw, this is a simple yet powerful way of making sense of confusing, upsetting episodes in our lives, giving us some closure and allowing us to move on.

Subsequent research has found that the writing exercise works best when two conditions are met: people gain some distance from the event, so that thinking about it doesn't overwhelm them, and they analyze *why* the event occurred. To understand this, take a minute to think of a time from your past when you felt a great deal of anger and hostility toward someone. Maybe it was an ex-lover who cheated on you, or the boss from hell who hovered over your desk and made every work day miserable. If you are like most people, when you think about episodes like these you immerse yourself in them as if they were happening again. You see the veins bulge on your boss's neck when he yells at you for no reason and recall in excruciating detail what it was like when he called you into his office and tore up the report you had spent weeks preparing. How are you feeling as you relive the episode? Research shows that this "immersion" strategy causes people to re-experience negative emotions and engage in repetitive, circular rumination about the event, and triggers unhealthy cardiovascular reactions, including an increase in blood pressure. Basically, people relive the event without making any further sense of it than they did before, and feel terrible as a result.

But suppose you adopt another approach. Instead of immersing yourself in the original experience, you take a step back and watch it unfold from the perspective of a neutral observer. Then you focus on *why* you feel the way you do, rather than on the feelings themselves. Here is an excerpt from the instructions people are given in research studies testing this *step-back-and-ask-why* approach (the full instructions are at the end of this chapter): "Go back to the time and place of the experience you just recalled and see the scene in your mind's eye. Now take a few steps back. Move away from the situation to a point where you can now watch the event unfold from a distance and see yourself in the event...As you continue to watch the situation unfold to your distant self, try to understand his/her feelings. Why did he (she) have those feelings?"

Several studies have tested the effectiveness of this step-back-and-ask-why strategy by using the experimental methods described in chapter 2. In one study, for example, participants were asked to think of a time they felt "overwhelming anger and hostility" toward someone, just as I asked you to do a moment ago. Participants were then randomly assigned to either immerse themselves in the experience or to adopt the distancing approach. Further, half of the participants in each of these groups were asked to focus on the feelings they experienced at the time, and half were asked to think about the reasons behind their feelings. There were thus four experimental groups: (1) those who immersed and focused on feelings, (2) those who immersed and thought about reasons, (3) those who distanced themselves and focused on feelings, and (4) those who distanced themselves and thought about reasons.

As it happened, only one of these groups benefited from the writing exercise: those who distanced themselves and thought about reasons. Only these participants were able to adopt a dispassionate approach whereby they reframed the event and found new meaning in it (e.g., "I see now that my boss's anger had more to do with his impending divorce than with anything about me, and now that I think about it, I have to admit that I could have done a better job on that report"). And, by reconstruing the event, participants in this group experienced fewer negative emotions, engaged in less repetitive rumination, and maintained a steady blood pressure. As simple as this sounds, it is an easy lesson to forget, because for most of us, our natural inclination is to immerse ourselves in past grievances and upsetting events, engaging in a "he said, she said" internal dialogue that makes us feel bad all over again. The next time you think about an upsetting event from your past, remember to take a step back and analyze it from a distance, and to think dispassionately about why it occurred. In short, don't *recount* the event, take a step back and *reconstrue and explain* it.[17]

George Bailey and the Pleasures of Uncertainty

What about when we recall pleasant events? Should we adopt the same distancing strategy, trying our best to understand why something good happened to us? There is a clear advantage to doing so; after all, by understanding why the attractive stranger smiled at us at the party, or why our boss liked our report, we are in a better position to make these events happen again. But herein lies a paradox—just as understanding and explaining negative events blunts their impact, so does understanding and explaining positive events. That is, as we have seen, reducing uncertainty about negative events, and understanding them as best we can, is a good way to bounce back from these events. But the same holds for the pleasures of life: if we reduce uncertainty about them, and understand them too well, we rob these events of the pleasure they bring us. My colleagues and I call this phenomenon the *pleasure of uncertainty* to convey the idea that a little mystery about positive events prolongs the pleasure we get from them.

In one study, for example, a research assistant approached a student studying alone in the library and gave him or her a card with a dollar coin attached to it. "Have a nice day," the assistant said, and walked away. Imagine you were the recipient of this unexpected gift. You would likely be perplexed as to why a stranger had just given you a dollar, and would search the card for an explanation. The text on the card wasn't much help: it said, "The Smile Society, a Student/Community Secular Alliance," and "We Like to Promote Random Acts of Kindness." That gives you a clue as to who gave you a dollar—it wasn't some religious cult trying to convert you—but it is still pretty perplexing. We suspected that this element of mystery would keep people's attention on the gift and prolong the pleasure they got from it. This seemed to be the case: when another research assistant approached the students and asked them to complete a short survey, they indicated that they were in a good mood—more so than people in a control condition who hadn't received a gift.

But how did we know that it was the mystery about the card that prolonged people's pleasure? We included another condition in which we gave people the same gift but tried to reduce the mystery surrounding it. We did so with a subtle alteration of the text, namely, the addition of questions to which the aforementioned phrases seemed like logical answers. For example, we inserted the question, "Who Are We?" which was answered with the same text as the other participants got: "The Smile Society, a Student/Community Secular Alliance." We also inserted the question, "Why do we do this?" to which the text "We Like to Promote Random Acts of Kindness" provided the answer. In other words, participants in this group got the same information as did participants in the first group, except that it was framed in a question-and-answer format that, we suspected, would give people the impression that they understood why a stranger had given them a dollar. We also assumed that this understanding would make people dwell on the event less—they would be more likely to return to their studying instead of thinking about the event, which would shorten the pleasure they got from the gift. Just as we thought, people in this question-and-answer condition reported a less positive mood when approached by the research assistant with the survey than did people who got the card with the answers but not the questions. (Other students who saw the cards confirmed our hunch that the ones with the questions and answers appeared to make more sense and seemed less mysterious.)[18]

In short, there seems to be a pleasure paradox: people want to understand the good things in life so that they can experience them again, but by so doing they reduce the pleasure they get from these events. Furthermore, the pleasure paradox helps explain why a popular way of increasing happiness—keeping gratitude journals, in which people write about the things in their lives for which they are thankful—does not always work. Although it seems like taking time to stop and smell the flowers in this manner would increase people's well-being, studies that have examined this technique have yielded mixed results. A few studies have found that keeping gratitude journals makes people happier, but many others have found that doing so has no impact on people's happiness. The reason gratitude journals can be ineffective, I think, is that people typically spend a lot of time thinking about the good things that have happened to them, and thus by the time they sit down to write about these events they have already achieved an understanding of them and robbed them of some of their mystery.

The first time I had an article accepted for publication in a professional journal, for example, I was thrilled. "Maybe I really can make it as a research psychologist," I thought, and I basked in the good news for days. But that first publication was followed by others, and in retrospect it doesn't seem all that significant in the grand scheme of things. I am thankful when I think about the article (which I haven't done in some time before writing about it now), but stopping and smelling that particular rose doesn't do much for my current mood, to be honest. In McEwan's words, "the extraordinary becomes commonplace."

Fortunately, there is a way around this problem. Instead of writing about something you are grateful for, like a career breakthrough, try writing about all the ways that that good thing might *not* have occurred. My colleagues and I call this the George Bailey technique: you may recall that, in the movie *It's a Wonderful Life*, an angel named Clarence Odbody shows George what the world would have been like if he had never been born. Rather than asking George to count his blessings, Clarence allows him to see a world in which those blessings never came about. Similarly, in our research we ask people to mentally subtract from their lives something they cherish. In one study, for example, happily married participants imagined what life would be like if they had never met their spouses, had never begun dating them after they met, and had not ended up together after starting to date. Other participants were randomly assigned to a condition in which they wrote about how they did in fact meet their partners, began dating, and ended up together.

Before I tell you the results of this study, think about which writing exercise you would rather do: would you prefer to spend time thinking about all the ways you might not have ended up with your partner, or to tell the story of how you did end up with him or her? If you are like our participants, you would overwhelmingly prefer the latter task and predict that it would make you happier. After all, who wants to dwell on the fact that they easily could have missed the party at which they met their future husband or wife? In fact, however, the participants randomly assigned to do just that—those in the George Bailey condition—reported greater happiness with their relationship than did people randomly assigned to tell the story of how they had met their spouses. The latter participants had undoubtedly told that story countless times, and telling it again had little impact. But imagining how one of the most important things in their lives might not have happened made it seem surprising and special again, and maybe a little mysterious—the very conditions that prolong the pleasure we get from the good things in life.[19]

To recap, a critical element to our well-being is how well we understand what happens to us and why. But so far we haven't said much about the *way* in which we understand positive and negative events, which is surely important. Consider the people who took the genetic test and found out that they had the Huntington's gene. The one who puts a positive spin on this, deciding to live life to its fullest and do all the things she always wanted to do, will be happier than the one who wallows in self-pity and decides that she must have done something to deserve this cruel fate. Similarly, as we saw in chapter 1, a student who does poorly on a test is better off explaining this as a sign that she needs to buckle down and work harder than she is assuming that she doesn't have what it takes to succeed in college. True, the worst state to be in is uncertainty about the nature of a negative event or why it occurred. But it is also true that some ways of understanding and explaining negative events are better than others, particularly if one can find a silver lining in the cloud of bad news.

HOPE: THE REAL POWER OF POSITIVE THINKING

Let's return to the student who did poorly on a test. Research shows that how he explains his bad performance is critical to his well-being and future performance. People who attribute negative events (such as failing a test) to things about themselves that are hard to change and that affect a broad spectrum of their lives experience learned helplessness, which puts them at risk for depression and poor health, gives them low expectations about the future, and makes them likely to give up easily on future tasks. People who attribute negative events to things that they can control and change, such as the time they spend studying for the next test, are less likely to be depressed, are less likely to have health problems, and are more likely to try harder when the going gets tough. We saw evidence for this in chapter 1 in my study with college freshmen: those who learned that many people experience academic problems in the first year of college, but do better thereafter, had reason to hope that they would do better in the future. And indeed they did, compared to a control group who did not get the message that the causes of bad grades are temporary.[20]

More generally, people who have a hopeful, optimistic outlook on life are happier and healthier than people who have a hopeless, pessimistic outlook. As an example, take a moment to answer the questions in the table opposite and compute your score. This questionnaire, called the Life Orientation Test (Revised), is the most commonly used measure of optimism.[21] Studies have shown that the higher people score on this test, the happier they are, because they are better at dealing with life's traumas. For example, optimists are less likely to experience postpartum depression and less likely to experience distress after coronary bypass surgery or following a diagnosis of cancer. And optimists tend to be healthier, as measured by the reports of their physicians and such things as survival time following a heart attack.

LIFE ORIENTATION TEST—REVISED

Instructions

Please answer the following questions about yourself by indicating the extent of your agreement using the following scale:

0 = Strongly disagree
1 = Disagree
2 = Neutral
3 = Agree
4 = Strongly agree

Be as honest and as accurate as you can throughout, and try not to let your responses to one question influence your responses to other questions. There are no right or wrong answers.

_____ 1. In uncertain times, I usually expect the best.
_____ 2. It's easy for me to relax.
_____ 3. If something can go wrong for me, it will.
_____ 4. I'm always optimistic about my future.
_____ 5. I enjoy my friends a lot.
_____ 6. It's important for me to keep busy.
_____ 7. I hardly ever expect things to go my way.
_____ 8. I don't get upset too easily.
_____ 9. I rarely count on good things happening to me.
_____ 10. Overall, I expect more good things to happen to me than bad.

Scoring

A. Reverse-code your answers to questions 3, 7, and 9. That is, if you answered 0, change it to a 4; if you answered 1, change it to a 3; if you answered 3, change it to a 1; and if you answered 4, change it to a 0.

B. Sum your answers to questions 1, 3 (reversed), 4, 7 (reversed), 9 (reversed), and 10. Ignore your answers to questions 2, 5, 6, and 8; those are filler items.

The higher your score, the more optimistic you tend to be. The authors of the scale found that the average score for college students was 14.3. Men and women did not differ significantly in their levels of optimism.

This research seems consistent with the message in many self-help books, such as *The Secret* and *The Power of Positive Thinking*; i.e., we simply need to think positive thoughts in order to get what we want. But it isn't just sitting in our armchairs and having positive thoughts that does the trick. Instead, research shows that there is an *optimistic way of behaving* that makes people happier. What really sets optimists apart is that they have better coping strategies in the face of adversity — they confront problems rather than avoid them, plan better for the future, focus on what they can control and change, and persist when they encounter obstacles instead of giving up. It is important to add that optimists do not have their heads buried in the sand. Obviously it would not be good for people to smoke cigarettes with abandon, eat whatever they like, and drive 120 miles per hour on the interstate because they are convinced that nothing bad will happen to them. Instead, optimists see the world the way it really is and recognize the obstacles in their path, but also believe that they can overcome these obstacles by planning for them and redoubling their efforts when they fail. In short, optimists don't just sit back and think positive thoughts — they have an adaptive, healthy way of coping with the world.[22]

All of this raises the question of whether it is possible to become more optimistic. If you are the kind of person who sees the glass as half empty, is there something you can do to change your outlook so that you see it as half full? The bad news is that optimism is, in part, a deeply rooted trait that is not completely malleable. In fact, there is evidence that it has a genetic component, just as happiness does.

But, as with happiness, there is room to maneuver — people can be trained to be more optimistic using story-editing techniques. In one study, college students participated in a group session in which they were taught to replace negative thoughts (e.g., "It's useless to engage in wishful thinking") with positive ones (e.g., "Wishful thinking can help people find alternative solutions to problems"); to engage in positive visualization, in which they vividly imagined positive outcomes (such as getting a desired job) and optimistic reactions to negative outcomes (such as not getting a desired job); and to complete a "silver lining" exercise, in which they found at least one positive aspect to a negative situation (e.g., "I didn't get the job in New York but at least I don't have to move far away from my family"). The students were instructed to practice these exercises on their own for a week. Compared to students who had been randomly assigned to a control group, at the end of the week those in the "optimism training" group reported more optimistic thoughts, felt better equipped to solve problems, and performed better on a task of creative problem solving.[23]

Although this intervention was successful, it required facilitators to guide people through the exercises. Fortunately, there is also a simple exercise that you can do on your own. Here's how it works: Think about your life in the future and write for twenty minutes, on four consecutive days, about how "everything has gone as well as it possibly could" and your life dreams have come true. (The exact instructions are at the end of this chapter, on page 73.) College students who completed this "best possible self" writing exercise, compared to students who were randomly assigned to write about a neutral topic, reported greater optimism on the questionnaire reproduced on page 65 and greater satisfaction with their lives—not just right away but three weeks later. And, in the five months following the study, the students who had written about their best possible selves visited the health center significantly less often than did students who wrote about the neutral topic.[24]

Can such a simple writing exercise really work? Well, we need to be careful how we do it, in order to avoid being like Stuart Smalley, who simply recites positive statements to himself. Smalley, a fictional character created by Al Franken on *Saturday Night Live*, looks in the mirror and repeats, "I'm good enough, I'm smart enough, and, doggone it, people like me!" (Smalley is reminiscent of the real-life Émile Coué, the French author who advised people, nearly a century ago, to repeat to themselves, "Every day, in every way, I'm getting better and better.") Unfortunately, it's not so simple, and in fact the Stuart Smalley approach can backfire among people who have low opinions of themselves—the very people who most need a boost. In one study, people with high or low self-esteem were randomly assigned to either the Stuart Smalley condition, in which they repeated the phrase "I am a lovable person" every fifteen seconds, or to a control condition, in which they did not repeat any phrases. People who already felt good about themselves showed a small benefit from repeating the phrase: compared to those in the control condition, their moods went up slightly. But those with low self-esteem became even more dispirited! For people with a low opinion of themselves, saying "I am a lovable person" reminds them of all the ways in which they are *not* lovable, pushing them further into the doldrums.[25]

Why doesn't repeating the phrase "I am a lovable person" work, when it is helpful to write for twenty minutes on four consecutive days about how "everything has gone as well as it possibly could"? The key difference is that simply thinking about how wonderful we are does not equip us with strategies to make ourselves so. But by imagining how well things will turn out in the future, we focus on ways of achieving those goals and think about what we need to do to get there. Indeed, research shows that people who focus on the *process* of achieving a desired outcome are more likely to achieve it than those who simply think about the outcome itself. Thus, Stuart Smalley would be better off writing for twenty minutes each day about the ways in which he could *become* good enough and smart enough instead of simply declaring it to be so.[26]

This research highlights a key problem with self-help books like *The Secret*. According to *The Secret*, all we have to do is sit in our armchairs and think about what we want and it will magically come to us. And therein lies the danger—people are told that they don't have to actually do anything, such as diet if they want to lose weight or study if they want to do well on a test. In fact, why diet or study if we can get what we want simply by thinking positive thoughts? Pass that bag of Doritos! In contrast, the optimism interventions we've just seen, such as the "best possible selves" writing exercise, don't simply instill positive thoughts, they change how people interpret events in ways that make it easier for them to *act* in beneficial ways. Optimists, for example, are more likely to stick to their diets because of their confidence that they can succeed. College students who believe they can improve their grades by studying harder actually do study harder.[27]

A SENSE OF PURPOSE

So far we've seen that happy people's narratives provide meaning, particularly about why bad things occur, as well as hopeful, optimistic outlooks on the future. Good narratives also have a strong protagonist, a leading woman or man who takes charge and works toward a desired goal. People who have such a narrative—who feel in control of their lives, have goals of their own choosing, and make progress toward those goals—are happier than people who do not. Thus we should strive to be like Indiana Jones pursuing the lost ark or Lara Croft seeking the Triangle of Light. We can't all be swashbuckling adventurers or multilingual tomb raiders, of course, but fortunately these aren't the only ways of feeling like effective, autonomous people who are good at what they do. There are accountants who feel this way, as well as teachers, doctors, lawyers, social workers—members of any profession, really, who love what they do. Nor do we have to find purpose in our professions as long as we have passions to follow elsewhere in our lives—through volunteer work, say, or our families, or a hobby. The important thing is to pursue goals that give us a sense of autonomy, effectiveness, and mastery. If we can do so in a way that draws us closer to other people, so much the better, given how important social relationships are to happiness.[28]

Not everyone has the freedom to pursue a life course of his or her own choosing, especially those who live in extreme poverty. Most of us, though, have some latitude in the goals we can set for ourselves. Consider college students deciding what career to pursue. As a college professor, I have talked to many students about what they want to do after they graduate. Not surprisingly, many students want to pursue careers that pay high salaries. I remember one student, for example, who told me that she would be applying to law school, not because of any particular interest in the law but because of the high salaries lawyers make. Compare her motives to another advisee of mine who applied to law school. Her father is a minister who founded a homeless shelter, and this student shares his commitment to helping people in need. A law degree would enable her to fulfill her goal of fighting poverty by providing legal services for people who could not otherwise afford them.

Let's fast-forward five years into the future and imagine what these students' lives are like. The first student has finished law school and has landed a job in a prestigious firm that pays her a six-figure salary. She has thus fulfilled her goal of becoming financially secure. But she has little control over her life and no sense of satisfaction in what she does. She is expected to work up to eighty hours a week and to answer e-mails from clients within an hour at any time of day or night, except when she is asleep (which, given her schedule, exempts her for only a few hours a night). She has little interest in the details of the cases she works on, which have to do with corporate acquisitions. She has few friends at work, and in fact finds herself in a competitive environment where several associates are vying for a limited number of partnership positions in the firm.

Student number two finishes law school and secures a job at a legal-aid office in her hometown. Although her salary is a fraction of what she could earn in a private law firm, she earns enough to live on. She has considerable latitude in the kinds of cases she selects; recently, she decided to bring a class-action suit against a landlord who owned a number of substandard housing units in a high-poverty part of town. There is an esprit de corps at her office; after all, no one is in it for the money and no one is competing for limited partnership positions. She becomes close to several of the other new attorneys and hangs out with them after work and on weekends.

Obviously, the first lawyer's wealth will give her opportunities the second lawyer doesn't have, such as the ability to buy a house in the best school district (should she have kids) and the opportunity to retire at a young age. But lawyer number two has a lot of advantages that the first lawyer doesn't have—advantages that young people often overlook when planning their futures. She has a greater sense of autonomy, effectiveness, and competence, as well as a closer connection to other people. Focusing on a full bank account can be important, but we shouldn't do so at the expense of a full life.

Another reason lawyer number two is likely to be happier is because of the do good, be good principle discussed in chapter 1. We are all observers of our own behavior and draw conclusions about ourselves by watching what we do. Just as most people would admire the second lawyer for devoting her life to helping others, at considerable financial cost to herself, so is she likely to admire herself. Indeed, research shows that people who help others are happier than those who do not. They are more likely to form bonds with others and to acquire an image of themselves as effective, worthy people. It is probably no accident that Gus Godsey, for example, volunteers a great deal of his time to many charities and community organizations, including the Juvenile Diabetes Research Foundation, the Richard Hassell Foundation, and the Virginia Beach Human Rights Commission. Twenty years ago, he started a Thanksgiving and holiday food and toy drive, and more recently he started the Mr. Happy USA Foundation, which raises money for seniors. Thus one of the best ways to achieve a sense of purpose is to find an activity you enjoy in which you are helping others.[29]

USING IT

In this chapter, we applied the story-editing approach to personal happiness. Happy narratives, we saw, are those that give people meaning, hope, and purpose. And there are a number of techniques we can use to revise our narratives in these directions, including simple writing exercises, maintaining a sense of purpose, and the do good, be good approach. Each of these techniques has been shown to make people happier. If you want to give them a try, here are specific instructions:

The Pennebaker Writing Exercise: Is there something in your life that you are particularly worried or upset about right now? If it has been on your mind for several weeks, and keeps bubbling back up to the surface of your thoughts, you might want to try the Pennebaker writing exercise. Find a quiet, private place to write. Commit to writing about your problem for at least fifteen minutes a day for three or four consecutive days—ideally, at the end of the day—and write without interruption each time. You can write longhand or on a computer, or even talk into a tape recorder instead of writing. You can find more specific instructions on James Pennebaker's Web page: http://homepage.psy.utexas.edu/homepage/Faculty/Pennebaker/Home2000/WritingandHealth.html.

The Step-Back-and-Ask-Why Approach: As we saw earlier in this chapter, there is another writing exercise that helps people get over events from their past that they find particularly upsetting or depressing. After recalling an upsetting or sad event, follow these instructions:

Close your eyes. Go back to the time and place of the experience you just recalled and see the scene in your mind's eye.

Now take a few steps back (in your mind). Move away from the situation to a point where you can now watch the event unfold from a distance and see yourself in the event. As you do this, focus on what has now become the distant you.

Now watch the experience unfold as if it were happening to the distant you all over again.

Replay the event as it unfolds in your imagination as you observe your distant self. Take a few moments to do this.

As you continue to watch the situation unfold to your distant self, try to understand his/her feelings. Why did he (she) have those feelings? What were the underlying causes and reasons?[30]

The Best Possible Selves Exercise: If you would rather not dredge up upsetting events from the past, and prefer to focus on the positive, try this writing exercise. Again, find a quiet, private place and follow these instructions on four consecutive nights: "Think about your life in the future. Imagine that everything has gone as well as it possibly could. You have worked hard and succeeded at accomplishing all of your life goals. Think of this as the realization of all of your life dreams. Now, write about what you imagined."[31]

Don't just think about what you have achieved (e.g., getting your dream job), but be sure to write about *how* you got there (e.g., doing an internship, going to graduate school). By so doing you might become more optimistic about your future and cope better with any obstacles you encounter.

Maintain a Sense of Purpose: In a classic *Peanuts* comic strip, Sally is merrily jumping rope when suddenly she bursts into tears. "What's the matter?" asks her friend Linus. Sally replies, "I was jumping rope...Everything was all right...When...I don't know...Suddenly it all seemed so futile."[32] When we find ourselves in Sally's boat, we should remind ourselves of our most important goals in life and find ways of making progress toward them. Caring for our families is the most important goal for many of us, and for many of us there are ways we can do it better. Others find meaning and purpose in their religions, professions, communities, or, as in the cartoon earlier in this chapter, in the world of cats. Whatever it is that gives us a sense of purpose, we should be sure to make time in our lives to pursue it. As obvious as this advice sounds, people sometimes forget to follow it when choosing careers or deciding how to spend their leisure time.

The Do Good, Be Good Principle: We can't all be as happy as Gus Godsey—after all, some of us inherited those curmudgeon genes, and some of us endure gut-wrenching blows such as losing our jobs or seeing a relationship disintegrate. But we can all *act* like Gus Godsey, by engaging in a lot of volunteer work, trying to find the positive in whatever we must endure, and connecting ourselves to other people. By so doing, our narratives will change to match our behavior and we will move a little closer to Gus on the happiness scale.

CHAPTER 4

Shaping Our Kids' Narratives
Becoming Better Parents

I was sitting in a rocking chair in the nursery of the hospital where my son had just been born—this wonderful, delicate, perfect little human being cradled in my arms. I could barely contain my joy as I waited to rejoin my wife, who was in the operating room recovering from the C-section birth. I guess my son wasn't quite as thrilled, because after a few minutes he began to fuss and cry. "Uh-oh," I thought. "What do I do now?" Just then a nurse walked by and handed me a pacifier, which my son readily accepted. He was happily sucking away when another nurse walked by, glanced at me disapprovingly, and said, "So— you've made the choice to use a pacifier, have you?"

"Oh my God!" I thought. "I've already made a critical parenting decision without even knowing it! You mean some parents don't give their babies pacifiers? They didn't cover this in our Lamaze class. What does the research say? Have I doomed my son to a life of oral dependency? What if he refuses to breast-feed? What am I going to tell my wife?"

As I learned, parents have to make a constant stream of decisions from the moment their babies are born. I also learned that it is easy to exaggerate the importance of these decisions. I don't think it mattered that I plopped a pacifier in my son's mouth; he easily learned to nurse, and my wife and I couldn't be prouder of the adult he has grown up to be (we are equally proud of his younger sister). Surely whether we give our children pacifiers, wrap them in disposable or cloth diapers, or put them down to sleep at 7:00 p.m. or 8:00 p.m. does not determine whether they live fruitful, happy lives or become juvenile delinquents. Some researchers even argue that parents don't make much difference at all. According to this viewpoint, our kids' futures are determined largely by their genes and their peers, and as long as we don't abuse them, they'll do just fine.[1]

But I think the pendulum has swung too far over to the "parents don't matter" camp. There is plenty of research showing that parents exert a huge influence on their kids' cognitive and emotional development. Consider, for example, the fact that children born into families of high socioeconomic status (SES) have higher IQs, on average, than children born into families of low socioeconomic status. Some researchers argue that this is due to genetic differences in intelligence, namely, the possibility that people with high IQs are more likely to "rise to the top" economically, to marry people with high IQs, and then to pass these "high IQ" genes on to their children. The social psychologist Richard Nisbett, however, has argued persuasively against this strict "hereditarian" view of intelligence, pointing out that one reason for the class difference in IQ is different child-rearing practices. Higher-SES parents talk a lot more to their children than do lower-SES parents—on the order of two thousand words per hour versus thirteen hundred words per hour. By the age of three, children of higher-SES parents know 50 percent more words than do the children of lower-SES parents. And it's not just the volume of words: higher-SES parents talk to their kids in a way that encourages them to question, analyze, and think about the physical and social world, which sharpens their thinking and prepares them for school.[2]

There is also plenty of research showing that parents exert a huge influence on their kids' social and emotional development. Effective parents are attentive to their children's needs and form close attachments with them, which allows the children to internalize healthy narratives about relationships—narratives that increase the likelihood that they will form trusting, loving relationships with others throughout their lives. Effective parents also know how to shape their children's behavior in ways that encourage them to internalize desired values and attitudes. But how do good parents learn how to do this?

Many mothers and fathers trust their instincts and hope for the best. Others rely on the wisdom of their elders, including their own parents and grandparents. Still others seek advice from the dozens of parenting books that are available. Indeed, the number of books advising parents on how to raise their kids is rivaled only by the tomes in the self-help section of bookstores. There are books on "scream-free" parenting, "simplicity" parenting, and "playful" parenting, as well as *Parenting by the Book: Biblical Wisdom for Raising Your Child* and *The Complete Idiot's Guide to Fatherhood*. There are countless books on how to discipline kids, including *Parenting with Love and Logic, Making Children Mind Without Losing Yours,* and *Parenting Your Out-of-Control Teenager.*

For many years, one of the most popular parenting books was Benjamin Spock's *Baby and Child Care*, originally published in 1946. Although Dr. Spock died in 1998, the book is still in print and has sold millions of copies. One reason the book has been so popular is that it conveys the message that parents should relax, trust their instincts, not worry so much about rigid feeding schedules, and by all means pick up a crying baby without fear of spoiling her or him. This message was novel in the 1940s, when parents were advised to stick to strict schedules and to avoid spoiling their children. Countless parents of baby boomers—mine included—had dog-eared copies of *Baby and Child Care* that were trusted sources of advice. (When I was in college,

I had the opportunity to hear Dr. Spock give a talk to a large audience of students. He began by opening his arms wide and proclaiming, "My children!")

But Dr. Spock also said that trusting our instincts isn't enough: "There may have been a time when parents knew exactly how to bring up their children or thought they did. But for most of us now there simply aren't clear-cut rules to follow. We have more options, but there are also more choices that have to be made...Everywhere you turn, there are experts telling you what to do. The problem is, they often don't agree with each other!"[3]

This conundrum is by now familiar to readers of this book— grandmothers and other experts give us advice, but much of it conflicts and little of it has been adequately tested. Many parenting practices can't be tested experimentally, of course; no scientist in his or her right mind would randomly assign families to a condition in which they were asked to hit their children or to a control condition in which they were not. But many other techniques can be tested, and when they have been, the answers are often surprising.

In 1997, for example, a company named Baby Einstein released videos for young children that were designed, as the name implies, to enhance the intelligence of the toddlers who watched them. The Baby Einstein website says that the videos "are designed as interactive tools for parents to use with their babies...allowing a parent to have two free hands while enjoying and experiencing the video with their little one." Many parents, however, interpreted this to mean that their child would benefit from watching the video by him- or herself—kind of like a PBS documentary for toddlers. Who wouldn't feel good letting their child watch this video while they got some housework done or made a few phone calls? Several companies now market videos for kids and millions of children have watched them. As a result, these kids are exceedingly smart, right?[4]

Unfortunately not, because it turns out that toddlers do not learn very well from disembodied voice-overs on videos. Consider a clever study done by colleagues of mine at the University of Virginia, in which parents of twelve-to-eighteen-month-old infants were randomly assigned to one of four conditions. In one condition, the infants watched a commercial educational video by themselves, at least five times a week for four weeks. The video was designed to increase toddlers' vocabulary by introducing them to new words. The parents were in the room with the infants but did not watch the video with them. In a second condition, the infants watched the video for the same amount of time, but a parent watched with them. In a third condition, the infants never saw the video. Instead, the parents were given a list of the vocabulary words featured in the video and were instructed to teach their kids the words in whatever way seemed natural to them. The fourth condition was a control group in which the parents neither showed the video to their children nor taught them the words from it.

At the end of the four weeks, the researchers tested the children's knowledge of the words featured in the video. The testers, who did not know what condition the children had been in, showed the kids a pair of objects and asked the kids to point to the one the testers named (e.g., "Can you show me the clock?"). If the child pointed to the correct object, and "clock" was one of the words featured in the video, then bingo, the child got credit for having learned that word. Which group of kids learned the most words?

It turns out that there is no substitute for good old parent-child interaction: the kids whose parents tried to teach them the words, without showing them the video, learned the most words. The kids who saw the video, with or without their parents watching with them, didn't learn the words any better than did the kids in the control condition. Interestingly, many of the parents *thought* their children had learned a lot from the videos. In fact, the more the parents liked the videos, the more they thought their children had learned from them. Unfortunately, our instincts about what works best for our kids are not always correct.[5]

Okay, maybe we're not experts in language development. But surely we have good instincts about how to nurture our kids and make them feel good about themselves: all we need to do is to shower them with love and praise, right? Well, yes and no. It is important to form close emotional bonds with our children, but showering them with praise is not always the best thing to do.

We will see why in this chapter, which focuses on how parents can shape the narratives of their kids in healthy ways—namely, with story-editing interventions that have been tested scientifically. This is not a chapter on general parenting advice: there won't be any tips on how to cure diaper rash, get your child to sleep through the night, or help him or her deal with bullies. These are important topics, to be sure. But perhaps the most important thing parents do is redirect their children's views of themselves and the world—the personal interpretations that are the topic of this book and the blueprints by which children will live their lives. I'll begin with how parents can get their kids to develop a sense of autonomy and purpose, which, as we saw in the previous chapter, is a key element of a healthy adult narrative.

AUTONOMY AND PURPOSE

A few years ago, when I was chair of the psychology department at the University of Virginia, I experienced the phenomenon of "helicopter parents" firsthand. As I entered the building one day, the receptionist took me aside. "There's a man here to see you," she said. "He says he flew down from New York this morning to talk to you about his daughter." There he was, sitting impatiently with his daughter, a fourth-year psychology major. When I invited them into my office, the man wasted no time getting started: "I think it is outrageous," he said, "that my daughter can't get into the seminar of her choice."

By way of background: all of our psychology majors are required to take at least one small seminar, usually in their fourth year. But psychology is a popular major, and the seminars are popular courses, and competition for them is fierce. Not all students get their first choice. Such was the case with the student in my office; she had wanted to take a particular seminar but it had filled up quickly and there were no more spaces available. "I pay a big chunk of change in out-of-state tuition," her father continued. "And I think my daughter should be able to take the course she wants."

I explained that we do the best we can to fulfill all students' requests but that we can't give everyone their first choice. But the man wasn't satisfied: after he left my office he marched over to the main administration building and demanded to see the president of the university. Officials there politely told him that there was nothing they could do, and, alas, his daughter had to take her second choice of seminar.

Incidents such as this are not uncommon on college campuses. A few years ago, Judith Shapiro, then the president of Barnard College, wrote an op-ed piece in *The New York Times* asking parents to back off. She gave these examples of helicopter parenting on her campus: one father called his daughter's career counselor to get a list of prospective employers so that he could contact them and bring them up to date on her sterling qualities. A mother accompanied her daughter to a meeting with a dean so that she could help with her daughter's "independent" research project. When it came time for one young woman to apply to colleges, her father took a year off from his job to shepherd her through the process.[6]

Clearly, these parents were just trying to help. But what message were they conveying to their kids? The father who flew down to see me was a take-charge kind of guy, used to getting what he wanted, and he probably thought he was teaching his daughter a valuable lesson—namely, that it is a dog-eat-dog world and you have to push to get what you want. But I wonder if she learned something else entirely: "Dad will step in when I need help, so there's no need for me to figure out things for myself."

In the previous chapter, we saw that a key to happiness is having a sense of purpose and autonomy—to be able to set goals for oneself and decide how to pursue them. One of the best things we can do for our children is to help them develop this sense of autonomy—even if that means that they experience a few bumps along the way, such as not getting their first choice of seminar. Hovering over our children from birth through the college years, making every choice for them, is hardly the way to accomplish this.

But let's look back at more formative ages, when children's narratives about autonomy and control are developing. What can parents do when their kids are taking tentative steps out of the nest and becoming more independent, as they do during the important middle-school years? I'll begin with what parents *shouldn't* do, namely, adopt a highly domineering style in which they attempt to control every step their children take. Several studies have found that an intrusive, controlling parenting style is associated with low autonomy in children and low overall well-being.

In one study, students who were starting seventh grade, in the United States and China, were asked how decisions were typically made in their families—namely, whether they were most likely to decide things for themselves or whether their parents decided for them. The questions covered several areas that are important to seventh graders, such as who they make friends with, how much time they spend with their friends, what time they go to bed, how much time they spend studying, and what they do in their free time. In both countries, some kids reported that they had considerable latitude in making these choices, some reported that their parents decided for

them in most of the areas, and some reported that it was in between—
i.e., that they decided what to do in certain areas and their parents
decided for them in others. The researchers then tracked the kids for
the next two years and measured their emotional well-being. The
main result was that the more controlling the parents were (at least in
the eyes of their kids), the worse off their children were emotionally
over the next two years. In other words, if kids reported at the beginning of the seventh grade that their parents made most of their decisions for them, they were more likely to show a decrease in emotional
functioning over the next two years.

Interestingly, this pattern of results was found among both the
American and Chinese adolescents. The issue of parental control in
different cultures has been a matter of debate: some have argued that a
controlling style is the norm in Asian countries, and that because this
parenting style is expected and accepted there it is less harmful. In the
study just mentioned, however, no such difference emerged: both the
Chinese and American kids who had controlling parents were likely to
suffer emotionally in subsequent years. I wouldn't say that this issue is
fully settled; researchers continue to look at the role of parenting styles
in different cultures. Further, we need to be careful in interpreting
correlational studies such as this one, in which researchers measure
the association of two variables rather than conducting an experiment.
The parents who were more controlling might have differed in any
number of other ways from parents who were less controlling (see the
discussion of unmeasured third variables in chapter 2). At a minimum,
though, the results show that controlling parenting styles are predictive of problems down the road for adolescents, at least among kids
from the United States and China.[7]

Other studies have shown the dangers of another type of controlling parental style—namely, doling out love and affection only when
our kids do what we want them to do. In a study of ninth graders in
Israel, researchers examined the extent to which parents use *conditional*

negative regard, a technique in which they attempt to control their kids' behavior by withholding their affection when their kids do something wrong. The ninth graders reported their level of agreement with statements such as "If I do poorly in school, my mother will ignore me for a while" and "If I show my fear, my father will express less warmth toward me for a while." Those who agreed with statements such as these were classified as having parents who use conditional negative regard. The downside of this strategy is that kids come to view their parents as punitive and overly controlling and tend not to internalize the goal to do well on their own. Indeed, kids whose parents used this style reported greater resentment toward their parents, and their teachers rated them as less engaged in school, as compared to kids whose parents did not use this style.

"Well," you might think, "I would never punish my kids by ignoring them or withholding love. Rewards work better than punishments, so better to shower my kids with love when they do well. What better way to teach them good habits?" If that's what you do, you are using *conditional positive regard*, a technique in which parents respond to their kids' good behavior with love and affection. In the Israeli study, kids who endorsed statements such as "I feel that when I'm studying hard, my father appreciates me much more than usual" and "If I am afraid but do not express my fear, my mother will express more love for me" were classified as having parents who use conditional positive regard.

This strategy is better than withholding affection, but the danger is that kids learn the lesson that they can earn their parents' love only when they do what their parents want them to do. In the academic realm, for example, kids might focus on getting good grades to please their parents but fail to develop an intrinsic interest in their studies. This is what the study of Israeli kids found: the kids whose parents used conditional positive regard were more interested in grades than in the academic material (as reported by their teachers).

Well, if it's not advisable to withhold affection or make it contingent on our children's successes, what are parents to do? Actually, there is a better approach, called *autonomy support*, in which parents try to see things from their children's perspective, helping them understand the value of the different alternatives with which they are faced and convey a sense that they, the children, are ultimately the ones choosing which path to follow. The idea is to gently guide one's kids in the right direction while giving them the sense that they are making the choices themselves. To measure this parenting style, the researchers in the Israeli study asked the ninth graders what typically happens when they disagree with their parents; e.g., when "I think that my investment in school is adequate, but my father thinks it is not." Teens who reported that their parents understand them, but also that their parents provide a rationale for their (the parents') perspective, were classified as receiving a high amount of autonomy support. As the researchers predicted, these kids were better off than the kids whose parents used the other two parenting styles. They reported the highest amount of control over their feelings and behavior, were better able to regulate their emotions, and their teachers reported that they had the most intrinsic interest in academics. Another study (done in the United States) assessed parenting styles by interviewing the mothers and fathers rather than relying on how their kids saw it. Consistent with the Israeli study, the parents who scored high in autonomy support were more likely to have kids who were well behaved in school and got high grades.[8]

"I'D BE A LITTLE ANNOYED . . ."

So, autonomy support is preferred to controlling parenting styles. But as any parent knows, it isn't always possible to reason with one's child and let her make her own decisions. Especially when kids are young, we have to set limits and make it clear what the consequences will be if they do something wrong. And when our kids do act out, we need to decide whether to punish them and, if so, how. If our five-year-old is hitting his little sister with a toy train, or trying to pry the safety cover off an electrical outlet with a fork, reasoning with him only goes so far.

Many parents believe that an effective strategy in such situations is to give their kids a swat on the rear. In a survey conducted by the non-profit organization Zero to Three, 61 percent of parents of young children endorsed spanking as a regular form of punishment, with 57 percent of the parents reporting that spanking helps children develop a better sense of self-control. Another survey found that 94 percent of parents have spanked their child at least once by the time the child is four years old. Spanking in the home is legal in all U.S. states, and some states allow corporal punishment in schools.[9]

The American Academy of Pediatrics and the National Association of Social Workers disagree, recommending against the use of corporal punishment by parents. Many countries have outlawed corporal punishment in public and private, including Sweden, Norway, Germany, Austria, and Hungary. What does the research say? Corporal punishment does succeed in getting kids to stop doing whatever it was that brought about the spanking. But it is also associated with a number of negative outcomes, including an increase in aggressive and anti-social behavior, a lower-quality relationship with parents, poor mental health, and an increased likelihood that the child will grow into an adult who abuses his or her child or spouse. Now, I should hasten to add that these are correlational findings, which makes it impossible to determine whether corporal punishment causes these negative outcomes. We can't rule out the possibility that there is some third variable, such as family pathology, that increases the likelihood of both corporal punishment and negative outcomes.

It is worth noting, though, that kids who have been spanked or slapped are bad at what psychologists call "moral internalization." Rather than learning that "I shouldn't hit my little sister because that's the wrong thing to do," kids learn that "I shouldn't hit my little sister because Mom will slap me if I do." This means that the child won't hit his little sister when his mom is around, but what happens when she is out of the room or at work? Watch out—the kid who behaves only to avoid Mom's wrath is now free to unload on his sister. Further, his mother has taught him that violence is a reasonable way to try to control someone else's behavior, so why shouldn't he use it himself? Studies have shown that kids are excellent imitators of the techniques other people use to get what they want, including aggression. In short, many parents who use corporal punishment focus too much on controlling their children's behavior and too little on what they are doing to their kids' narratives. Ultimately, we want our kids to *internalize* appropriate values and attitudes, rather than obeying in order to avoid being punished.[10]

Issues such as these concerning discipline are some of the most difficult ones parents face and are the focus of many parenting books. Dr. Spock stated the dilemma well. On the one hand, he said, "You can create a harsh system of rewards and punishments so that, like good little robots, your children will behave perfectly most of the time. But what would be the effect on the child's spirit, on his sense of self-worth, on his personal happiness, on his feelings toward others?" On the other hand, he continued, "Imagine a child whose every whim is indulged, whose every action, good or bad, is lavishly praised. Such a child might have a certain measure of happiness, but most people wouldn't want to be within ten feet of him." Most of us would agree that there should be a happy medium between these two extremes, but exactly how do we accomplish this? The answer is to use the story-editing approach, which isn't in any of the many parenting books I've perused, including Dr. Spock's.[11]

To understand how parents can use this approach, consider this example: you and your eleven-year-old daughter are making some cookies for a bake sale at her elementary school. The two of you have a good time mixing the dough, spooning it onto a baking sheet, and smelling the wonderful aroma that wafts from the oven. When the batch is done, you and your daughter treat yourselves to a cookie with a glass of milk. "Can't I have another one?" your daughter pleads. "No," you say. "It would spoil your dinner, and besides, if we eat more we won't have enough for the bake sale. Why don't you start your homework while I go pay some bills?" Your daughter sits there sulkily, casting none-too-subtle looks at the cookies cooling on a rack on the counter.

You are about to leave your daughter in a highly tempting situation; she could easily sneak a cookie while you are out of the room. Say you've been having a little trouble getting her to obey your wishes of late; just the other night she snuck out of bed and got on her computer after you told her to turn out the light, and a couple of days before that she spent the evening texting her friends instead of doing her homework. You decide it's time to crack down. "Look," you say. "If you take another cookie while I'm paying the bills, you'll be in big trouble—I'll take your cell phone away for a week and let you use your computer only to do your homework—no more Facebook." "That ought to do it," you think. "It's high time she learned to obey the rules." Just to be sure, you count the number of cookies on the rack, and when you return later you are relieved to see that they are all still there.

It might seem like Mission Accomplished. Your daughter didn't spoil her dinner and learned a valuable lesson about avoiding temptation and doing what she was told. Or did she? Was your threat commensurate with the potential transgression, or did you go a little overboard? Even if you did, is that so bad? After all, you succeeded in getting your daughter to obey the rules. But again, the issue isn't just one of *compliance* but of *internalization*. Have you directed her narrative in a good or bad direction?

The answer is suggested by a two-session experiment that was done with children in the second grade. At the first session, a researcher left a child alone in a room in a tempting situation, not unlike the one with your daughter and the cookie. In this case, there were a bunch of toys in the room and the researcher told the child not to play with one of the best ones. He then varied the severity of the threat he delivered to the child. In one condition he was harsh, not unlike the mother threatening to take away her daughter's cell phone and ban her from Facebook: "Now, while I'm gone," he said, "you can play with all of the toys except the robot. It would be wrong to play with the robot, and if you play with it, I would be very upset and very angry with you." In another condition, the researcher dialed back his comments, giving only a mild threat. Instead of saying he would be "very upset and very angry," he said he would be "a little bit annoyed" if the child played with the forbidden toy. Then he left the room for a few minutes.

A key result is that both threats were successful: no child actually played with the forbidden toy while the researcher was gone. From a story-editing perspective, however, the critical question is how the children explained to themselves *why* they weren't playing with the toy. In the severe threat condition, the kids were likely to attribute their behavior to the threat. "I'm not sure why that guy was so bent out of shape about the robot," they probably thought, "but I'm sure not going to find out by playing with it. He'd be really mad at me." In the mild threat condition, however, the children could not as easily use the threat to explain why they didn't play with the robot. After all, the researcher only said he'd be a little annoyed, so what's the big deal?

The fascinating thing about the mild threat is that it was strong enough to prevent the kids from playing with the toy, but not so strong as to convince them that it was the *reason* they weren't playing with it. Instead, the kids inferred that they must not like that robot as much as they thought. That is, they assumed that they weren't playing with it because they didn't really like it very much—not because of the researcher's threat. We know this because at the end of the experimental session, the kids in the mild threat condition reported that they liked the robot significantly less than did kids in the severe threat condition.

The kids in the mild threat condition didn't stop with devaluing the robot. They found another reason to explain their good behavior, namely, that they must be especially honest kids who are good at avoiding temptation. After all, they could have played with the robot—the researcher would only have been a little annoyed—so why didn't they? In addition to deciding that the robot wasn't all that great, they concluded that they were good, honest kids who obey the rules.

The way we know this is that the researchers brought the kids back to the lab three weeks later and put them in another tempting situation. A different researcher, who didn't know which condition the children had been assigned to in the first session, asked the kids to play an electronic bowling game in which they could win prizes such as a doll, flashlight, or magnifying glass if they got a score of thirty-five or above. Then the researcher left the room and told each child to keep score him- or herself until the bowling game turned itself off. Lo and behold, the game ended when the child had earned only thirty-three points, just shy of a winning score. The researcher returned and asked the children how many points they had gotten. Were they honest or did they add a couple of points to their score in order to win a prize?

As the researchers expected, it depended on what condition the kids had been randomly assigned to in the initial session three weeks earlier. Very few kids who had received the mild threat cheated on the bowling game, whereas a substantial number of kids who received the severe threat did. This supports the idea that kids in the mild threat condition saw their good behavior in session 1 as a sign that they were honest kids who obeyed their elders, whereas kids in the severe threat condition simply said to themselves, "Hey, I didn't play with the robot because that guy would be really upset—not because I'm a particularly honest kid."

As discussed earlier, these kinds of changes in people's narratives are not fully conscious. The kids in the toy study did not sit there and scratch their heads, verbalizing to themselves the reasons they weren't playing with the robot. Instead, the mild threat seems to have led to a change in the kids' implicit self-narratives, which made them behave honestly when left alone with the bowling game three weeks later.[12]

The toy study and others like it have clear implications for what our hypothetical parent should have done in the cookie example. The threats to take the daughter's cell phone away and ban her from Facebook were probably too severe. Yes, these threats succeeded in getting her to obey, but in all likelihood they were so strong that they prevented any internalization. The daughter probably resisted temptation in order to avoid the punishment, rather than convincing herself that she is an honest kid who believes in doing the right thing. It would have been better to dial back the threat, keeping it strong enough to work but weak enough so that the daughter attributed her compliance to her own honesty. For example, the parent might have said, "I'd be annoyed if you snuck a cookie," though he or she would need to determine the exact level of threat that is both mild and effective.

Some parents might question the use of threats at all. Isn't it better to shower our kids with praise and to reward them for good behavior than to threaten them? Instead of telling our daughter that we would be annoyed if she disobeyed, for example, might it have been better to reward her for obeying? It depends on how strong those rewards are and how they are used, as we will now see.

SHOW ME THE MONEY

Consider another parenting dilemma: you would like your ten-year-old son to read in his free time instead of playing video games and watching television. You take him to the bookstore and buy him some age-appropriate books, and that works to some extent. He enjoys *How to Eat Fried Worms* by Thomas Rockwell, but he goes back to playing video games and the other books collect dust on his nightstand. Feeling a little exasperated, you decide on a new approach: rewarding your son for reading. You tell him that for every ten books he reads, you will buy him a new video game of his choice. And it works! Your son devours *The Boys from Brooklyn*, *Lawn Boy*, and the other books you bought him. Mission accomplished, right?

Well, maybe not. There is no doubt that rewarding kids can change their behavior in dramatic ways. Indeed, parents use incentives all the time. "If you eat two more bites of your carrots you can have dessert," moms and dads say, or, "If you practice the piano I'll take you out for ice cream." As long as the incentives are strong enough, then bingo, the carrots disappear and the piano gets played. Reward programs for kids have become institutionalized, such as the long-standing Book It! program sponsored by the Pizza Hut restaurant chain. According to the Book It! website (http://www.bookitprogram.com/), the goal of the program is to "motivate children to read by rewarding their reading accomplishments with praise, recognition, and fun!" When kids read a number of books set by their teacher (twenty books in my kids' elementary school), they receive a coupon for a free personal pan pizza. "The restaurant manager and team congratulate every child for meeting the monthly reading goal and reward them with a free, one-topping Personal Pan Pizza, Book It! card, and backpack clip," the website says—noting that more than ten million students participate in the program each year.

Programs such as these follow the most basic law of economics, namely, that people do what they do because of incentives. How can you go wrong by offering kids incentives to do what you want them to do, such as practicing the piano or reading more books? But again, it depends on whether our goal is compliance or internalization. If we want kids to read more, then rewarding them can work—as long as the incentives continue to be available. Rewards can produce compliance, just as threats of punishment can. But as in our example of teaching kids to be honest, we want our kids to internalize desired attitudes and values, in this case a love of reading. After all, we can't reward them for reading a book for the rest of their lives. What happens when summer comes and the Pizza Hut program ends?

"Well," an economist might answer, "we hope that kids will learn to like the activities after doing them for a while, so that they keep doing them after the rewards stop. But if they don't, the worst that can happen is that when the rewards aren't available anymore, kids go back to their original level of reading. No harm, no foul."

But it turns out that there is a possible foul: rewards can *undermine* kids' intrinsic interest in an activity by convincing them that they are doing it for the reward and not because the task is enjoyable in and of itself. This "overjustification" effect has been found in dozens of experiments. One of my favorites took place in an elementary school with fourth and fifth graders. The teachers wanted to increase students' interest in math, and they figured that a reward program was worth a try. First, the teachers introduced four new math games during class and observed how much the students played with each one during this baseline period. The answer was some but not much. Next, the teachers introduced a reward program. For every three hours the kids spent on the math games, they earned credits that they could use to get trophies and other prizes. These rewards were popular and effective: the time the kids spent on the math activities shot up.

So far so good. But what happened after the reward program ended? To find out, the teachers announced that, to be fair to the rest of the students in the school, they had to terminate the reward program, but that the math games would still be available for kids to play with, just as before. Now that there was nothing in it for the kids, their interest in the games plummeted to a level below where it had been during the pre-reward baseline period. In other words, it didn't just go back to where it had been before the reward program was instituted, as an economist might have predicted—the kids were now *less* interested in the games than they were when the program started. (The researchers determined, by comparing these results to those in a control condition, that it was the rewards that undermined kids' interest in the math games, not boredom with the games as time went by.) This study and others like it show that giving people strong rewards for an activity convinces them that they are "doing it for the money" and not because they have any intrinsic interest in the activities, and that in fact rewards can undermine interest that was there at the outset.[13]

Does this mean that parents and educators should abandon all rewards, throwing out their drawers full of gold stickers, prizes, and lollipops? Not at all. First, there isn't much risk of undermining kids' intrinsic interest when it is zero to begin with. If your child shows absolutely no interest in reading—he hasn't touched a book in months—then a small reward to get him started can't do any harm. Parents are in a position to know what their kids like and dislike, and thus to know when to use rewards. The problem with programs such as Book It! is that they are implemented throughout entire schools, where some of the kids will already be interested in reading and thus will be at risk for having that interest go down as a result of being rewarded with pizzas for something they already like to do. (In chapter 8, we will discuss programs that have tried—without much success—to close the achievement gap by paying disadvantaged kids to do well in school.)

Second, note that in the math game experiment the kids earned rewards simply for playing with the math games, regardless of how well they performed. Many rewards, such as good grades in school, are contingent on doing well—people get them only if they perform at a high level. Rewards of this type are less likely to undermine intrinsic interest because they convey to people that they are good at the activity being rewarded. But even rewards like grades can be problematic, to the extent that they focus people's attention on the incentives and raise anxiety about being evaluated.

Another approach is to use rewards but downplay their power and significance. Now, this might seem odd: if the goal is to get kids to do what we want, why wouldn't we use powerful incentives? But, as we saw, the problem with strong rewards is that they can undermine the very interest we are trying to foster. What if we adopted the same approach that I recommended for the use of threats, namely, dialing them back so that they are just strong enough to be effective? The goal would be to make them strong enough to get kids to perform the desired activity but not so strong that the kids latch onto the rewards as the sole explanation for their behavior.

A study with preschool children in Canada did just that. Four-year-old children were taken to a room and told that they could play with a drum, which is a highly popular activity with kids that age. In the salient reward condition, the researcher told the kids that they would receive a prize if they played with the drum, and the prize was introduced in such a way that kids could hardly think about anything else: the researcher said that the prize was under a box that was directly in front of the child, and told the kids that they couldn't lift up the box to see what the prize was until after the drum-playing time was over. Think about what this would be like for four-year-olds—they are sitting there playing the drum and staring at the box, constantly wondering what the prize is, their excitement mounting as time goes by. In the nonsalient reward condition, the kids were also told that they would get a prize after they played the drum but the researcher didn't say anything more about it; there was no box with a prize under it to capture kids' attention. Finally, there was a control condition in which the kids played the drum with no mention of any rewards.

The researchers measured the children's subsequent interest in the drum in a variety of ways, including asking them to name their favorite toy in the room and observing how much time they spent playing with the drum during a "free time" period both right after the initial session and several weeks later. On each of these measures, the kids in the salient reward condition showed a drop in intrinsic interest relative to the kids in the control condition. For example, they were less likely to name the drum as their favorite toy and they spent less time playing with it during the free play times. "I did it to get the prize," they seemed to have said to themselves, "and now that no prize is being offered, I'll play with the tinker toys instead of the drum, thank you very much." What about the kids in the nonsalient reward condition? They, too, got a prize for playing with the drum, but because their attention was not as focused on the reward, they seem not to have assumed that that was the only reason they played with it. In fact, compared to kids in the control condition, their subsequent interest in the drum was slightly higher—the prize added some excitement to playing with the drum but was not viewed as the sole reason for playing with it.[14]

The moral of all of this is what the social psychologist Mark Lepper calls the *minimal sufficiency principle*. If the goal is to get kids to internalize desired attitudes and values, then parents should use threats and rewards that are minimally sufficient to get kids to do the desired behaviors, but not so strong that the kids view the threats or rewards as the *reason* they are acting that way. Minimally sufficient threats and rewards are an effective story-editing technique, convincing kids that they are doing the right thing because they *believe* in doing the right thing.

Although this is great in theory, I have to say that in practice it isn't always easy to pull off. The problem is that we don't always know in advance what a minimally sufficient threat or reward will be. How much of a reward is enough to get a preschooler to practice the piano? How much of a threat is sufficient to get a teenager to avoid smoking? Further, there is a danger to erring on the low side. If the threats or rewards are too weak, our kids won't do what we want them to do. This can backfire, because the kids might become even more enamored of the undesirable behavior. If teens decide to smoke even though their parents would be annoyed, for example, they are likely to infer that smoking must be a really attractive thing. Similarly, if they decide not to practice the piano, even though they could have gotten some candy for doing so, they are likely to infer that piano playing must be really boring. The best approach is to start with threats or rewards that are strong enough to get kids to do the desired behavior, but then, on future occasions, dial them back a bit, making it harder for kids to attribute their actions to the threat or reward.

Another possible objection to the minimal sufficiency principle is that it might seem devious or controlling. Is it right to "trick" our kids into thinking they are doing something because they want to? Parents will have to decide this one for themselves, though in my view it is our job to get our kids to internalize desired attitudes and values. The irony is that this can be done more effectively with mild threats and small rewards than with severe threats and large rewards. Isn't it more controlling to take an overly authoritarian stance, one that will ultimately lead to less internalization of desired attitudes and values?

"YOU ARE SUCH A HELPFUL CHILD . . ."

There is a more straightforward way to get kids to internalize desired values, one that uses the story-prompting approach: simply providing kids with the right label for their behavior. Let's go back to the cookies example. Say you tried the minimal sufficiency principle, telling your daughter that you would be a little annoyed if she snatched a cookie while you were out of the room. But it turns out that your threat wasn't strong enough. When you return there is one less cookie on the plate and some telltale crumbs on the edge of your daughter's mouth. She sees the look of disappointment on your face and clearly feels bad for disobeying you. But what lesson has she learned, exactly? If she interprets her feelings as guilt, she might internalize the lesson that she should avoid future transgressions—after all, she doesn't want to disappoint you again. But if she says to herself, "Darn, I can't *believe* I got caught," she has learned a very different lesson—that next time she should do a better job of rearranging the cookies on the plate and brushing the crumbs off her mouth.

It turns out that adults can help kids label feelings such as these. Consider a rather devious experiment conducted with second graders. A researcher took each kid to a room in which a toy race car was moving slowly around an oval track and asked him or her to make sure that the car didn't jump the track. He showed the child how to stop the car if it started going too fast, and then left the room. Unbeknownst to the child, there was an accomplice in another room who was controlling the race car, and, lo and behold, when the child's attention wandered to other toys, he sped up the car and made it jump the track.

Soon thereafter, the first researcher returned, looked at the errant car, and noticed with dismay that it was broken. Now imagine you are the second grader. The man had just asked you to do something but you really screwed up. You are probably feeling pretty bad. But how exactly do you interpret these feelings? Do you feel guilty or annoyed over getting caught? For the kids in the race-car study, it depended on how the researcher labeled their feelings. Some of the children were randomly assigned to a *guilt* condition, in which the researcher communicated that they probably felt guilty for doing something wrong. "I bet you feel a little bad now that the car fell off," he said. "I've seen other kids feel bad when they weren't able to do exactly what they were supposed to do." Other kids were randomly assigned to what we might call a *dang, I can't believe I got caught* condition. Here, the researcher altered his comments slightly, labeling the kids' feelings as disappointment over being discovered. "I bet you feel a little bad now that *I found out* the car fell off," he said. "I've seen other kids feel bad when *someone found out* they weren't able to do exactly what they were supposed to do."

To see if his comments had sunk in, the researcher gave the kids a new race car, showed them how to put it back on the track if it came off, and asked them to keep an eye on it while it went around the track.

As he left, he emphasized that no one would come into the room for several minutes. Then the researchers surreptitiously measured how much time the kids spent focusing on the car while they were alone, making sure that it didn't jump the track, and how much time they spent looking at the other toys in the room.

It turned out that the label the researcher had provided did sink in. The kids who had been encouraged to attribute their earlier transgression to guilt spent significantly more time watching the race car than did the kids who had been encouraged to attribute their behavior to disappointment over being caught. The former kids seemed to be thinking, "I'd better keep an eye on the car, because I sure would feel guilty if I screwed up again, even if no one finds out." But the latter kids seemed to be thinking, "So what if the car jumps the track—no big deal. I can just put it back on the track before that guy comes back." If you want your kids to internalize the motivation to be good, then when they screw up, label their feelings as guilt.

What about when kids do the right thing? Here again, the way in which we label the behavior can make a difference, as shown in a study that tried to get fifth graders to be good citizens and not throw their trash on the floor. In one randomly chosen classroom, over a period of eight days, the teacher and principal consistently labeled the kids as people who did not litter. On one day, for example, the teacher pointed to a piece of trash that had been left by students from another class and noted, "Our class is clean and would not do that." On another day, the teacher put up a poster in which a cartoon character was saying, "We are Andersen's Litter-Conscious Class." On yet another day, the principal came into the class and commented on how clean the room was and how orderly the students were.

In another randomly chosen classroom, the teacher and principal took a different tack. Instead of labeling the kids as nonlitterers, they used standard persuasive appeals to convince them to keep the room clean. On one day, the teacher lectured the students on ecology and the dangers of littering, and on another she told the students how important it was to put candy wrappers in the trash instead of throwing them on the floor. On still another, the principal visited the classroom and told the students how important it was to keep the classroom tidy. Finally, a third randomly chosen classroom served as a control group and didn't receive any communications about littering.

After the intervention, the researchers observed how much the kids in each classroom littered. For example, two weeks later, the teachers gave each student a puzzle that was wrapped in a small disposable container. The researchers kept track of the number of kids who threw the containers on the floor and the number of kids who put the containers in the trash. It turned out that kids in the first, "labeling" condition internalized the message the most; they were the least likely to litter on the follow-up tests, even when they didn't know that their behavior was being monitored. For example, only about 15 percent of the kids in this classroom threw their puzzle containers on the floor, whereas in both the classroom that got the persuasive messages and the control classroom, about 70 percent of the kids threw the containers on the floor.[15]

Does this mean that we should lavish our kids with praise, as a way of giving them positive labels for their behavior? If you are like me, you have a strong desire to compliment your kids when they excel at something, such as doing well in school. "Great job on the multiplication test," you might say. "You sure are good at math." Nothing wrong with a verbal pat on the back, right?

Well, it depends on the message that the pat conveys. As we've seen, the labels adults provide matter, and the danger with praise is that it might convey the wrong label—what social psychologist Carol Dweck calls a *fixed mindset*, which is the idea that we are born with a fixed amount of talent in a specific area, such as math or soccer or music. We either have that talent or we don't, according to this viewpoint, which is fine as long as we continue to do well (e.g., get As on math tests) but can be devastating when we don't. Suppose that in middle school we do poorly on our first algebra test—what are we to conclude? If we believe that everyone is born with a fixed amount of mathematical ability, we can only surmise that we have reached the limit of ours and that there is no use in studying hard for the next test. "I'm just not a math person" is the logical conclusion.

But suppose we adopt what Dweck calls a *growth mindset* about math, the idea that we can learn to be good at something if we try hard and practice, that abilities are like muscles that get stronger with use. When we have a setback, such as that poor grade on the algebra test, we are more likely to take it as a sign that we didn't study hard enough and that we need to try harder next time.

Note that fixed versus growth mindsets are narratives that kids adopt and do not necessarily reflect how talented they actually are. Talent isn't irrelevant, of course. Some people, like former basketball great Michael Jordan, have far more natural ability than the rest of us. But the importance of practice should not be underestimated, and this is determined largely by people's mindsets. You might be surprised to learn, for example, that Michael Jordan was cut from his high school basketball team the first time he tried out. But rather than giving up, he redoubled his efforts, leaving home at 6:00 a.m. in order to practice for an hour before school started. Eventually, he did make his high school team and played well enough to earn a scholarship to the University of North Carolina, which has one of the premier college basketball programs in the country. But even then he didn't stop practicing. When North Carolina's season ended with a disappointing loss in the NCAA tournament, Michael Jordan's response was to go to the gym right after the game and practice his jump shot. Clearly, he had a growth mindset about his basketball abilities.

Where do these mindsets come from? Parents play a key role. When Michael Jordan's mother heard that he hadn't made his high school team, she told him to "go back and discipline yourself"—which is classic "growth mindset" feedback. Rather than saying, "You were robbed, I'm going to talk to the coach" or "Maybe you should try soccer instead," his mother conveyed the message that you have to work at something in order to be good at it—even if you are Michael Jordan.[16]

By the same token, parents should be careful about how they label their kids' successes. As tempting as it is to praise our children's outstanding talents—after all, we want to think of them as gifted—doing so can convey exactly the wrong message. In the second panel of the cartoon below, for example, Sally makes a classic mistake: she conveys a fixed mindset to her daughter, the idea that people do well in school because they are "gifted." What will her daughter conclude if she doesn't do well on her exams? It is better to compliment our kids for the hard work they put in, to send the message that success comes from hard work, not innate abilities. "Great job on the multiplication test," you might say. "I really admire how much time you spent studying for it. It really paid off."[17]

CORE ATTACHMENT NARRATIVES

What else can parents do to promote healthy narratives in their children? In the previous chapter, we discussed the importance of having a coherent core narrative that answers key questions about our existence and place in the world. An important feature of core narratives we haven't yet encountered is the way they portray our relationships with other people. What are other people like? Can they be trusted? If we get close to people, will they be there when we need them, or will they

eventually leave us for somebody else? Many people have core relationship narratives that provide heartening answers to these questions;
they believe that most people are trustworthy and can be counted on.
Other people aren't so sure—their core relationship narratives portray people as untrustworthy and not to be depended on.

Where do these relationship narratives come from? According to
attachment theory, these narratives—or "attachment models"—have
their roots in our relationships with our primary caregivers in the first
years of life. Say that your primary caregiver was your mother. If she
was attentive and responsive to your needs, and provided consistent,
dependable, and prompt care, you likely developed a secure model of
attachment. If she wasn't, you might have developed a less healthy
model of attachment. If she tended to ignore you when you were crying or in distress, you are likely to have developed an avoidant attachment style, whereby you have difficulty getting close to and trusting
others. If she was inconsistent in her attention, vacillating between
attentiveness and neglect, you are likely to have developed an ambivalent/
resistant attachment style, whereby you fear that your loved ones will
abandon you and therefore you tend to smother them with affection. If
you felt both frightened and comforted by your primary caregiver,
because he or she vacillated between threats and reassurance, you are
likely to have developed a disorganized attachment style.

These attachment styles form the blueprints by which we understand our relationships with other people, the narratives that we use to
interpret other people's behavior and guide our behavior toward them.
One study found that infants who were securely attached to their
mothers at twelve months of age were more skilled at making friends
in elementary school (as rated by their teachers), were more secure
about their friendships at age sixteen, and had more positive and supportive romantic relationships in their early twenties, than were
infants who were not securely attached at age twelve months.[18]

Does this does mean that if we were insecurely attached as infants we are doomed to unhappy relationships for the rest of our lives? Well, it does raise the odds, but, as we have seen, people's narratives can change. Children with insecure models of attachment can, through successful interactions with caregivers, acquire more secure models. Some studies show that the quality of a person's adult romantic relationships is largely related to his or her *current* attachment model—the way he or she views relationships as an adult—which is not necessarily the same as the model he or she had as an infant.

This raises the question of how best to redirect attachment narratives. Perhaps we could target mothers and infants who seem to be having difficulty forming close attachment bonds and help them in some way. This might seem like a daunting task, because mothers and their children can be caught in a vicious cycle in which the mother is insensitive to her baby's needs (perhaps because of her own insecure model of attachment), which lowers the probability that her baby will develop a secure model, and so on—part of a long chain of insecurity breeding insecurity. How can we possibly break this chain, short of major psychotherapy?

As we have seen, a fundamental assumption of the story-editing approach is that small interventions can reap huge benefits, if they succeed in redirecting a key element of a person's narrative. There is evidence that this can work to break the insecurity chain of attachment. One intervention, which involved only three home visits by a researcher, targeted mothers in the Netherlands who had firstborn infants who were high in irritability. Highly irritable infants were selected because it can be difficult for parents to establish secure bonds with babies who fuss and cry a lot. In fact, parents of these kinds of babies are especially likely to get caught in a vicious cycle in which they respond more and more passively to their babies—partly because the babies are less likely to smile and coo than nonirritable babies and partly because the more passively parents respond, the less likely they are to trigger a crying spell in their babies. Consequently, parents become less attentive to their children's needs and are less likely to become securely attached to them.

The researcher tried to interrupt this negative cycle, beginning when the infants were six months old. During each of three two-hour visits, she attempted to get the mother to be more attentive to the signals the infant was giving about his or her needs, to interpret the signals correctly, and to respond appropriately. When the baby fussed and cried, the mother was encouraged to try a variety of techniques to soothe him or her, because some babies prefer close contact and others do not. Mothers were encouraged to engage their babies in positive ways, rather than respond only to negative signals. For example, mothers were taught to make eye contact with their babies and coo at them when their babies held their gaze (because eye contact is a sign that the baby is engaged and interested in interacting), but to be silent when the babies looked away. The intervention was tailored to each individual mother-infant pair, with the overall goal of getting the mother to be more attentive to her baby's signals and needs.

Compared to mothers randomly assigned to a control group, those who received the intervention did indeed become more responsive to their infants' needs. As a result, their infants became less irritable, more sociable, engaged in more exploration, and were better able to soothe themselves when upset. At twelve months of age, only 22 percent of the infants in the control group were classified as securely attached to their mothers, but this number nearly tripled to 62 percent in the intervention group—an amazing difference given that the intervention consisted of only three home visits.

Even better, mothers in the intervention group were still more responsive to their children, compared to mothers of children in the control group, three years later. At age three and a half, children in the intervention group were more secure and cooperative than were children in the control group. These positive effects, it turned out, were brought about by the change in the child's attachment relationship with the mother, which supports the idea that establishing a secure internal working model of relationships is key to child development, and that at least for some parents (e.g., those with highly irritable children), a simple, short-term intervention can reap large benefits in attachment. And, like many other story-editing interventions, this one worked in part because it was self-sustaining. Once a mother learned to read her baby's signals better, the baby fussed less and was more responsive to her. This positive outcome encouraged the mother to stick with the program and try harder to be sensitive to her baby's needs.[19]

PREVENTING CHILD ABUSE

"That's all well and good," you might think, "but would story editing work with families that are even more at risk than the ones studied in the Netherlands?" There is a lot of social pathology out there and some parents do terrible things to their children. Surely they can't be helped with one of these tiny little story-editing interventions. Or can they?

Well, consider child abuse, which is surely one of the most heinous of crimes. Unfortunately, it is far from uncommon. Approximately 900,000 children are found to be the victims of abuse or neglect each year in the United States. In 2007, 1,760 of these children died as a result of abuse or neglect.[20]

In the 1990s, the United States Department of Health and Human Services declared that child abuse was a national emergency and urged that prevention programs be implemented. One organization, Prevent Child Abuse America (PCA America), believed that a home visitation program founded in Hawaii would work. The Hawaiian Healthy Start Program, which had been in operation since the 1980s, screened new parents in the hospital and offered counseling and home visits to those deemed at risk for abusing their children. The program was thought to be so effective that it was adopted as a national model by PCA America.

It was renamed Healthy Families America and now has chapters in more than 440 communities in the United States. Parents of newborns who are believed to be at risk for abuse are referred to the program and receive home visits by trained staff who provide support, parenting tips, and anger management training. Federal and state governments spend millions of dollars a year on this well-intentioned program.[21]

There is only one problem—it doesn't work. Like other common-sense interventions we have encountered, Healthy Families America was implemented on a mass scale before anyone tested it with rigorous experimental techniques. Once it was tested, the results were disappointing. In one study, for example, Hawaiian families were screened as usual for the Healthy Start Program. Those deemed at risk were randomly assigned to participate in the program or to a control group that did not participate. It turned out that there was no difference between the two groups in the percentage of children referred to child protective services because of child abuse (these percentages were very low in both conditions); no difference in mothers' reports of corporal punishment or physical aggression; no difference in the percentage of mothers who relinquished their role as primary caregiver (8 percent in both groups); and no difference in the percentage of children who required emergency health care, such as emergency room visits. In short, there was little or no evidence that the Healthy Start Program was having any impact at all on the behaviors it was designed to prevent. Other reviews of home visitation programs have reached similar conclusions.[22]

As well-intentioned as the Healthy Start Program is, and as likely as it seems that it would work, there are a number of reasons why it doesn't. For example, it ignores some of the key variables that increase the risk of child abuse, such as spousal abuse, parental depression, and parental substance abuse. Another possible reason it doesn't work comes right out of the story-editing approach: the program fails to target the way in which parents interpret their children's behavior, which may be a key contributor to child abuse.

In fact, social psychologists have noticed something curious about parents who abuse their children: they seem to blame the children for being difficult. When their kids act up, these parents often think, "It's his fault"—he has a bad disposition, he's stubborn, he was born that way, or he is deliberately trying to provoke them. Parents who don't abuse their children are more likely to attribute their kids' crankiness to something about the situation that is easily addressed—the child is hungry, tired, or needs a hug. Further, researchers suggest that these attributions are not necessarily conscious, and in fact may be part of parents' implicit narratives that they cannot fully verbalize, even to themselves.[23]

If so, then it might work to get mothers to redirect these narratives with a story-prompting intervention. To find out, researchers at the University of California, Santa Barbara, recruited families to participate in the Healthy Start Program, but gave some of them prompts to change their explanations about why their kids were acting up.

Here's how it worked: as with the Healthy Start Program, the Santa Barbara researchers targeted parents who were deemed at risk for being abusive to their children. For example, in one of their studies, 50 percent of the parents reported that they had been physically abused when they were growing up. In another, the participants were low-income women whose children were born with medical problems. These families were randomly assigned to one of three conditions. Some were in a control condition that received information about available community services but did not receive any home visits. Others took part in the standard Healthy Start Program, in which they received an average of seventeen home visits from trained staff over the course of the first year of their babies' lives. The visits followed the procedures of the Healthy Start Program; for example, they included parent education, anger management training, and parenting tips.

The third group also took part in the Healthy Start Program, but in addition received a story-editing intervention that tried to reduce the extent to which the mothers blamed their babies for caregiving problems and to increase the extent to which they attributed these problems to causes that could be fixed. Rather than simply giving the parents a new explanation for their babies' conduct, the home visitors encouraged parents to come up with these explanations themselves. First, they asked parents to think of examples of times when their children were difficult to care for and why they thought this was the case. Typically, the parents would attribute the problems to factors that were difficult to change, and would often blame their children. For example, a mother might say that her baby cried inconsolably after being fed in the evening and that the reason was that the baby was mad at her or trying to provoke her. At that point, the home visitor asked the mother whether she could think of any other reasons why her baby might cry, continuing with this line of questioning until the mother came up with an explanation that did not blame the child and was easier to remedy. After a while, for example, the mother might say, "Well, maybe my baby gets indigestion in the evening." This line of questioning would continue until the mother came up with a new strategy for solving the problem; for example, "I could try a different kind of formula and spend more time burping him after he eats." At the next visit, the home visitor inquired about the success of the strategy the mother came up with, discussed changes in the strategy if it wasn't working, and then repeated this process with a different caregiving problem. The hope was that after several such interactions, parents would blame their children less and identify solutions to behavioral problems that they could easily implement.

At the end of the yearlong program, parents reported on the health of their children and on how often they used abusive or harsh parenting techniques, such as hitting, shaking, or slapping. Consistent with previous studies, the Healthy Family home visits alone had little impact. Twenty-three percent of the children in this condition were physically abused, compared to 26 percent in the control condition — a difference that is not statistically significant. But, as the researchers predicted, the story-editing intervention worked: only 4 percent of the children in this condition were physically abused. Similar results were found on measures of corporal punishment that do not meet the legal definition of abuse, namely, slapping and spanking: 42 percent of parents in the control and Healthy Families group reported using these punitive techniques, compared to only 18 percent of parents in the story-editing condition. In follow-up studies, the story-editing intervention was found to reduce child injuries, lower the levels of cortisol in the children (cortisol is a hormone that is an indicator of stress), and improve cognitive functioning in the children. Consistent with many other story-editing interventions, redirecting people's narratives—in this case, encouraging parents to reinterpret why their children act up—reaped huge benefits down the road.[24]

USING IT

If you are a parent, grandparent, or someone who spends a lot of time with children (a teacher, say), I hope you learned some practical lessons from this chapter. Here are some techniques to remember when trying to redirect your children's narratives.

Avoid an Overly Controlling Parenting Style: Parents who are too controlling prevent their children from developing a sense of autonomy and purpose. I certainly wouldn't recommend that you go to the opposite extreme, becoming so lax that your kids fail to learn any limits or self-control. We've all seen parents who are incapable of using the "no" word and who end up at the mercy of their kids' every whim and wish. One way to find a happy medium is to use the *minimal sufficiency principle*, whereby you dole out rewards and punishments that are strong enough to get your kids to do what you want them to do, but not so strong that the kids think the rewards and punishments are the reason for their behavior. If you use this principle, your kids are likely to internalize good values and character traits, rather than believing that they are "doing it for the money" or to avoid the wrath of Mom and Dad. As I mentioned, this is sometimes easier said than done, because it can be hard to tell in advance what will be "minimally sufficient" to get our kids to do what we want them to do. What level of threats will be sufficient to keep our teenagers from texting while they are driving, for example? Saying we would be "a little annoyed" might be too weak, with disastrous results. Better to err on the side of too strong a threat about such dangerous actions, at least at first, while recognizing the risks of going too far overboard.

Label Your Kids' Behavior Appropriately: Once your kids are behaving appropriately, it can help to provide them with a favorable label for those behaviors. "You sure are a safe driver," you might say, or "Looks like you're the kind of person who loves to read." Again, don't go overboard. My kids were fond of making fun of my clumsy attempts to label their behavior, repeating in a singsong voice, "We know, Dad, we're not eating our vegetables in order to get dessert, we *love* vegetables." Further, be mindful of the kinds of labels you use. As Carol Dweck's work shows, it is harmful to label your kids' successes in ways that imply a fixed mindset ("You are such a talented athlete!"). Better to label them in ways that imply a growth mindset ("Your practice really paid off!").

Foster Secure Attachment Models: In the last part of this chapter, we saw the importance of core attachment narratives. Beginning the moment your child is born, be attentive to his or her needs and respond consistently with appropriate love and care. Doing so will foster a secure attachment model in your children, which will serve them well as they grow older and help them form bonds with others in their lives. Along with a sense of autonomy and purpose, there may be no greater gift we can give our children than the narrative that they can form close, trusting relationships with others.

Chapter 5

Just Say . . . Volunteer

Preventing Teenage Pregnancies

S ome people claim that the best parents can do is hold their breath when their children become teenagers and exhale when they enter their twenties. The teenage years are notoriously difficult, for both teens and their parents. Many sweet, innocent ten-year-olds transform into surly, moody thirteen-year-olds who would rather do anything than be seen with their parents. Not all adolescents rebel so dramatically, of course, but the teen years are a time of transition as kids go through puberty, become more independent, seek the approval of their peers, and experience increased academic pressures at school. Not many of us would choose to relive those years.

If parents were to list their biggest worries about their teenagers— the reasons they hold their breath—three dangers would make everyone's list: pregnancy, violence, and substance abuse (including alcohol). Countless promising lives are thrown off track by one or more of these problems, and a great deal of parental and societal efforts go into preventing them. In this chapter we will consider teenage pregnancy, which occurs at a very high rate in the United States. Millions of dollars have been spent on prevention programs that don't work.

Meanwhile, programs that incorporate the story-editing approach have been shown to be effective.

Let's begin with Amanda Ireland, a 2008 graduate of Gloucester High School in Massachusetts, who has some advice for her younger friends: don't become a teenage mother. Amanda speaks from experience, because she gave birth to a daughter when she was in the ninth grade. Sometimes classmates came up to her in the hall to tell her how lucky she was, but Ireland set them straight: "It's hard to feel loved when an infant is screaming to be fed at 3:00 a.m." Christen Callahan, another teen mother from Gloucester High, concurs. "I don't think it's the best idea for anyone, including myself," she says. "You lose everything."

But Ireland's and Callahan's advice didn't seem to sink in, if what happened with a group of younger girls at Gloucester High is any indication. In June of 2008 these girls made international headlines for having allegedly formed a pregnancy pact, each vowing to get pregnant as soon as possible. Although school officials deny that there was any such pact, one thing is clear: there was a fourfold increase in pregnancies at the high school over the previous year. Seventeen girls became pregnant, none older than sixteen years of age.

Pundits were quick to point their fingers and give reasons for the spike in pregnancies. Liberals blamed the school for not providing sex education and for banning contraceptives from its health clinic. Conservatives pointed out that Massachusetts had rejected federal funds to provide abstinence-centered education. Others suggested that the girls were imitating teenage celebrities such as Jamie Lynn Spears, who became pregnant at age sixteen (and, coincidentally, gave birth to a baby girl the same week that the Gloucester High story hit the news).[1]

Whatever the cause, the problem is not limited to Gloucester High. At T. C. Williams High School in Alexandria, Virginia, seventy teenage girls were pregnant or became mothers in the fall of 2008. Nancy Runton, the school nurse, claims that not all these pregnancies were accidental. "I've known girls who've made 'I'll get pregnant if you get pregnant' pacts," she says. "It's a status thing. These girls go around school telling each other how beautiful they look pregnant, how cute their tummies look." Then reality sets in. Cynthia Quinteros, a T. C. Williams student, gave birth to a boy when she was fifteen. A year later, this is her typical day: she gets up at 6:00 a.m., feeds and dresses her son, Angel, and drops him off at a day care center located in the high school so that she can start classes at 7:50 a.m. After school she plays with Angel and starts her homework, then leaves Angel with her mother while she works as a cashier at a supermarket from 5:00 p.m. to 10:00 p.m. She returns home, finishes her homework, and goes to bed, only to repeat the routine at 6:00 a.m. the next day. "I love Angel," she says. "But if I didn't have him I wouldn't have to work after school, I could study more, I could be a normal teenager."[2]

When reading about young mothers such as Amanda Ireland and Cynthia Quinteros, it is hard not to engage in some tongue-clucking. What were these girls thinking? And let's not forget the fathers of their children. Didn't these boys and girls know the risks they were taking and the consequences of becoming teenage parents? But before pointing fingers, it might be useful to remember that nearly anyone could have been in their shoes. How many of us have had experiences like this when we were teenagers? We are alone with our first love, experiencing a rush of emotion and passion more intense than we ever thought possible. Maybe we're in our parents' empty house, in a deserted park, or in the backseat of a car. We fumble with buttons and clasps and zippers and—well, here is where the story diverges. Some of us put on the brakes, deciding to wait until we were older before having sex. But that was probably a minority of us. According to recent statistics, one-third of teens report that they have had sex by the ninth grade and 65 percent have had sex by the twelfth grade. (If these percentages seem high, it should be noted that they have actually dropped a bit over the past fifteen years.)

Some of us who chose to have sex when we were teenagers did so with careful planning—for example, by purchasing and using condoms. Many of us, however, did not. Today, 38 percent of teens report that they did not use a condom the last time they had sex. We don't need statistics to tell us how this plays out: a pair of fifteen-year-olds don't make careful plans before having sex, and when they are alone in a house or in the backseat of a car, they think, "Surely nothing bad will happen—it's just one time, right?" Lots of teens are lucky and don't get pregnant or contract a sexually transmitted disease (how many of us, reading these words, just said a silent word of thanks to the gods of reproduction?). But many teens are not so lucky. Today, nearly one in three girls becomes pregnant before the age of twenty in the United States, resulting in more than 400,000 births a year. The rate at which teenagers become pregnant, contract sexually transmitted diseases, and have abortions is much higher in the United States than in most other industrialized nations, including Canada, England, France, Japan, and the Netherlands. The costs are high: teenage mothers are more likely to drop out of high school, to remain single parents, and to live in poverty, and their children are more likely to be victims of abuse, to be placed in foster care, to have below-average general knowledge, math, and reading skills when they enter kindergarten, to drop out of high school, and to go to prison as teenagers or young adults—even after we take into account the socioeconomic status of the mothers and other relevant factors.[3]

Teenage pregnancy is not a new problem, of course, and for decades many schools have offered sex education to try to reduce it. Depending on your age and where you went to school, you might have attended a single furtive session conducted by an embarrassed gym teacher or several classes on reproduction and birth control as part of a comprehensive family life curriculum. Many localities also have programs to support teen mothers and reduce the likelihood that they will have another child in their teens, because repeat births among teen mothers are disturbingly common. The question is, do these programs work? And what does the story-editing approach have to offer? As we will see, there are some surprisingly effective strategies that can be easily adopted by schools and parents.

SEX EDUCATION

The history of sex education in the United States can be traced back to the beginning of the twentieth century, when Victorian taboos against public discussions of sexuality began to change. By the 1920s, more than twenty-five hundred high schools in the United States offered some form of sex education, though the approaches varied widely. In some schools, students were subjected to graphic pictures of the ravages of sexually transmitted diseases, whereas other schools adopted a more quaint approach. (In high schools in Kansas, students took field trips to local jewelers to learn how to shop for wedding rings.) By the 1930s, some colleges offered rudimentary sex education. At Russell Sage College, for example, a women's college in New York State, the college president and his wife met with students to have frank discussions about family life.[4]

Sex education was always controversial, but it became even more so in the turbulent 1960s. Mary Steichen Calderone, a physician who was the medical director of Planned Parenthood, pushed for a more open discussion of sex and birth control, rather than an exclusive emphasis on abstinence. In 1964, she succeeded in reversing a policy by the American Medical Association that prohibited doctors from discussing birth control with their patients. Meanwhile, against the backdrop of the 1960s counterculture movement and its advocacy of "free love," conservative groups became alarmed at changing societal mores about sex and the open dissemination of information about birth control and abortion.

The battle over sex education continues to this day. In 1996, the

United States Congress passed Section 510 of Title V of the Social Security Act, which provided money to states for sex education, but only if the approach was abstinence-based. The act defined abstinence education as a program that "has as its exclusive purpose, teaching the social, psychological, and health gains to be realized by abstaining from sexual activity," and stated that, among other things, "sexual activity outside of the context of marriage is likely to have harmful psychological and physical effects." (These were the funds that Massachusetts refused to accept, which, according to some, led to the increase in pregnancies at Gloucester High School.) Today, sex education continues to be part of the culture wars in the United States. To liberals, the idea that hormone-intoxicated teenagers will "just say no" when half clothed in the backseat of a car is naive. To conservatives, it is parents—not the schools—who should decide what kind of information teens get about sex. And some are concerned that providing information about contraception will make premarital sex more tempting to teens.[5]

The politicization of sex education reached absurd heights in the 2008 presidential campaign, when a television ad for John McCain claimed that Barack Obama was in favor of teaching "comprehensive sex education" to kindergarteners. "Learning about sex before learning to read?" the ad intoned. "Barack Obama. Wrong on education. Wrong for your family." The truth is that when President Obama was an Illinois state senator he supported a bill mandating "age-appropriate" sex education, which would have given kindergarteners information about inappropriate touching and sexual predation, not descriptions of intercourse and offers of free condoms. And there was an opt-out clause allowing parents to exclude their children from the sessions if they wished.[6]

Instead of trying to score political points, we should use the scientific method to find out what works and what doesn't when it comes to preventing teenage pregnancies. Yes, people disagree on moral grounds about the appropriateness of premarital sex and birth control. But regardless of where one stands on these issues, it is to everyone's benefit to find out whether educational programs increase or decrease the likelihood that teens will have sex and whether they prevent unwanted pregnancies. The Obama administration endorsed this approach, making federal funds available for sex education programs that have been "proven effective through rigorous evaluation."[7]

Unlike some of the other problems we will encounter in this book, teenage pregnancy has been the subject of rigorous research in recent years. Several well-designed, experimental tests of sex-education programs have been conducted. The reason for this, I suspect, is that because many people view teenage pregnancy and sexually transmitted diseases as medical problems, they are amenable to scientific tests of programs designed to prevent these outcomes. Nonetheless there are many examples of "blistering" in this area (the term I use for programs that common sense tells us should work but that in fact do not; see chapter 1).

DOES "KNOW" MEAN "NO"?

Let's begin with the question of whether abstinence education makes teens less likely to engage in sexual intercourse. A paper published by the Heritage Foundation, a conservative think tank, concludes that it does: "Authentic abstinence programs are . . . crucial to efforts aimed at reducing unwed childbearing and improving youth well-being." A careful look at the evidence, however, reveals that this conclusion is at best premature.[8]

In 1997, researchers examined all published studies that tested the effectiveness of different kinds of pregnancy-prevention programs. They did so using a technique called meta-analysis, which statistically

combines the results of individual studies to produce an overall estimate of effectiveness. The results were encouraging: girls who participated in the prevention programs were significantly less likely to get
pregnant than girls who did not. When the type of program was
examined, however, it was discovered that the programs that discussed
and distributed contraception did better than abstinence-based
programs.[9]

The same year this review was published, the United States Congress authorized an evaluation of abstinence-based programs, namely,
those that were funded by the law that mandated abstinence-only sex
education. One might question whether the cart was put before the
horse here—providing fifty million dollars a year for a program and
then evaluating it—but in any event, an evaluation was conducted by
Mathematica Policy Research, a nonpartisan private research firm.
The study used a true experimental design: at four different schools,
two thousand adolescents were randomly assigned either to participate
in an abstinence program or to a control group that did not participate. The bottom line? None of the programs had a detectable effect
on the participants' likelihood of abstaining from sex or on the age at
which they first had sex. For example, on a follow-up survey conducted
between forty-two and seventy-eight months after the abstinence programs began, the percentage of teens who said they were virgins was
identical among those who took part in the program and those who
did not (49 percent in both cases).[10]

We should acknowledge a weakness of all studies of teenage sexual
activity: they rely on teens' reports about their sexual behavior. Obviously, the researchers cannot follow adolescents into their bedrooms
or the backseats of cars and observe what they actually do. Participants
may not be completely forthcoming about their sexual escapades,
making the effects of the programs hard to evaluate. Researchers
attempt to deal with this problem by ensuring that participants'

responses are completely confidential; and, indeed, many teens do report sexual activity on surveys.

Another limitation of the Mathematica study is that it looked at only four abstinence programs. Although the researchers attempted to choose programs that were exemplars of the abstinence approach, perhaps there are other programs that are doing a better job. To provide a broader picture, a different set of researchers conducted interviews with a nationally representative sample of more than seventeen hundred teenagers who ranged in age from fifteen to nineteen. They divided the teens into three groups: those who had never received any sex education (10 percent), those who had received abstinence-only sex education (23 percent), and those who had received comprehensive sex education that included both abstinence messages and information about birth control (68 percent). The results? Teens in the abstinence-only group were no less likely to abstain from sex, and were no less likely to get pregnant, than teens who didn't receive any sex education. However, teens who had received the comprehensive sex education, which included information about birth control, were somewhat less likely to engage in sex and much less likely to get pregnant.[11]

An advantage of a national survey is that it includes a representative sample of all Americans, allowing us to generalize beyond a few specific programs. A disadvantage, of course, is that the participants are not randomly assigned to receive one or the other type of sex education. Although the researchers statistically controlled for variables that might influence the results, such as gender, age, race, family makeup, socioeconomic status, and area of residence, we can't rule out the possibility that unmeasured variables biased the results (as discussed in chapter 2). But in conjunction with the Mathematica study that randomly assigned teens to receive abstinence education or to a control condition that did not, this survey certainly calls into question whether abstinence training has any effect.

To be fair, the absence of a statistically significant effect is a null finding and does not prove that the approach is ineffective (for example, maybe the sample sizes in the studies were too small to detect any benefits). Perhaps the fairest summary of abstinence-based programs comes from an in-depth report issued by the National Campaign to Prevent Teen and Unplanned Pregnancy, a nonprofit group devoted to lowering the rate of teen pregnancy in the United States. This report concluded that "studies find no strong evidence that any particular abstinence program delays the initiation of sex, although they hint that future studies may find a positive effect for one or more programs."

In fact, one recent study found that a version of an abstinence program was effective. In this study, African American sixth and seventh graders attended two four-hour sessions that stressed the importance of abstinence. The kids also received education about sexually transmitted diseases and training in how to resist peer pressure to have sex. The authors of this study were quick to point out that their intervention would not meet federal guidelines for abstinence education. It was not moralistic or religious, and it stressed that kids should avoid sex until they were ready to handle the consequences, rather than mandating that they wait until marriage. Further, the program did not disparage the use of condoms; instead, it corrected any misconceptions the kids had about condoms' effectiveness. In a way, then, this intervention was a hybrid of abstinence education and sex education. The mixture was effective: about one-third of the teens who received the intervention reported that they had sex over the next two years, compared to 47 percent of the teens who had been randomly assigned to a control group.[12]

Many other studies have found that educating teens about birth control prevents pregnancies. Further, fears that giving teens information about birth control will make them hop into bed with their friends are unfounded. There is no evidence that sex-education programs make teens more likely to have sex.

PREVENTING REPEAT TEEN PREGNANCIES

Lameesha Lee, a resident of High Point, North Carolina, gave birth to a healthy baby girl when she was fourteen years old. At an age when many teenage girls are discovering boys, social networking sites, and high school algebra, Lameesha dropped out of school to raise her child on her own (her boyfriend was in prison at that point). As we have seen, having a child in one's teens puts both the child and the mother at risk for all sorts of bad outcomes. These problems are compounded when teen mothers have a second child, which is not a rare occurrence. In the United States, about 25 percent of teen mothers give birth to another child before reaching the age of twenty.[13]

Some programs have thus targeted teen mothers in an attempt to prevent second pregnancies. Two such programs, one in North Carolina and another in Colorado, came up with an approach that would be applauded by economists: pay teen mothers not to get pregnant. The North Carolina program, called Dollar-A-Day, was the brainchild of members of the School of Nursing at the University of North Carolina, Greensboro. The Colorado program, also called Dollar-A-Day, was founded by the local chapter of Planned Parenthood. As their names imply, the programs pay teenage mothers a dollar for each day they are not pregnant. There are also weekly meetings at which the young moms can socialize, talk about their problems, and get advice from professionals and other older adults.

Do the programs work? Lameesha Lee, who took part in the North Carolina program, thinks so. "I know I don't want any more kids for a good long while." The authors of an article about the North Carolina program also think so: they describe their effort as "a model program for others to emulate." Jean Workman, a public health educator, agrees: "We have found that those who remain in the program and faithfully attend don't have second pregnancies. The girls who miss two to four weeks are the ones who get pregnant again." A more formal evaluation of the North Carolina program reached the same conclusion, finding that ten of the sixty-five girls who took part (15 percent) became pregnant during the first five years of the program, a rate that "was substantially lower than the...30–35 percent rates reported for other programs."[14]

Now even I, a professional skeptic about the ways in which social interventions are evaluated, find this pretty impressive—at first glance. But if we learn nothing else from this book, we should learn to take a closer look at such data. Doing so, unfortunately, leaves considerable doubt about whether these programs have any effect. First, Jean Workman's observation is a clear case of correlation without causation. The fact that girls who stick with the program don't get pregnant doesn't mean that the program is responsible for that desirable result. It could be a classic case of a "third variable": things that increase the girls' risk of a second pregnancy (e.g., psychological problems, drug use, their family situation) also make them more likely to drop out of the program; or, put differently, girls who are unlikely to get pregnant in the first place are more likely to stick with the program. The fact that only 15 percent of the girls who took part became pregnant is suggestive, but without a control group we can't be sure that the program was responsible for this low rate. In fact, it is not clear how low the rate actually is: as mentioned, the rate of second pregnancies appears to be closer to 25 percent than the 30–35 percent the authors of the evaluation used as their comparison point.

Unfortunately, there is further reason to be skeptical of these programs. Researchers conducted an experimental test of the Colorado Dollar-A-Day program and the results were disappointing. They randomly assigned teenage girls who had recently given birth to their first child to one of four conditions: the standard program in which mothers attended weekly support meetings with other teenage mothers and received a dollar for each day they were not pregnant; a group-only condition in which the girls attended group meetings but were not paid (the paid and unpaid mothers attended different meetings); an incentive-only condition in which they received a dollar for each day they were not pregnant but did not attend any meetings; and a control condition in which they did not attend meetings or receive any money.

The incentives worked to increase attendance at the group meetings. In the group-only condition, in which no incentives were offered, only 9 percent of the young mothers invited to participate attended one or more of the meetings. When offered a dollar a day, 58 percent attended one or more meetings. So far so good—the money got the girls (many of them, at least) to show up. But did the meetings have the desired effect of preventing repeat pregnancies? Unfortunately, there is no evidence that they did. Nor is there any evidence that the incentives alone reduced pregnancies. By the end of a two-year follow-up, 39 percent of the girls had become pregnant again, with no significant differences in the percentage of pregnancies between any of the four conditions. It didn't matter whether the researchers looked at all the mothers randomly assigned to the four conditions or only at those who actually attended the group meetings. Consider, for example, the girls who were randomly assigned to the dollar-a-day-plus-group-meetings condition *and* who actually attended the meetings. About one-third of these girls became pregnant again, which was not statistically different from the percentage in the control group. The researchers even hint at a negative effect of the group meetings: "Some of the young mothers...tended to reinforce one another's inconsistent contraceptive behavior and ambivalence about postponing future childbearing." Bringing together at-risk teens in a way that backfires is a phenomenon we will encounter again (see the next chapter, on adolescent behavioral problems). The verdict: Dollar-A-Day pregnancy prevention programs are an example of blistering, and possibly of bloodletting as well (a commonsense approach that does more harm than good).[15]

THE BENEFITS OF VOLUNTEER WORK

Suppose that school officials in Gloucester, Massachusetts, hired us to help reduce the pregnancy rate, or that officials in North Carolina and Colorado asked for our advice on how to help teen mothers postpone future pregnancies. By now we know that abstinence-based programs are unlikely to work by themselves; nor will offering teen moms a dollar a day to attend weekly meetings have the desired effect. We also know that providing information about contraception will prevent pregnancies, but this is a political hot potato, particularly in a town like Gloucester, which is predominantly Roman Catholic. Even if we could convince the school district and parents to start with comprehensive sex-education classes, what else might we do?

According to the story-editing approach, we should try to change teens' narratives in a way that will make them less likely to engage in unprotected sex. Well, what sort of narrative places teens at risk for becoming pregnant, or for getting someone pregnant? Research shows that teens who feel disengaged from their school and community and feel alienated and socially excluded are particularly at risk. Now, I don't mean to imply that unprotected sex is a deliberate, conscious way in which teenagers rebel. Rather, feeling alienated is likely to put kids at risk in many ways, influencing who they hang out with and how much they plan for their futures. Put differently, kids who feel like they have a stake in their communities and have clear goals for the future are less likely to put themselves at risk by having unprotected sex.[16]

How, then, can we change teens' narratives from a sense of alienation to one of engagement—from the belief that "I don't fit in here" to "I'm a valued member of my school and community"? It turns out that an effective approach is to have teenagers engage in regular volunteer work in their community. Now, at first blush this might seem a little hard to believe. What does volunteering at a soup kitchen or a nursing home have to do with teenage pregnancy? What it does is take advantage of the do good, be good principle discussed in chapter 1, namely, the idea that one of the best ways of changing people's self-views is to change their behavior first. Involving at-risk teens in volunteer work can lead to a beneficial change in how they view themselves, fostering the sense that they are valuable members of the community who have a stake in the future, thereby reducing the likelihood that they engage in risky behaviors, including unprotected sex.

There are at least three well-tested programs showing that this approach works. The first to make this discovery, the Teen Outreach Program, was founded in 1978 by Brenda Hostetler, a St. Louis school administrator. Teen Outreach is typically implemented in high schools in grades nine through twelve and has two components: supervised community service and weekly classroom sessions in which the students discuss their volunteer experiences and issues related to teen development. The students choose their volunteer activity from a wide range of alternatives, including working as aides in nursing homes and hospitals, taking part in walkathons to raise money for charities, and peer tutoring. They are asked to perform a minimum of twenty hours of volunteer service over the course of the year, though most put in many more hours than that.

The classroom sessions involve group discussions, role-playing, guest speakers, and class exercises. In addition to providing an opportunity for students to discuss their volunteer experiences, the meetings focus on such issues as teen relationships, values, communication, peer pressure, goal-setting, and sexuality. As part of the latter discussion, teens receive sex education, including information on contraception and sexually transmitted diseases. However, the researchers involved in testing the program stress that sex education is not the central focus of the program and that it in fact takes up less than 15 percent of the classroom curriculum.[17]

After its debut in St. Louis, Teen Outreach spread to other cities, with the sponsorship of the Association of Junior Leagues International and the American Association of School Administrators. To the great credit of its founders and sponsors, the program was tested more rigorously than most social interventions, including an experiment in which students at twenty-five sites were randomly assigned to take part in Teen Outreach or to a control group that did not. The results of this experiment were promising: the girls who took part in the program were half as likely to become pregnant as girls in the control group. The program works equally well in preventing first pregnancies as well as second pregnancies in teenage mothers. The program also had positive effects on the kids' academic performance.

Teen Outreach increases teenagers' sense of autonomy and connection with adults and peers, especially among young teens. That is, the volunteer work changes the participants' narratives about themselves, fostering the view that they are valued members of the community. Remember, the teens who are most likely to get pregnant are those who feel disengaged from their school and community and feel alienated and socially excluded. Volunteer work can be an effective remedy for such alienation, making teens feel more engaged and connected.

The astute reader, however, will have noted that Teen Outreach involved community service *and* a classroom component, making it difficult to tell whether it was the volunteer work per se that was responsible for its success. The classroom component involved sex education about contraception, which we already know can help reduce pregnancy rates. Maybe it was the classroom instruction alone, and not the volunteer work, that was the key to the program's success.

Fortunately, another program, Reach for Health Community Youth Service (RFH), provides an answer to this question. RFH was implemented in the early 1990s in a New York City middle school that primarily served African American and Latino students. Like Teen Outreach, the main component of the program was community service, in which seventh- and eighth-grade students spent an average of three hours a week doing volunteer work in a variety of community settings, including nursing homes, senior citizen centers, medical clinics, and day care centers. As in Teen Outreach, the students participated in weekly classroom sessions that covered issues about teen development, including sex education. But the program differed from Teen Outreach in that the students in the control condition received the classroom curriculum as well. That is, classes (eighteen in all) were randomly assigned to receive just the classroom component of the program or the classroom component plus the volunteer service, which allows us to assess the added benefits of the volunteer work.

The results were encouraging. First, the researchers looked at the proportion of students who reported that they were virgins before the program and remained abstinent after the program. By the tenth grade—two years after they took part in the RFH program in middle school—50 percent of teens in the community service condition reported that they were still virgins, compared to only 37 percent of teens in the control condition. Second, the researchers asked the teens, when they were tenth graders, whether they had had sex in the previous three months. Forty-one percent of teens in the community service condition reported that they had, compared to 58 percent of teens in the control condition. Both of these results are statistically significant. Thus, engaging in volunteer work delayed the age at which teens had their first sexual experience and reduced the frequency of sex two years after the program had ended.[18]

LESSONS UNLEARNED

Another intervention that incorporated community service was the Quantum Opportunities Program (QOP). In 1989, a pilot program funded by the Ford Foundation targeted at-risk youth in five American cities. Beginning in the ninth grade, and continuing through high school, the kids received 250 hours per year of educational assistance (for example, homework help, peer tutoring) and 250 hours per year of developmental assistance (for example, life/family skills training, help with job applications, planning for college). In addition, the students engaged in 250 hours of community service per year, receiving a small stipend for their participation. The intervention was tested with an experiment, in which teens from families receiving public assistance were randomly assigned to take part in the program or to a control group that did not. The results? Compared to the kids in the control group, those who participated in the program were less likely to have children, more likely to finish high school, and more likely to go to college.[19]

Given these encouraging results, the Ford Foundation and the United States Department of Labor funded an even larger-scale intervention in seven different American cities. Whereas the pilot program included only 125 students, the full program included nearly six hundred students (between fifty and one hundred teens per site). These teens were randomly selected from a larger pool of eligible participants and took part in the program while attending grades nine through twelve.

Unfortunately, the full program did not replicate the beneficial effects of the pilot study. There were no significant differences between the teens who participated and those randomly assigned to a control condition, either in educational outcomes (e.g., the likelihood of finishing school) or in behavioral outcomes (e.g., the likelihood of becoming a teen parent). In fact, there was some evidence that the program backfired: the teens who took part in QOP were *more* likely to be arrested or charged with a crime than were teens in the control group, qualifying it for my bloodletting award. Thus, rather than having the intended beneficial effects, the program turned at least some kids into criminals.

What happened? It turns out that each site was given a fair amount of latitude in how they implemented the QOP program, and none of the sites adopted the entire curriculum. In particular, most of the site managers decided to focus on the mentoring aspects of the program and *none fully implemented the community service component*—the very component that we know, from the Teen Outreach and Reach for Health programs, has beneficial effects! Sadly, more than $15 million was spent on a five-year intervention in which a key ingredient (community service) was eliminated. Even more sadly, the program retained a component—bringing at-risk teens together on a regular basis—that had already been shown to have negative effects, as we will see in chapter 6 (possibly explaining the increase in crime rates in the intervention group).[20]

The fact that policy makers learned so little from past research—at huge human and financial cost—is made even more mind-boggling by being such a familiar story. Too often, policy makers follow common sense instead of scientific data when deciding how to solve social and behavioral problems. When the well-meaning managers of the QOP sites looked at the curriculum, the community service component probably seemed like a frill compared to bringing kids together for sessions on life development. Makes sense, doesn't it? But common sense was wrong, as it has been so often before. In the end, it is teens like Amanda Ireland, Christen Callahan, Cynthia Quinteros, and Lameesha Lee who pay the price—teen mothers who might have been helped by relatively inexpensive interventions proven to work.

USING IT

There are clear lessons here for school administrators who want to reduce teenage pregnancy: abandon abstinence-only sex education (at least the moralistic version that refuses to discuss birth control), implement sex education that includes a discussion of contraception, and encourage teens to engage in volunteer work. If you have children in school, you should find out what kind of sex education and volunteer programs the school offers, and ask what the evidence is for the effectiveness of the programs in use.

But what about you and me in our everyday lives? There are some pretty interesting implications for those of us who are parents of teenagers. The clear message is that we must do what we can to prevent our kids from feeling alienated and disengaged. This isn't exactly new advice, of course—it's making it happen that can be hard. Alienation is as much a part of adolescence as acne, as epitomized in the movie *The Wild One*, in which Marlon Brando's character, Johnny, the leader of a motorcycle gang, is asked what he is rebelling against. "Whatta ya got?" he responds.

But alienation isn't inevitable. The key is to make your teen feel like part of a larger whole that is making a difference. One way to do this is to get your teen involved in volunteer work. But ladling soup at a homeless shelter is by no means the only way for a teen to feel connected. Working on a national political campaign can work well, too (witness the passion of young Obama volunteers in 2008 and the fervor of young conservatives in 2010). Teens can also become involved in any number of local civic and political issues. A side benefit is that they will make friends with peers who are also involved in the community, rather than with people like Johnny, the leader of the motorcycle gang (or his modern equivalent).

That's all well and good, you might say, but what about teenagers who spend all their time in their rooms texting their friends or playing video games and who show no interest in soup kitchens or political campaigns—especially (gasp!) if their parents suggest it? Good question, because the more people feel like they are forced into something, the less likely they are to enjoy doing it and want to keep at it (see chapter 4). Although there are no magical solutions here, there are things parents can do. One is to steer children toward their interests.

If they love sports, help them find volunteer opportunities in that area, such as becoming a referee or assistant coach in a league for disadvantaged children. If they love music, they can organize a group to play at nursing homes or day care centers. Another approach is for parents to do volunteer work with their children. We sometimes forget how much we are role models for our kids; they are keen observers, and often learn more from what we do than from what we say.

CHAPTER 6

Scared Crooked

Reducing Teenage Violence

T odd Walker had to do something. In his fifteen years as a youth
football coach in Oakland, California, he watched kid after kid get
into trouble. Many ended up on the streets and became victims of violence. "I was losing too many kids to homicide," Walker lamented.
"Instead of going to graduations, I was going to funerals." As Walker
knew, violence strikes the young disproportionately. In 2006, homicide
was the second leading cause of death among youths ages ten through
twenty-four, second only to accidents. Among African American youth,
homicide was the number one killer. Often, the perpetrators of these
violent acts are other teens. The number of violent crimes committed by
juveniles has been falling since 1995, but in recent years it has begun to
creep up again.[1]

Walker wondered how he could get through to these kids. What
would convince them to stay off the streets and away from crime and
violence? Maybe, he thought, the answer is to scare the living daylights
out of them. Walker founded a program called Restoring Inner City
Peace (R.I.P.) that shows teens, very graphically, where they might end
up if they start selling drugs and hanging out with the wrong people.

He takes groups of young people to local cemeteries and funeral homes and cajoles them into touching a gurney used to roll bodies into the mortuary. "When you're dead, we strap you on here, stick a tag on your toe," he tells them. "Then we put you in the freezer." The kids hear from embalmers who explain how they prepare bullet-ridden bodies for funerals and from former convicts who talk about life in prison. Is the message sinking in? Tyris Bamba, a fifteen-year-old participant in the program, thought so. "It was a reminder of where I don't wanna be," Tyris said. "Now I think I'm more conscious of the friends I hang out with, and the places that people want to go to—where you know bad things are gonna happen. I just stay away."[2]

Walker is one of those admirable people who act on their good intentions, doing something about the problems they see instead of simply complaining about them. He even went so far as to take a second job delivering bodies to a local funeral home so that he could take his kids there and show them the gurneys and coffins. But there's just one problem with his "scared-straight" approach: it doesn't work. In fact, it probably does more harm than good, increasing the likelihood that Walker's kids will commit crimes in the future.

The term "scared straight" was popularized in 1978 by an award-winning documentary of the same name that depicted a program run by a group of inmates at Rahway State Prison in New Jersey. The inmates, all of whom were serving sentences of at least twenty-five years, wanted to do something good for the community and hit upon the idea of meeting with at-risk kids and showing them what prison was really like, with the idea that this "shock experience" would scare the kids away from crime. With the cooperation of the prison superintendent, the local police chief, and a juvenile court judge, the Juvenile Awareness Project was born, in which small groups of teens, typically between the ages of twelve and eighteen, visit the prison and meet with the "lifers." In a typical session, they are subjected to a verbal harangue from the inmates, including graphic descriptions of rape and murder

within the prison walls. After the documentary was aired on television, more than thirty similar programs were founded in and outside
of the United States.

In 1999, another television documentary was aired, called *Scared
Straight! 20 Years Later*, which further extolled the virtues of the intervention. The kids who had taken part in the original visit to Rahway
State Prison, now in their thirties, were interviewed, and most said
that the program had helped them. Arnold Shapiro, the producer of
both the original and the new documentary, was not surprised. Since
the original film was shown, he noted, "I can't tell you how many
people have come up to me and said, 'I was a juvenile delinquent, and
when I saw this, I stopped, I changed.'"[3]

In chapter 2, in which I talked about how to evaluate interventions,
I suggested that we institute a don't ask, can't tell policy, in which we
stop relying on testimonials about whether a program works. People
often don't know how much a program has helped them; after all, they
don't know how well-off they would be if they hadn't participated in it.
Instead, we need to conduct rigorous tests of social programs such as
Scared Straight. The only way we can tell what effect they have is by
randomly assigning kids to a group that goes through the program or
to a control group that does not. Several studies have done just that,
and the results are remarkable in both their consistency and direction:
not only do scared-straight programs fail to reduce the likelihood that
kids will commit crimes, they actually *increase* criminal activity. A
review of seven experimental tests that measured how likely participants and nonparticipants were to commit crimes, in time periods
ranging from three to fifteen months after a scared-straight intervention, found that the kids who attended the interventions were more
likely to commit crimes than were kids in the control groups *in every
single study*. The increase in criminal activity among the scared-
straight kids ranged from 1 percent to 30 percent, with an average of
13 percent.

The program at Rahway State Prison (now called East Jersey State Prison) still exists, and has now served more than fifty thousand at-risk kids over a thirty-year period. Let's do the math—using the 13 percent figure, we can estimate that the program has caused 6,500 kids to commit crimes they otherwise would not have committed. Scared-straight programs thus merit my bloodletting award: they do more harm than good.[4]

Why does taking part in a scared-straight program make kids more likely to commit crimes? The story-editing approach suggests an answer, by asking how these programs change kids' interpretations of why they should stay out of trouble. The problem is that the programs provide kids with *external* motivation—wanting to avoid the horrors of prison—that can, paradoxically, undermine their *internal* motivation to take the straight path. A number of years ago, Daniel Lassiter and I demonstrated this phenomenon in a two-session experiment with college students. At the first session, we gave the students twenty trivia questions and told them that the answers were written on a blackboard, hidden behind a piece of cardboard. Because the participants took the quiz alone, they could have easily cheated by moving the cardboard and peeking at the answers, but none of them did, indicating that they had little intrinsic motivation to cheat in this situation. After all, it was a just a trivia quiz with no consequences for being right or wrong.

There were two conditions at this first session, one of which was just as I've described—those students took the quiz and decided not to peek at the answers. The second group received a strong external reason not to cheat—the experimenter told them that the data would be ruined if they peeked at the answers and that if they did they wouldn't receive their credit for doing the experiment. Remember, no one was interested in cheating in the first place—and no one in either condition did—so this threat was superfluous.

A week or so later, the participants took part in what they thought was an unrelated study in a different location, where they took a very difficult achievement test that contained questions similar to those on the Graduate Record Exam. The experimenter instructed participants to spend about a minute on each question and then to move on to the next question without returning to previous ones. Because this was a difficult, diagnostic test, we expected that participants would be more tempted to cheat in this situation. And indeed, many did, by returning to earlier questions after moving on to later ones.

The question was whether the condition that the students had been in at the first session influenced how much they cheated in the second session. The participants who had received the strong superfluous threat not to cheat on the trivia quiz, we reasoned, might have attributed their lack of cheating during the first session to the threat rather than to their intrinsic honesty. That is, they might have said to themselves, "The reason I'm not peeking at the answers is because I might get caught and lose my experimental credit." As a result of attributing their compliance to the threat, rather than to their lack of desire to cheat in the first place, they might have underestimated how intrinsically honest they were. If so, they might be more tempted to cheat at the second session, because they have come to view themselves as people who are not very honest. This is exactly what we found: the students who had received the superfluous threat at the first session spent more than four times as long reworking their answers on the second test than did the students who had not received the superfluous threat.[5]

How might this explain why scared-straight programs backfire? Some of the teens who take part in these programs probably have little interest in hanging out with gang members or selling drugs in the first place. But because they are considered "high risk," they are put in the program and subjected to hardened convicts screaming in their faces that they will be raped and maimed in prison if they become delinquents. They receive strong threats not to do something they don't want to do in the first place, which, as we saw, can have paradoxical effects. These participants get the message, "Hmm, maybe I *am* tempted by a life of crime if these convicts are going to such extreme measures to talk me out of it." That is, just as with the college students in our cheating study, strong external threats at one point in time can increase interest in the forbidden activity at a later point in time. In this manner, scared-straight programs redirect teens' narratives down the wrong path, making them more likely to give in to temptations and pressures from their peers in the ensuing months.

If this explanation is right, then it should be the case that scared-straight programs are especially likely to backfire with kids who were not interested in criminal activity in the first place, because these kids are most at risk of having their narratives changed from "I'm not very interested in a life of crime" to "Maybe it would be cool to hang out with the guys on the corner." And, indeed, the original scared-straight program at Rahway State Prison was especially likely to backfire among kids who did not have a criminal record at the outset.

GETTING EVEN TOUGHER

Maybe there is another reason why scared-straight programs fail— they don't deliver a strong enough message. What if we got even tougher with at-risk teens? We could send them off to "boot camps" modeled after basic training in the military, where they learn a thing or two about discipline, hard work, and respect for authority. Wouldn't that hammer some sense into them?

This approach has been tried without success, though that hasn't stopped teen boot camps from proliferating. Boot camps became popular in the 1990s and there are now more than fifty such programs in the United States and other countries. Most are for first-time juvenile offenders who are assigned to boot camps instead of prison or other detention facilities. The juveniles typically attend for two to six months, during which time they wear uniforms, follow strict schedules, participate in military-style drills, engage in physical exercise, and perform assigned duties and chores. Although there are very few good studies of their effectiveness, those that have been conducted show that boot camps don't work to reduce criminal recidivism. It's easy to think of reasons why boot camps don't work—maybe they are too punitive, maybe they catch kids too late in the game, or maybe they focus too much on discipline and too little on providing counseling or giving the kids useful skills such as job training. Or, like the scared-straight approach, maybe they don't pay enough attention to teens' narratives about who they are and why they might want to avoid a life of crime.[6]

A KINDER AND GENTLER FLOP

Instead of getting tough with kids, maybe we should provide them with love, understanding, and positive role models. Such was the belief of Harvard physician and ethicist Richard Clarke Cabot, who in 1935 set in motion one of the most ambitious projects ever conceived to prevent juvenile delinquency. This project, which came to be known as the Cambridge-Somerville Youth Study after the cities in Massachusetts in which it was conducted, targeted a group of more than five hundred underprivileged boys. The researchers did virtually everything they could think of to add positive influences to the boys' lives. The boys—who entered the program at the age of ten and a half, on average—were each assigned a counselor. The counselors established relationships with the boys and their families, and referred the boys to a variety of services as needed, including academic tutoring, psychotherapy, family interventions, and recreational activities. The boys received a great deal of individual attention over a five-year period;

indeed, every possible problem area in the boys' lives was addressed. The counselors also helped the boys' families with such things as employment assistance and day care arrangements.

To the great credit of the researchers, they randomly assigned half the boys to a treatment condition that received all or most of the benefits just described or to a control group that received none of these benefits, thereby allowing an experimental test of the intervention. This project remains one of the most ambitious interventions ever tested with an experimental design in the social sciences. Unfortunately, it also ranks as one of the most spectacular failures. A thirty-year follow-up revealed that men who had been in the treatment program were *more* likely to have died at a young age, *more* likely to have committed repeated crimes, *more* likely to show signs of alcoholism, and *more* likely to have had serious mental illnesses than were the men in the control condition. Moreover, the longer the boys in the treatment group had participated in the program, the more likely they were to have negative life outcomes.[7]

What happened? One possibility is intimately related to the story-editing approach. In chapter 4, we saw how vulnerable children are to having their feelings and behavior labeled by adults. This can be a good thing if adults provide a positive label, such as "You are responsible kids who do not litter." But by being selected for the Cambridge-Somerville study, kids were labeled by researchers, teachers, and counselors as "potential delinquents." The researchers may have inadvertently given the kids the wrong story prompt, redirecting their narratives from "I'm a good kid" to "I'm a troublemaker," or at least a potential one.

Another problem with the study, according to some experts, is that it brought the at-risk teens together on many occasions, such as on overnight camping trips. Some of the boys were also sent to summer camps, where they had a ready audience of other teens. This can be a problem, the argument goes, because teens learn from one another and reinforce negative patterns of behavior. In fact, the kids in the Cambridge-Somerville study who did the worst were those who went to summer camp two or more times.

This evidence is circumstantial, of course, but other studies have confirmed that giving at-risk teens the opportunity to hang out with and impress their peers produces negative outcomes. In one program, for example, at-risk teenagers met in groups once a week for twelve weeks. The researchers were trying to instill prosocial goals and teach the kids about self-regulation, but in fact the intervention had unintended negative effects: compared to teens randomly assigned to a control condition that did not meet in groups, those who met in groups were *more* likely to engage in delinquent behavior and to use tobacco products. If you want at-risk teens to act out and become even more deviant, it turns out that one of the best things you can do is to arrange for them to hang out together on a regular basis.[8]

This is probably another reason why scared-straight programs do more harm than good, and why I think we need to worry about Todd Walker's approach of taking groups of teens to the funeral home. These kids are at precisely the age where the opinion of the sixteen-year-old standing next to them matters a lot more than anything the old dude screaming in their face has to say. And remember the Dollar-A-Day programs we encountered in chapter 5, in which teen moms are paid to avoid getting pregnant again? One reason these programs don't work might be that they bring at-risk teens together.

SUBTRACTING THE BAD FROM THE GOOD

What if we gave at-risk kids a lot of attention without bringing them together with their peers? We could assign them an adult mentor who meets with them alone rather than with other at-risk kids. As it happens, this is exactly what the Big Brothers Big Sisters of America program does, and it works. This organization has its roots at the turn of the last century in New York City. In 1902, a group of women began mentoring girls who appeared in Children's Court, and this eventually became the Big Sisters organization. In 1904, a court clerk named Ernest Coulter began matching volunteer mentors with boys who appeared in his courtroom, and this eventually became the Big Brothers organization. The two groups spread rapidly to other cities throughout the United States, and, in 1977, merged to become Big Brothers Big Sisters of America. Today, there are chapters of Big Brothers Big Sisters in all fifty states and in twelve countries around the world.

The goal of the program is to foster a close relationship between a mentor and a child. Mentors are carefully screened and trained and then matched with a disadvantaged teen. The mentor meets individually with his or her mentee, typically for three to five hours a week, for an average time period of two and a half years. A case manager supervises and develops a plan for each mentoring relationship: for example, he or she might set goals related to school attendance and academic performance. But there are no required activities; rather, the emphasis is on the mentor and mentee finding things to do that they both enjoy and developing a close relationship. In a way, the program embodies Richard Clarke Cabot's ideal of doling out love and friendship to at-risk kids while avoiding the parts of the Cambridge-Somerville Project that may have done it in (e.g., providing opportunities for kids to hang out with other at-risk teens).

The Big Brothers Big Sisters program was evaluated with a scientifically sound study in the 1990s. In eight American cities, kids ages ten through sixteen were randomly assigned either to get mentors right away or to be placed on a waiting list (the latter group got mentors after the evaluation ended; the time they had to wait was about equal to the normal waiting period for the program). After eighteen months, the youths in the mentoring group were doing better academically, had better relationships with their parents, were less likely to have started using drugs or alcohol, and were less likely to have hit someone than were the kids in the control group. These beneficial effects were especially evident among the youths who were in mentoring relationships for a year or longer.[9]

WHAT ELSE WORKS?

The Center for the Study and Prevention of Violence (CSPV) at the University of Colorado has done an excellent job of reviewing the literature and publicizing programs that have been shown to work, according to a strict set of criteria. In addition to the Big Brothers Big Sisters program, the CSPV identified a variety of other effective interventions. These programs target kids of different ages and use different approaches, though it is important to note that all avoid the problem of bringing at-risk teens together. It is worth describing the ones that work, because some (though not all) incorporate story-editing principles.

The Nurse-Family Partnership Program intervenes at the earliest point, namely, before children are born. Disadvantaged women who are pregnant with their first child are assigned a nurse who visits them at their homes two to four times a month, beginning when the women are pregnant and continuing for two years after the child is born. The nurses focus on prenatal care and health, the development of the child once he or she is born, and the personal development of the mother. In addition to advice on health care, for example, the nurses give child-rearing advice; encourage the mothers to develop plans for the future (e.g., educational and employment plans); and advise the mothers on family-planning methods and the timing of additional children. The program has been evaluated with three random clinical trials, each of which has demonstrated positive effects on prenatal health and early child development.

The oldest of the three studies followed the children until they were fifteen years old. Among children born to poor, unmarried women, the program succeeded in preventing adolescent delinquency. At age fifteen, the kids whose mothers had been part of the program were less likely to have run away, less likely to have been arrested or convicted of a crime or parole violation, and less likely to have abused alcohol or drugs, compared to the kids whose mothers had not been part of the program.[10]

Why has this program been so successful when other home-visitation programs have not? In chapter 4, for example, we saw that the Healthy Families America program, designed to prevent parents from abusing their children, doesn't work. Although there are many differences between the Nurse-Family Partnership Program and Healthy Families America, two in particular stand out, both of which involve story editing. First, the Nurse-Family Partnership Program attempts to increase mothers' *self-efficacy*, which is their belief that they have what it takes to carry out desirable actions. Specifically, moms are told that they have the ability to bring about desired changes in their own lives and their children's lives, which probably helps to break a self-fulfilling cycle of negative thinking. In this respect it is similar to the interventions discussed in chapter 4 that do reduce child abuse. Second, the Nurse-Family Partnership Program has some similarities to the skill-based treatment program in the Netherlands (also discussed in chapter 4), in that it attempts to get mothers to attend more closely to their children's needs and to foster secure mother-infant attachment relationships. Its success may thus be due in part to the fact that it incorporates some of the best features of other proven interventions.

The Promoting Alternative Thinking Strategies (PATHS) program targets young children in a classroom or preschool setting. The curriculum, which involves half-hour lessons taught three times a week, focuses on increasing and improving children's self-control, emotional understanding, self-esteem, social relationships, and interpersonal problem-solving skills. Studies that randomly assigned classrooms to receive PATHS or not found that children in the PATHS classrooms exhibited superior self-control, had fewer conduct problems, tolerated frustration better, and better recognized other people's emotions.[11]

As its name implies, the Olweus Bullying Prevention Program (OBPP) is designed to prevent bullying in schools. It targets kids at a wide range of ages, namely, those in elementary school through junior high school. The program, which is coordinated by a committee of school administrators, teachers, counselors, students, and parents, begins with an anonymous student questionnaire to gauge the extent of bullying in the school, followed by a conference day at which the results of the survey are presented to students, teachers, and parents. Teachers set firm guidelines against bullying and intervene swiftly when they see it in the classroom or the playground. They meet with bullies, their victims, and parents to come up with a plan to end the bullying. The program has been evaluated in at least four countries with positive results—in schools in which the program was implemented, there was a decrease in students' reports of bullying.[12]

What about mental health services? Two forms of family therapy have been shown to be effective, both of which target teenagers who are exhibiting conduct problems. Multisystemic therapy (MST) targets teenagers who are at risk for being placed outside of the home. A therapist sees the juvenile and his or her family in their home for several hours per week, typically for four to five months. A major focus of MST is to teach parents and other caregivers better parenting skills. Another focus is to reduce the juveniles' contact with deviant peers and increase their contact with peers who are better role models. That is, the therapy specifically targets the problem we encountered earlier with other interventions, namely, that contact with peers increases deviant behavior, especially like-minded peers. One recent study, for example, randomly assigned juvenile sex offenders to receive either

MST or therapy provided by the juvenile probation department. A year after beginning the treatment, those who received MST were significantly less likely to be engaging in delinquent behavior in general and sexually deviant behavior in particular. The more the kids' parents improved their parenting skills in the MST group, and the less time the teens spent with at-risk friends, the better the outcomes. There have been at least fourteen experimental tests of MST involving more than thirteen hundred families; these studies have shown that MST improves family functioning, increases school attendance, reduces criminal activity, and reduces the use of alcohol and drugs.[13]

Functional family therapy (FFT) also targets teens that have conduct disorders, but takes less time (a total of eight to twenty-six hours, depending on the severity of the case) and can be delivered by people with a variety of training (such as probation officers and mental health professionals) in a variety of settings (including the home and juvenile court). It has three phases: engagement and motivation, in which the leader builds trust with teens and their families and targets areas to change; behavior change, in which leaders try to improve parenting skills, family communication, and conflict management; and generalization, in which the leader attempts to maintain positive changes, in part by connecting the family to community resources. Experimental tests of FFT have yielded encouraging results: the criminal recidivism rate among teens who got FFT was 26–73 percent lower than it was among teens who did not get FFT. The intervention even reduced the arrest rate of the siblings of the treated teens.[14]

What if teens have already committed offenses that put them at risk for incarceration? The Multidimensional Treatment Foster Care (MTFC) program is an alternative to incarceration in which teens are placed in foster families. The families receive twenty hours of training in ways to manage a teenager who has conduct problems, and once the child is placed in a family there are a lot of services available. There are weekly meetings of foster parent families, individual therapy sessions for the teens, and group therapy sessions for the teens' parents or other caregivers. The teen's case manager monitors his or her progress at school, maintains daily contact with the foster family, and administers an individual program that each teen is expected to follow. Psychiatric care and medication are arranged as needed. Teens typically spend between six and nine months with the foster family.

MTFC has been evaluated in a number of experiments and has been found to have beneficial effects for both boys and girls. In most studies, teens are randomly assigned either to the program or to the normal course of care in their state, which typically involves group residential facilities. Those who get MTFC are less likely to run away, less likely to be arrested, and less likely to use hard drugs than are those in group residences. One recent study confirmed that an important component of MTFC's success is the fact that case managers monitor the contact the teens have with other teens and do their best to minimize it, thus limiting the amount of time teens spend with their delinquent peers.[15]

VOLUNTEERING AND VIOLENCE

There are other ways to reduce violence that involve story editing more directly. In chapter 5, we saw that teens who feel alienated from their community are most at risk to become pregnant or get someone pregnant. It seems reasonable to assume that alienated, disengaged kids are also more likely to go down the path to delinquency. If so, then the same story-editing interventions that reduce teenage pregnancy—getting kids involved by having them do volunteer work—might also reduce delinquent behavior, including violence.

There is evidence that this is indeed true from two of the programs we encountered in chapter 5, Teen Outreach and Reach for Health (RFH). Not only were students in Teen Outreach less likely to become pregnant, they were significantly less likely to fail a course or be suspended from school, suggesting that the benefits of the program extend beyond preventing teenage pregnancy. Furthermore, eighth graders who participated in the RFH program became less violent. On a survey administered six months after the program, these students reported that they got into fewer fights, were less likely to have threatened someone, and were less likely to have a knife or gun than were students in the control group. This same reduction in violence was not found among seventh graders who were in the program, possibly because they engaged in less extensive volunteer work than the eighth graders did.[16]

Here is how one of the eighth graders in the Reach for Health program described the experience of volunteering in a nursing home: "The elders benefit because they get to talk to people. Some of them are lonely. And they tell us some great stories. This one guy was telling me all about his experiences in World War II. I love going there and I know that they love us being there." Or consider this report from a teacher who helped supervise the volunteer work: "We take this one kid who is one of the most violent kids in our school. He's always getting into fights. And then you see him at this nursing home. There's this patient who is paralyzed in one arm from a stroke. She can't feed herself. And for three hours, this boy sits next to her and just feeds her. One spoon after another. And he looks straight into her eyes. You can see how much he loves her."[17]

Now, as I've suggested at several points in this book, we can't rely on testimonials alone to evaluate a program. But we know from good experimental studies that volunteering reduces teen violence, and these quotes may provide clues as to why—teens change their view of themselves as a result of their volunteer work. Someone who thinks, "Mrs. Johnson is looking forward to my visit next week, and I'm looking forward to seeing her" is probably a lot less likely to get into a fight and risk getting suspended than someone who feels no connections at all.

BROKEN WINDOWS

In 1982, James Wilson and George Kelling published an influential article in *The Atlantic* magazine entitled "Broken Windows: The Police and Neighborhood Safety." The major premise of the article was that appearances matter when it comes to preventing crime. Minor signs of disorder, such as broken windows and graffiti, signal to people that a neighborhood is deteriorating and that it is permissible to break the law—leading to an increase in more serious crimes. A number of police departments took this to heart by adopting "zero tolerance" approaches to petty crimes, such as drinking in public, graffiti, and vandalism, with the assumption that preventing highly visible minor crimes would decrease people's tendency to commit more serious crimes.

The "broken-windows" theory adopts a classic story-editing approach because it attempts to alter people's interpretations of their environment by changing relatively minor story prompts (e.g., graffiti on public buildings), under the assumption that doing so will lead to big changes in behavior (reduced crime). Whether it really works has been a matter of debate. Supporters point to the fact that when New York City adopted this approach in the 1990s, the crime rate dropped dramatically. Critics point out that the crime rate was dropping throughout the country at this time, even in cities that did not adopt the broken-windows approach.

As we have seen, there is nothing like a good experiment to settle the question, and researchers in the Netherlands obliged by experimentally manipulating the existence of public signs of lawlessness and observing whether this influenced people's criminal behavior. In one study, for example, they put a five-euro bill in an envelope that had a cellophane window and placed the envelope halfway out of a mailbox, so that the bill was clearly visible to passersby. Then, from a hidden location, they observed how many passersby stole the envelope. When there were no visible signs of lawlessness, only 13 percent of the passersby gave into temptation and pocketed the envelope. But when the researchers added signs of lawlessness—graffiti painted on the mailbox or litter scattered on the ground below—this percentage doubled.

This study shows that signs of disorder, such as graffiti and litter, can cause people to reinterpret a situation as one in which other kinds of disorder are permissible, such as stealing money. People are highly sensitive to social norms (information about what other people are doing and what they approve of), and subtle indicators of these norms can have dramatic effects on people's behavior (we will encounter this lesson again in the next chapter). When there are signs that lawlessness is the norm, people are more likely to act lawlessly.

But does it work for police to clean up signs of disorder and enforce laws against petty crimes? There is evidence that it does. Researchers identified thirty-four high-crime areas in Lowell, Massachusetts, and randomly assigned half of them to receive the broken-windows strategy of policing. The police eliminated signs of disorder and petty crime in these areas by cleaning up vacant lots, improving lighting, finding shelters for homeless people, making arrests for drug dealing and drinking in public, and increasing foot and car patrols. During the next year, there were significantly fewer serious crimes, such as robbery and assault, in the areas that received the broken-windows policing strategy than there were in the areas that did not. Signs that lawlessness is the norm—such as vandalism and public drunkenness—do appear to breed more serious crimes.[18]

USING IT

I have the greatest admiration for the Todd Walkers of the world, people who see a problem in their communities and devote their lives to solving it. Walker's Restoring Inner City Peace program required a great deal of time and effort to put into place and it certainly meets the "common sense" criterion. How can it hurt to scare some sense into at-risk kids by taking them to funeral homes? Well, we've seen that it can hurt in at least two ways, by giving at-risk teens more of an opportunity to hang out together and by encouraging the teens to think, "Maybe I am attracted to a life of crime if it takes visits to a funeral home to scare me out of it."

What might Walker and other inspired people do, instead of trying to scare kids? It turns out that there are several existing programs that work, such as Big Brothers Big Sisters of America. Matching kids with effective, caring mentors through this organization, or others like it, will do more good than taking them to a funeral home. Involving the kids in volunteer work in their communities is another effective approach.

There is a larger lesson here for all parents, namely, that we should care a lot about who our kids are hanging out with. It is hardly newsworthy, of course, that peer pressure can be very strong among adolescents. I think we sometimes forget, however, how powerful these influences are. (They certainly were a surprise to the researchers who designed programs to help at-risk teens, only to find that the programs backfired by bringing the teens together.) As parents, we can't control everything our teens do, nor should we try to. It's not like we get to pick our kids' friends, especially when they get to middle school and beyond. But by encouraging kids to engage in some activities and not others, we can influence the pool of teens from which our kids will pick their friends. This is one way that volunteer work can help — by exposing kids to like-minded peers who are interested in helping others. Volunteering also helps kids, as we have seen, by fostering the narrative that they are effective people who have a stake in their community.

Finally, we saw that people are sensitive to signs of what other people are doing and what they approve of, and that such things as graffiti and litter can signal to people that criminal behavior is permissible. Keeping one's neighborhood clean and orderly will encourage others to frame it as a place where they ought to behave well.

CHAPTER 7

Everybody's Doing It . . . Or Are They?

Reducing Alcohol and Drug Abuse

A t Penn State University, drinking is as much a part of college life as dining-hall food and choosing a major, which is one reason Penn State topped the 2009 Princeton Review list of best party schools. On Friday nights students line up outside of East Halls, a complex of freshman dorms, to take shuttle buses to fraternity parties across the campus. Many students have already "preloaded" in their dorms before going out, drinking shots of hard liquor or mixed drinks to prepare for the evening. When reporters from the radio show *This American Life* visited, and boarded the bus to interview students, they found one group of women who were on their second loop around campus because they had forgotten to get off at their stop the first time around. Many of these women were wearing cheap, ratty jackets over their mini–tube dresses, an incongruous combination until you realize what often happens to those jackets later—they get soaked with beer or worse. "They get like puked on—you don't want that back," said one student. These disposable garments have acquired a name of their own—"frackets."

It is not just the students who drink. As at many universities, tail-gating before football games is an institution at Penn State. Alumni gather as early as 8:00 a.m. on game days to start drinking and social-izing. One Saturday, after a huge snowstorm, Penn State University did something it had never done before, at least for as long as anyone could remember: it canceled all tailgating outside of its football sta-dium before a game. Although conditions were treacherous, many fans were not deterred, tailgating in their homes or on porches instead. Several families took refuge on the fourth story of a parking garage, setting up their tables and grills in the frigid spaces next to parked cars.

One middle-aged couple was there celebrating their daughter's twenty-first birthday by, to put it bluntly, getting her drunk. Another couple in their fifties, who were also tailgating in the garage, decided to join the fun by giving the birthday girl a drink from their stash, which she readily accepted. When a *This American Life* reporter asked the couple why they had joined the party, the husband replied, "We have to keep ourselves entertained somehow, right?"

"Watch the twenty-one-year-old get plastered, that's the enter-tainment?" asked the reporter.

"Exactly, exactly!" the man replied, accompanied by gleeful giggles from his wife.

Before going any further, I should point out something that is probably obvious to many readers — people at Penn State have a lot of fun. This comes through clearly in the *This American Life* episode. Students sing together, party together, and blow off steam together, at a time in their lives when the burdens of adulthood are just over the horizon. As we've seen, hanging out with close friends is one of the most important ingredients of personal happiness, and although people don't have to drink to achieve this, one has the sense that at Penn State it sure helps. As Ira Glass, the moderator of *This American Life*, put it, it seems like the motto at Penn State is "Drinking together is what we do." Yes, some people overdo it, just as some people drive their cars too fast and cause accidents. But that doesn't mean we should return to the days of Prohibition or the horse and buggy.[1]

But drinking seems to have reached a new level from what I remember from college. In my day, there were keg parties and some people overindulged. Occasionally, someone drank to the point of getting sick, but not so often that we felt the need to wear frackets. Today, the number of students who abuse alcohol is staggering. About 40 percent of college students engage in binge drinking (the figure is above 50 percent at Penn State), which the National Institute on Alcohol Abuse and Alcoholism defines as consuming enough alcohol to reach a blood alcohol concentration (BAC) of .08 percent or above. The number of drinks it takes to reach this level depends on your gender and body weight, and how long you have been drinking, but a good rule of thumb is five drinks in a two-hour period for men and four drinks in a two-hour period for women. People who binge-drink have an increased prevalence of serious injuries, accidents, cardiovascular disease, liver damage, neurological damage, sexually transmitted diseases, unwanted pregnancies, and sexual dysfunction.[2]

At Penn State, one-quarter of the students say that drinking has interfered with their academics. For some, it even interferes with their ability to find their way home. It is not unusual for intoxicated students to enter the houses of town residents and pass out on empty beds. So common, in fact, that the local police have a name for it: "drunk in the house." And, like many college campuses, Penn State has its share of medical problems due to alcohol poisoning. In the first three months of 2007, for example, 109 students were taken to the emergency room with an average blood alcohol level of .245 — three times the legally defined level of intoxication.

Many kids start to drink long before they get to college. Seventy-five percent of teens have tried alcohol at least once, and 23 percent have started drinking before the age of thirteen (think about it — one out of every four thirteen-year-olds you see at the mall has already begun to drink). On a recent survey, one in four high school students said they had engaged in binge drinking at least once in the previous thirty days and nearly one in three said they had driven with someone who had been drinking. Car accidents are the leading cause of death for teenagers in the United States, and 23 percent of teens who die in crashes have blood alcohol levels of .08 grams percent or more (.08 is the legal limit in all fifty states).[3]

Numbers only tell part of the story, of course, and one only has to type "teenage drinking stories" into a Web browser to read tragic accounts of what alcohol has done to the lives of many young people. There is no point in repeating those stories here; I imagine that readers are all too familiar with the havoc alcohol abuse can cause, and many have undoubtedly lost loved ones in drunk-driving accidents or other alcohol-related tragedies.

There is one death, however, that was so senseless and tragic—and close to home—that I haven't been able to get it out of my mind. It happened in 1997 at the University of Virginia, where I teach. Now, before I talk about this incident, I feel compelled to point out that the University of Virginia (UVa) has done a lot to combat alcohol and drug abuse over the years. A 1996 report identified UVa as having one of the twelve best campus alcohol strategies in the nation. In 2003, John Casteen, then president of UVa, was the first recipient of the President's Leadership Group Award, given by the Higher Education Center for Alcohol, Drug Abuse, and Violence Prevention to college and university presidents who have excelled in combating alcohol and drug abuse on their campuses. President Casteen initiated a number of programs, including one that is now named the Center for Alcohol and Substance Education in the Dean of Students Office. In short, UVa has done more than many universities to reduce alcohol and drug abuse.

But in any large group of eighteen-to-twenty-two-year-olds, there will be some who abuse alcohol. This is epitomized at UVa in a practice called the fourth-year fifth, whereby some seniors attempt to drink a fifth of alcohol on the day of the last home football game. To put it in perspective, that's seventeen one-and-a-half-ounce shots of alcohol. A 185-pound male who drank that much in three hours would have a blood alcohol level of .33 — close to the level at which coma and death occur. A 125-pound woman who drank that much in three hours would have an astounding blood alcohol level of .57, well above the level that causes death.

Most of the students who subject themselves to this self-poisoning survive it, probably by spreading out the drinking over several hours. But not everyone does. Leslie Baltz was a talented art major at UVa who had spent a semester abroad in Florence and was writing an honors thesis on the sculptor Elie Nadelman. She had been on the dean's list every semester and her GPA in her major was a nearly perfect 3.97. By some reports, Leslie was not much of a drinker. But on November 29, 1997, the Saturday of the last UVa home football game, Leslie was drinking heavily. It is unclear whether she was attempting the fourth-year fifth, but by the time the football game started she was so intoxicated that her friends left her on a couch in an upstairs apartment. When they returned that evening, they found Leslie comatose at the bottom of the stairs, where she had fallen headfirst. Her blood alcohol level was .27.

That same afternoon, another UVa senior, Ryan Dabbieri, went to a tailgate party and started drinking shots of bourbon. By the time he got to the football game, he was so drunk that he began vomiting in the stands. Two female friends managed to get him to their car, intending to drive him home and put him to bed. But one of the women, who had had first-aid training as a lifeguard, changed course at the last minute and took Dabbieri to the emergency room. It was a decision that saved his life, because just after she and her friend maneuvered Dabbieri into a wheelchair and pushed him through the doors of the ER, he stopped breathing. The doctors managed to get him on a respirator and resuscitate him, and by the next day he was out of danger. Not so Leslie Baltz, who lay critically ill with severe head injuries in the same intensive care unit where Dabbieri was being treated. Her injuries were not survivable, and Baltz's parents made the wrenching decision to take her off life support that Sunday and signed the forms to donate her organs. Her body was cremated later in the week.

Thankfully, the allure of the fourth-year fifth appears to be diminishing. One survey found that 13 percent of fourth-year students attempted it in 2001, but that number had dropped to 10 percent in 2004. In 1991, Peer Health Educators—students trained to educate their classmates about health matters—started an alternative activity called the Fourth-Year 5K, a benefit race that takes place on the morning of the last home football game. In 2007, 143 fourth-year students participated in the race. But, if the 10 percent figure is correct, then twice as many of their classmates were drinking themselves into a stupor (and possibly an emergency room visit) that very same day.[4]

DON'T YOU D.A.R.E.

I wonder how many of those UVa students had D.A.R.E. T-shirts tucked away in their dressers at home, left over from middle school? D.A.R.E. (Drug Abuse Resistance Education) is by far the most common school-based program to combat the use of alcohol, drugs, and tobacco. It began in 1983 in Los Angeles, as a joint venture of the police department and school system. Police officers from the LAPD came into elementary schools for an hour a week and taught kids about the dangers of alcohol and drugs and how to resist peer pressure. The program soon achieved phenomenal popularity. It was expanded to junior high and high school grades and was adopted by school districts throughout the country, including the schools my children attended. Both of my kids sported black D.A.R.E. T-shirts that they received after completing the program, and they were not alone. According to the D.A.R.E. website, 75 percent of the school districts in the United States use the program, and it has spread to forty other countries as well. Recent presidents of the United States seem to agree that D.A.R.E. is a fine program; they have all designated a day in April as National D.A.R.E. Day.[5]

There is only one problem—D.A.R.E. doesn't work. A number of well-controlled experiments have shown that the program has no effect on students' use of tobacco, alcohol, or other drugs. In 2003, the United States General Accounting Office surveyed the evidence and reached the same conclusion. (Apparently, the White House doesn't pay close attention to reports from the General Accounting Office, or at least not this one.) Amazing amounts of time, effort, and money (more than one billion dollars annually) have been devoted to a program that was not adequately tested and, when it was, turned out to be ineffective.[6]

Some D.A.R.E. officials have chosen not to believe the scientific evidence. When fifth graders at the St. Joseph School, in Medford, Massachusetts, attended a D.A.R.E. graduation ceremony, Domenic DiNatale, the Massachusetts state D.A.R.E. coordinator, asked the children, "When people say D.A.R.E. doesn't work, what do you say?" Unsatisfied with the muted responses, he said, "Louder!" To which the children replied in unison, "It does!"[7]

But shouting won't make it work, and in 2001 the D.A.R.E. organization decided to revamp the program. With funding from the Robert Wood Johnson Foundation, D.A.R.E. developed the Take Charge of Your Life curriculum, which was tested experimentally in six U.S. cities. Eighty-three schools were randomly assigned either to a group that used the new curriculum or to a control group that did not. The results were decidedly mixed. Among students who were already using marijuana, those who took part in the program showed a greater decrease in use of that drug than did students in the control group. That's the good news. Among students who were not smoking cigarettes or drinking alcohol at the beginning of the study, those who took part in the D.A.R.E. program were *more* likely to be smoking and drinking by the eleventh grade than were students in the control group. This qualifies the program for my bloodletting award, because it seems like it should work but actually does more harm than good. Based on these results, D.A.R.E. abandoned the Take Charge of Your Life curriculum in favor of yet another approach called keepin' it REAL, which has yet to be tested.[8]

On the one hand, I admire the D.A.R.E. organization for (finally) paying close attention to the evidence and trying new approaches. But doesn't it seem odd that a program would first be implemented in 75 percent of our schools and then tested to see if it works? This is especially mind-boggling given that there are many other programs that have been proven to work. Although most of these programs were not conceived with the story-editing approach in mind, we will see that they have common elements that are consistent with that approach. And, by looking at them carefully, we will get some clues about why the D.A.R.E. program has failed so miserably.

LIFESKILLS TRAINING

LifeSkills Training (LST) was developed in the early 1980s as an anti-smoking program and was soon expanded to target the use of alcohol and drugs as well. It is a school-based program that begins in the sixth or seventh grade, the point at which kids are most likely to begin experimenting with alcohol, cigarettes, and drugs. Students attend fifteen class sessions of forty-five minutes each, followed by ten sessions the next year and five sessions the year after that. The curriculum is multifaceted, including units on personal self-management skills, social skills, and information about various drugs and their dangers. In the personal self-management unit, for example, the students engage in a self-improvement project in which they choose something about themselves that they want to change and then work on doing so. In the social skills unit, students work on how to get along better with others and receive tips on how to overcome shyness and be more asser-tive. In the drug-related information unit, students learn about drugs and how to resist influence from their peers and the media (e.g., ciga-rette advertising). In addition, students receive information about two kinds of social norms: the actual levels of drug use by adolescents and adults (which are often lower than people think) and the fact that social approval of cigarette smoking and other drug use is declining. As we will see shortly, conveying these norms to people is an impor-tant part of story-editing interventions.

LST has been evaluated extensively with positive results. One study took place in fifty-six suburban junior high schools in New York State, some of which were randomly assigned to implement the LST program and others to a control condition that did not. Students who took part in LST were significantly less likely to smoke cigarettes, drink alcohol, or use marijuana or other drugs at the end of high school. Similar results were found in a study that took place in inner-city schools in New York City that primarily enrolled African Ameri-can and Hispanic students.[9]

LST helps kids avoid alcohol, tobacco, and other drugs in at least three ways. First, it is not enough to tell kids to "just say no"; it's impor-tant to teach them *how* to say no, and LST does this by teaching asser-tiveness skills. Second, the program imparts a general sense of well-being in kids, which makes them less interested in using drugs. And finally, as mentioned, the program helps combat the notion that using alcohol, tobacco, and other drugs has social benefits. That is, kids who take part in the program are less likely to believe that their peers think it is cool to smoke and drink and use drugs.

PROJECT TOWARDS NO DRUG ABUSE

Project Towards No Drug Abuse (Project TND), developed in the 1990s, targets high school students. Students attend twelve class sessions over a four-week period. Like LifeSkills Training, Project TND is multifaceted; the twelve sessions attempt to explode myths about drugs, improve kids' assertiveness and decision-making skills, and correct kids' impressions about the popularity of drugs. The program has been evaluated in at least three experimental studies in which schools were randomly assigned to receive Project TND or to control groups that did not. These studies found that teens who participated in Project TND were significantly less likely to smoke and use marijuana and were somewhat less likely to drink alcohol than were teens in the control schools.

Enthusiasm about these results must be tempered, however, by a recent failure to replicate them in high schools for at-risk kids in California. Researchers randomly assigned classes to one of three conditions: one received Project TND; one received a new version of Project TND in which small groups of students were formed and led by student leaders who had been nominated by their peers; and one was a control group in which there was no program. The teens who received the standard version of Project TND were no less likely to smoke, drink, or use other drugs than kids in the control condition at a one-year follow-up. It is not clear why Project TND didn't work in this study when it did in the earlier investigations, especially given that some of the earlier studies also included schools for at-risk kids.

The results for the teens in the peer-led version of Project TND were even more interesting. It turned out that this program helped some kids and hurt others, depending on the extent to which the teens' friends were substance abusers. If teens hung out with friends who did not smoke, drink, or use drugs, then participating in the peer-led Project TND curriculum was beneficial: they became even less likely to use these substances, relative to teens in the control condition. But if teens hung out with friends who did smoke, drink, and use other drugs, then participating in the peer-led Project TND curriculum backfired: it made them *more* likely to use these substances. The researchers refer to this as a "peer acceleration" effect, because the peer-led substance-abuse program seems to have accelerated the influence of the peer group. If a kid's friends were on the straight and narrow, he or she became even less likely to imbibe. But if a kid's friends were smokers, drinkers, or potheads, the program made him or her even more likely to join them. This finding is reminiscent of the main conclusion from the previous chapter on teen delinquency: when teens hang out with other teens who are engaged in risky behaviors, they tend to imitate those risky behaviors.[10]

MIDWESTERN PREVENTION PROJECT

As powerful as school-based programs can be, they are obviously limited by the fact that they can reach kids for only a brief amount of time in the school environment. What if we targeted teens' parents and the general community as well? This is the goal of the Midwestern Prevention Project (MPP), an ambitious intervention developed in the 1980s. It includes a school-based program like that offered by LST, namely, one that begins in the sixth or seventh grade, teaches kids how to resist peer pressure, and conveys information about the dangers of drugs. MPP goes beyond LST, however, by including interventions outside of the school. There are sessions for parents that teach communication and child-rearing skills, plus community and government leaders are consulted and encouraged to offer drug prevention services and to coordinate those services across community agencies. Finally, there is media coverage of the program in the form of public service announcements, press conferences, newspaper articles, and interviews with the staff on television and radio.

The main evaluation of the program was conducted in the Kansas City school system, which randomly assigned schools either to receive MPP or to a control group that did not. By the end of their senior year, teens who took part in the program were smoking less, using less marijuana, and, to some extent, drinking less alcohol. A follow-up was conducted in schools in the Indianapolis area a few years later with some modifications. Again, the program was effective, especially among sixth and seventh graders who were already smoking, drinking, or using marijuana at the outset of the program. Like LST, the program works in part by changing teens' perceptions of how popular smoking and drinking are among their friends. They come to believe that their friends would be less receptive to these activities, which makes them less inclined to smoke or drink.[11]

SOCIAL INFLUENCE INSIDE OUR HEADS

The success of the three programs just reviewed is no doubt due to the fact that they are multifaceted. Because substance abuse has many causes, it is important to attack it from many angles, and each of the programs does just that. One of the main reasons that kids begin smoking or drinking, however, is because their friends pressure them into it. Virtually all teens are desperate for approval from their friends, and if Tyler or Taylor, the coolest kid they have ever met, gives them a cigarette and dares them to smoke it, it can be incredibly hard to say no. Many teens succumb to pressure from their friends to smoke, drink, take drugs, have sex, drive too fast, and any number of other activities that make their parents' hair stand on end. It is thus no coincidence that all the effective programs attempt to blunt peer influence by providing assertiveness training, role-play exercises, and the like.

But there is another kind of peer pressure that can be equally powerful, and that is the pressure that exists inside our heads. Yes, we may find ourselves in situations in which Tyler is twisting our arms to get us to smoke or drink. But there are plenty of times when Tyler isn't around and yet we *imagine* what he would want us to do. We all have perceptions of what the social norms are, namely, what we think the people we care about are doing ("Tyler is probably out partying as we speak") and what we think they would want us to do ("Tyler would think it would be really cool if I got drunk"). Even when no one is around to twist our arms, we are subject to imaginary arm-twisting by conforming to what we think others would want us to do. One way to reduce smoking and drinking, then, is to change people's perceptions of what others approve of—in other words, to use the story-editing approach to change people's perceived social norms.

TYLER AND TAYLOR AREN'T DRINKING AS MUCH AS YOU THINK

Most of the programs just reviewed try to change kids' impressions of what their peers are doing and thinking and correct misperceptions about the popularity of drugs and alcohol. But because these programs are multifaceted, we can't be sure how much of their success is due to this kind of story editing. An intervention that has been used primarily with college students, called the social norms approach, focuses exclusively on students' perceptions of what their peers are doing and thinking, with some success. The idea is that if we can correct college students' misperceptions about the prevalence of drinking, maybe that will reduce the pressure in their heads to follow suit.

On a recent survey, for example, 75,000 students at 130 colleges reported how many alcoholic drinks they had consumed the last time they had "partied" or socialized. The amount of drinking varied widely at the different colleges, with the average number of drinks ranging from zero to seven. Most schools (56 percent) fell in the three-to-four-drink range. What was especially interesting was that students at virtually all the campuses overestimated how much their peers drank. When asked to guess how many drinks the typical student at their institution had consumed the last time he or she "partied" or socialized, most students—71 percent—overestimated the amount of drinking on their campus. Only 14 percent guessed the correct number (15 percent guessed too low).

This tendency to overestimate how much one's fellow students drink has been found on survey after survey, on virtually all college campuses, among virtually all subgroups of students (e.g., men and women, different racial groups, students who are or are not in fraternities or sororities). Students also tend to overestimate how much their peers use other recreational drugs. Why do students get it wrong? Those who drink excessively stick out more than those who drink moderately (or not at all), and we thus are more likely to notice and remember them. When walking across campus on a Saturday night, for example, we are more likely to notice the inebriated students who are shouting loudly and carrying on than the sober students who are walking quietly to their dorms. Also, the overt act of drinking is easier to observe than someone's private doubts about the practice: just because we see someone drink a couple of beers at a party doesn't mean that that person is comfortable with what he or she is doing or will necessarily drink at the next party. And finally, films, television shows, and advertisements often glorify alcohol use and convey the impression that it is more common than it actually is.

For all these reasons, students overestimate how much others drink. Given the power of peer pressure, this mistaken belief can be quite consequential. In the survey of 75,000 college students, for example, the researchers looked at who drank the most. Some of the results were just as we would expect—members of fraternities or sororities drank more than nonmembers, men drank more than women, and students who attended schools where there was a lot of drinking drank more than students who attended schools where there was less drinking. By far the biggest predictor, however, was how much students *thought* their peers drank, independent of the *actual* amount of drinking at their school. Thus, if you want to know how much college students drink, ask them how much they think their peers drink.[12]

In other words, many people overestimate how much their peers drink, which makes them drink more than they otherwise would in order to conform to this imagined (but mistaken) norm. This doesn't mean that everyone drinks as much as they think their peers are drinking; if that were the case, then the real norm at their university would be the same as people imagined it to be. For example, if people believe that the norm is to have five drinks when socializing, and as a result they have five drinks, then the average *would* be five drinks and people's perceptions of the norm would be accurate. Instead, people ordinarily might not drink at all or have one or two drinks, but because they think other students are having five drinks, they up their consumption to three or four to be closer to the norm. If so, then we might succeed in reducing drinking by correcting students' impressions about how much their peers drink.

This is the reasoning behind the social norms approach, which has become a popular way of addressing alcohol abuse at colleges and universities. College administrators try to disseminate information about the actual amount of drinking on their campuses in the hope that this will correct students' misperceptions and that they will drink less as a result. One reason for the popularity of this approach is that it can be administered cheaply on a mass scale. Administrators place ads in college newspapers, distribute computer mouse pads with messages printed on them, and put posters up around campus (an example of one used at the University of Virginia is shown on the next page). In one particularly creative campaign at the University of Virginia, called the Stall Seat Journal, posters are placed on the insides of doors in bathroom stalls around the university.[13]

It will come as no surprise to readers that the social norms approach was implemented widely before it was adequately tested. In recent years, though, there have been some rigorous experimental tests of its efficacy. One study was conducted at eighteen colleges and universities in the United States. First, a random sample of students at each institution completed a survey on which they indicated how much alcohol they typically drink. Then, half the institutions (randomly assigned,

Traditions at UVA?

10,000 students attended the last home football game
7,503 students participate in community service
Have 0-4 drinks during the week

2 out of 3 UVA students have 0-4 drinks per week.*

of course) conducted a social norms campaign for three consecutive semesters, in which they publicized the average amount of drinking on their campus using newspaper ads, posters, and e-mails. Finally, students at all the institutions were surveyed again about how much they typically drink. The results showed that the social norms campaigns worked: students at schools that implemented the campaigns, compared to students at the schools that did not, lowered their perception of how much their peers drink and drank less alcohol themselves.

So far so good. Unfortunately, though, a follow-up study by the same team of researchers failed to replicate these encouraging results. The researchers selected an additional fourteen colleges and universities and again randomly assigned half to a treatment condition that implemented a social norms campaign for three semesters, and half to a control condition that did not. Even though the seven institutions in the treatment condition used social norms campaigns that were as intensive as in the previous study, these campaigns did not succeed in changing students' estimates of how much their peers drink, nor did they lower the amount of actual drinking. It is unclear why the social norms campaigns failed at the new sample of universities, though one clue comes from the fact that the amount of drinking at the new sample of universities was higher than at the original universities. Perhaps the more people drink initially, the harder it is to correct their misperceptions about how much their peers drink. Another possibility is that some of the universities may not have publicized their social norms programs widely enough.[14]

Perhaps the best summary of social norms campaigns is that they are promising but need to be refined and tested further. One problem with disseminating information through posters and the media, for example, is that these messages are easy for students to ignore. And even if students do pay attention, they might not connect the information to themselves. An alternative approach is to present people with individualized feedback, rather than counting on them to see an ad in the newspaper or a poster in a campus building. This has been done by having students answer questions, anonymously on a computer, about how much they drink and how much they think others drink. They then receive feedback about exactly how far off their estimates are. Some colleges have tried this approach with success.[15]

Another problem with the social norms approach is that the general message might not be appropriate for all students. Remember the survey of 75,000 students? Although most students overestimated the amount of drinking on their campus, 15 percent of the students *underestimated* the amount of drinking. If a social norms campaign were conducted on their campus, these students would discover that other students actually drink more than they thought, which might not have the desired effect. "Wow," these students might think. "If I want to be popular, maybe I should start drinking as much as Tyler and Taylor do."

To illustrate this point, I need to digress for a moment to another topic, namely, how to get people to conserve energy. Researchers in California used the social norms approach to try to get people to reduce their use of electricity. They took readings from the electricity meters at 290 houses twice within a two-week period, in order to get a baseline measure of how much electricity each house was consuming. Then they left a flyer on the doorknob of each house that showed how much electricity that household had been using and the average amount of electricity that their neighbors were using. Think about what this would be like: you come home one day and see the flyer on your doorknob, and read that you are using more electricity than your neighbors. "Whoa," you might think. "I guess I'm more of an energy hog than I thought." This probably makes you feel a little embarrassed, and so you stop leaving lights on when you leave a room and maybe even use your air conditioning a little less. This is just what the researchers found: people who discovered that they were above-average electricity users decreased their use of electricity over the next few weeks.

But what about the people who found out that they were using *less* electricity than their neighbors? The feedback had the opposite effect, leading to an increase in power use. "Why should I skimp on the air conditioning," these folks seemed to say, "when the Joneses and the Smiths are pumping out a lot more cool air than I am?" Thus we see the danger of social norms campaigns: they can backfire among people who find out that they are doing better than average. Perceived norms are a powerful thing. If we think we're conserving more energy than others, we slack off on our electricity use; if we find out we are drinking less than others, we might down a few more beers at the next party.[16]

WHAT DO TYLER AND TAYLOR *WANT* ME TO DO?

Maybe we can get around this problem by examining people's perceptions of what their peers want them to do, in addition to what they think their peers are actually doing. Social psychologists have, in fact, distinguished between these two kinds of social norms. Up to now, we've been talking about *descriptive norms*, which are people's perceptions of how others actually behave in a particular situation (e.g., how much others are drinking or how much electricity our neighbors are using). The alcohol studies we've seen so far address descriptive norms by trying to correct students' beliefs about how much their peers drink.

Injunctive norms refer to people's perceptions of what others approve or disapprove of in a given situation (e.g., the amount of drinking or electricity use that we think our peers find acceptable and approve of). Often, descriptive and injunctive norms are the same: for example, few people crack open a beer and take a swig in the middle of a church service (the descriptive norm is low) and if they did they would be subjected to icy stares and verbal rebukes (there is an injunctive norm against such behavior). But just because a behavior is unusual doesn't mean people disapprove of it: for example, most people don't eat a salad for breakfast, but no one would particularly care if they did. And just because a behavior is common doesn't mean that people approve of it. It seems like more and more drivers in my town run red lights, for example, something that most of us disapprove of. Thus, descriptive and injunctive norms are not always the same and it might help to convey information about both when trying to change people's behavior.

Maybe we could bolster social norms campaigns by disseminating information not only about what people do (they drink less than you think), but also about what people approve of (your peers don't condone drinking as much as you think). Would this be a more powerful way to change their behavior? The study of electricity consumption in California suggests that it might be. With an additional group of homes in that study, the researchers made a small addition to the flyer they left on the doorknob: if the homeowner was using less electricity than average, the researchers drew a little happy face on the flyer (☺), whereas if the homeowner was using more electricity than average, the researchers drew a sad face (☹).

In this simple way, the researchers conveyed an injunctive norm—people approve or disapprove of what you are doing—and this mattered a lot for the people who had been using less electricity than average. In addition to finding out that they were energy savers compared to their neighbors, they also got a little pat on the back, a smiley face that conveyed the message, "Good job! We approve!" This was enough to keep them on track: they maintained their low usage over the next few weeks, unlike those who got the feedback alone (without the smiley face) and took this as license to become energy hogs. The sad face didn't have any effect among those who were using more electricity than average, because finding out that they were energy hogs was enough to shape them up all by itself.

Would conveying information about injunctive norms work in a social norms campaign on college campuses? I doubt that many students would be swayed by smiley or sad faces on posters, but it shouldn't be that hard to find more effective ways of conveying the message that many students disapprove of binge drinking. Some social norms programs have in fact begun to include information about injunctive norms, and while the jury is out on how well this approach works, there is some evidence that this approach is effective.

One study, for example, conveyed information about injunctive norms by associating drinking with an unpopular group, thereby implying that only "uncool" people like to drink a lot. Researchers at Stanford University figured that many students beginning their first year would not want to be associated with older, geeky grad students who spend all their time in the library. At the beginning of the academic year, the researchers posted flyers in a freshman dorm that showed a graduate student holding an alcoholic drink. "Lots of graduate students at Stanford drink and lots of them are sketchy," the flyer said. "So think when you drink...Nobody wants to be mistaken for this guy." In another freshman dorm, the researchers posted flyers that portrayed the negative health effects of drinking alcohol but made no mention of graduate students. Then, two weeks later, the students in both dorms completed a survey on which they reported how many alcoholic drinks they had had in the previous week. They also indicated how much they would want other people to think that they were like graduate students.

It turned out that the "geeky graduate student" flyer had a dramatic effect on the drinking of students who did not want to be associated with graduate students. Among this group of freshmen, those in the "geeky" flyer condition had only had two drinks the previous week, whereas those in the health flyer condition had six drinks the previous week. (The flyers didn't have any effect on freshmen who admired grad students; interestingly, they didn't drink much to begin with.) Young people have a keen eye for what their peers approve of, and associating drinking with a geeky, disapproved-of group proved to be a powerful deterrent.[17]

Two of the programs we reviewed earlier that worked with high school students did so in part by changing injunctive norms. Teens who took part in the LifeSkills Training program were less likely to believe that their peers think it is cool to smoke, drink, and use drugs. And one way the Midwestern Prevention Project works is by changing teens' perceptions of how receptive their friends would be to smoking and drinking. The teens come to believe that their friends would be less receptive, which makes them less likely to imbibe.[18]

These findings offer a clue about why the D.A.R.E. program does not work. A distinctive feature of the D.A.R.E. program is that it is run by police officers from the local community, whereas the LifeSkills Training Program and the Midwestern Prevention Project are administered by teachers. Now, on the one hand, bringing police officers into the classroom in a teaching role might be a wonderful way to improve relations between the police and community members and break down kids' stereotypes about the police. But if the goal is to change kids' beliefs about what their peers approve or disapprove of, police officers may not be in the best position to accomplish this goal. Think about a kid who is already feeling a bit alienated and believes that smoking or drinking is going to make him popular with the Tylers and Taylors in his class—the cool kids. It won't be an easy sell for a police officer to convince him otherwise, because to an at-risk, disengaged kid, the police represent the authority they are rebelling against. It may be easier for a teacher, armed with an effective curriculum, to reach these kids.

I don't mean to suggest that police officers could never be effective in the classroom. But the fact remains that D.A.R.E. has had little success in reducing alcohol, tobacco, and drug use, whereas LST and MPP are effective. And these successful programs work in part by convincing kids that drinking, smoking, and taking drugs are not going to make them as popular as they think.

VOLUNTEER WORK AND SUBSTANCE ABUSE

What else does the story-editing approach have to offer, other than targeting teens' interpretations of what their peers are doing and thinking? In chapters 5 and 6, we saw that teens who feel disengaged and alienated are especially likely to become pregnant and commit violent acts. We also saw that an effective way of changing their self-views, making them feel more engaged and connected to their communities, is to get them to do community service. Might this also work to reduce substance abuse? No one would argue that getting teens to volunteer at a nursing home is the sole solution to drinking, smoking, and drug abuse. But it might help.

One study, for example, found that teens in inner-city schools who believed that they had few prospects in life—that is, that they had few friends they could count on and had little chance of going to college or getting a good job—were especially likely to engage in binge drinking. And the more they engaged in binge drinking over time, the more their view of their prospects sank. These kids were caught in a self-defeating thinking pattern that we've encountered several times in this book.[19]

I don't know of any research that has tested the hypothesis that engaging in community service will reduce substance abuse. There is a promising hint from one study, however, that surveyed more than 27,000 students at 119 colleges. The more volunteer work students reported doing, the less likely they were to say they abused alcohol. Although this is a correlational finding, it at least raises the possibility that encouraging students to volunteer will reduce problem drinking.

There was another intriguing finding from this study. Independent of the amount of volunteer work students themselves did, the amount of volunteer work that *other* students at their university did predicted lower alcohol use. Students who attended universities at which there was a culture of volunteering were less likely to abuse alcohol than were students who attended other universities. Thus we can predict whether a given college student abuses alcohol, at least to some extent, by knowing how much other students at his or her university volunteer, independent of how much that particular student volunteers. Colleges and universities have unique cultures, and ones that value volunteer work, it seems, devalue alcohol abuse. (Given that I focused earlier on alcohol abuse at the University of Virginia, I should mention that (a) most students at UVa don't abuse alcohol and (b) many engage in volunteer work. In fact, in 2009, UVa won an award from the Corporation for National and Community Service for its emphasis on community service and for having a high percentage of students who engage in service activities.)

The fact that an individual student's decision about how much to drink is influenced by the culture at his or her university is another indication that people are very sensitive to what their peers think and do. Imagine a student who finds out that many of her friends and acquaintances are going to spend spring break doing a service project in New Orleans instead of partying on the beaches of Florida. This student has learned something important about the norms at her university, norms that play a very important role in shaping her behavior.

USING IT

I hope that parents who have read this chapter will be proactive in a number of ways. If your kids go to one of the 75 percent of schools that has adopted the D.A.R.E. program, you might contact your school administrators and ask politely, "Why are you using a program that doesn't work, when you could easily be using a program that does?" You might direct them to the websites of programs such as LifeSkills Training (http://www.lifeskillstraining.com/).

Another clear message from this chapter and the two previous ones is that parents and teachers should do what they can to prevent kids from feeling alienated and disengaged. This is hardly news, though the ways of accomplishing it—such as getting kids involved in community service—are. Another solution, as we've seen, is to correct misperceptions about two types of social norms: what kids think their peers are doing and what they think their peers approve of. If parents and teachers can set kids straight about the prevalence of smoking, drinking, and drug use (or the lack thereof), these activities are likely to seem less alluring.

How can we best accomplish this? No one said it was easy, but there are things we can do. One way that kids learn about what is cool is through television and movies, many of which, unfortunately, glamorize smoking and drinking. About 70 percent of movies made in the United States depict someone smoking, and it is often the sexy, affluent, glamorous stars who light up and appear to enjoy it (we don't see their yellowing teeth or hear their hacking coughs). And research shows that the more kids watch movies in which people smoke, the more likely they are to try smoking. One study randomly assigned ninth graders to see the movie *Reality Bites*, either with or without the smoking scenes edited out. In the unedited version of the movie, the lead characters, played by Winona Ryder and Ethan Hawke, smoke in several scenes. In the edited version, the researchers removed these scenes while preserving the story line. The kids who saw the unedited version—with the smoking scenes—reported that smokers were cooler people and expressed more of an intention to smoke themselves than did the kids who saw the edited version.

What, then, can parents do? We can monitor the movies our kids see and boycott the ones that glamorize smoking and drinking. We can also lobby the movie industry to end this glamorization (see, for example, http://smokefreemovies.ucsf.edu/). If our kids do watch movies that glamorize smoking, we can talk to them about the dangers of smoking in advance and show them antismoking ads. The experiment mentioned above, for example, included an additional condition in which ninth graders first saw an antismoking advertisement and then saw *Reality Bites* with the smoking scenes. The antismoking advertisement worked as a prophylactic: the kids in this condition did not glamorize smoking and reported no more of an intention to smoke than did kids who saw the movie with the smoking scenes removed.[20]

Kids don't learn about social norms only from the movies, of course; they are hugely influenced by their peers. We might be tempted to lock our kids in their rooms until they turn twenty, but that is hardly the solution. After all, part of growing up is finding close friends we value, trading information about music, books, and movies, and carving out a niche for ourselves that is independent of our parents. Would you rather that your fourteen-year-old son have a tight-knit group of friends who influence his tastes and preferences, or that he spend every weekend night holed up in his room by himself? Of course we want our kids to have friends, but peer influence comes with the territory. What we don't want is for kids to have the wrong friends—ones who feel like they have no future or prospects and will tempt our kids with alcohol, cigarettes, and drugs. And although we can't control this completely, we can monitor who our kids are hanging out with and, above all, talk with our kids. You can ask them how many of their friends smoke and drink, and while you might not always get an honest answer, you can point out that for every kid who is smoking and drinking, there are probably several others who are uncomfortable with it but afraid to speak up. In essence, you could conduct your own mini–social norms campaign, in which you correct any misperceptions your kids have about how cool their peers think smoking and drinking is.

CHAPTER 8

Surely They Won't Like Me — Or Will They?

Reducing Prejudice

O f the many problems in the world today, one of the most perni-
cious is people's inability to get along with others whom they see
as different from themselves. Sunni Muslims, Shia Muslims, and Kurds
can't get along in the Middle East; Irish Catholics don't mix with Irish
Protestants; Serbs fight Croats; and in central China, the Han majority
clash with the Muslim Hui minority. Then there is the color of our skin,
the dividing line that has haunted America at least since the first European settlers reached our shores and treated Native Americans as curi-
osities or subhumans to be eradicated. The enslavement of Africans soon
followed. The onset of slavery can be traced to a fateful August day in
1619, when English settlers in Jamestown, Virginia, purchased "20 and
Odd" Africans from Dutch traders in return for food and supplies. Slavery was not formally recognized in Virginia until 1662, but the evil, cor-
rupting practice of human beings owning human beings had gained a
foothold in the New World.[1]

As recently as sixty years ago, many states denied basic freedoms to
African Americans, limiting whom they could marry, where they

could live, and where they could send their children to school. Today, such laws are a thing of the past, reflecting a broad change in attitudes in America. For example, in 1958, only 37 percent of white Americans said that they were willing to vote for a well-qualified black presidential candidate, whereas in 1997, 93 percent said they were willing to do so. In 2008, of course, this became a reality when Barack Obama was elected president of the United States.

Nonetheless, the color of our skin still matters. Consider what happened in Jena, Louisiana, in August of 2006. No one wants to stand under the hot glaring summer sun for too long in this small southern town. This was a problem at the local high school, because there was only one shade tree where students could escape the sun during recess, and by tradition it was reserved for whites only. That's the way it had always been, at least until Kenneth Purvis, an African American student, got tired of sitting in the sun and asked the principal if he might be allowed to rest beneath the tree. (The fact that he had to ask is telling.) The principal told Purvis that he could sit wherever he liked, but not everyone reacted kindly to Purvis's request. When students arrived at school the next morning, they were greeted by three nooses dangling from the oak tree, starkly evocative of the countless lynchings of African Americans in the not-so-distant Southern past. After a good deal of controversy over this incident, including a fight where six African American students were arrested for severely beating a white student, the town leaders decided that the best solution was to cut down the tree.

Such blatant racism is not limited to the deep South, as illustrated by what happened at a swim club in suburban Philadelphia in the summer of 2009. A city day camp contracted with the club to use its pool on Mondays, because budget cuts had shut down the public pool they had been using. But when the sixty-five black and Hispanic kids got off the bus and walked into the club, towels in hand, most of the white kids got out of the pool. The white kids' parents "were standing there with their arms crossed," said Alethea Wright, the director of the day camp. "I was hearing comments like, 'They won't be back here.'" One of the campers, nine-year-old Kevina Day, heard a white mother complain about the influx of campers. "She was saying a lot of racist words," Kevina reported. "The lady who said the bad things is a grown woman. We're just kids." A few days later, the director of the pool refunded the day camp's money and told them not to come back. "There is a lot of concern that a lot of kids would change the complexion...and the atmosphere of the pool," he said. Three hundred and eighty-seven years after the Jamestown settlers purchased the first slaves in America, race continues to divide Americans.[2]

Lest you think these are isolated instances of discrimination, consider studies that the United States Department of Housing and Urban Development has conducted since the 1970s on housing bias. Trained testers visit real-estate agencies to inquire about renting or buying houses and apartments that had been randomly selected from newspaper ads. The testers present nearly identical credentials—similar incomes, debt levels, educational backgrounds, employment status, and family circumstances. The only way they differ is in their race or ethnicity—some are white, some are black, and some are Hispanic. Even in the most recent testing, in the year 2000, a sizable percentage of the blacks and Hispanics were treated more negatively than whites. When inquiring about rental units, for example, whites were favored over blacks 22 percent of the time and over Hispanics 26 percent of the time.[3]

It is thus imperative to find ways to bridge the racial divide, and to do so, business leaders, educators, and psychologists have developed all sorts of interventions and workshops, like the Theatre at Work program discussed in chapter 2. Do they work? The answer is by now familiar: many well-known interventions either have not been adequately tested or have been shown to be ineffective, whereas techniques developed by social psychologists, using the story-editing approach, show great promise.

Let's begin by considering a well-known intervention that was implemented at a small liberal arts college a few years ago. An attractive student with striking blue eyes, whom I will call Lauren, showed up bright and early at a campus building for a group exercise on intergroup relations. At the beginning of the meeting, the group leader, a middle-aged woman, noticed that Lauren did not have a notebook or pencil to take notes and spent several minutes belittling her for her forgetfulness. Here is what happened next:

LEADER: You're acting angry.

LAUREN: I am angry.

LEADER: What are you angry about?

LAUREN: I'm angry that you are yelling at me.

LEADER: [Turning to the other students] Do you hear me yelling?
[Turning back to Lauren] THIS IS YELLING! Have I done that yet?

LAUREN: Okay, you're using a stern voice.

LEADER: Are you... are you defining ME?

LAUREN: No I am not defining you.

LEADER: [To the other students] Is she defining me? Did she say I am yelling when I am not? Perception is everything. [To Lauren] Do you feel like I'm yelling at you?

LAUREN: Yes.

LEADER: Yes—why?

LAUREN: Because you are using a stern voice.

LEADER: A stern voi... Honey, it isn't my fault you are stupid.

LAUREN: Would you like me to go get my paper and pencil?

LEADER: I wouldn't like you in any way, shape, or form.

LAUREN: Okay then, that's fine.

LEADER: Let's get that understood here.

Lauren: Okay.

Leader: It isn't a matter of whether I like you or not.

The group leader then asked Lauren to repeat an increasingly long string of phrases until she stumbled and failed. The leader harangued her again about not having her pencil and paper.

Leader: Did you learn anything?

Lauren: [Barely audible] Yes.

Leader: Do you appreciate what you just learned?

Lauren: [Barely audible] Yes.

Leader: Did you like the way it was taught?

Lauren: [Lips trembling] No.

Leader: Nooo—any of the rest of you ever taught in that fashion?

Scattered voices: Yes.

Leader: Yes. And did you have to express appreciation for it?
    Yeah…[Lauren is openly crying at this point.] Did you learn
    something from her example? [To Lauren] What are you crying
    about?…What are you crying about?

Lauren: My feelings were hurt.

Leader: How were your feelings hurt?

Lauren: [Inaudible]

Leader: Should I feel sorry for her?

Lauren: [Crying openly] I don't expect you to.

Leader: [To other students] Should I feel sorry for her? Some of you
    are thinking that this is too harsh for this young woman.

Although this might seem like a clear case of abuse on the part of the leader, in fact it was an exercise designed to raise awareness about prejudice and racism. The group leader, a woman named Jane Elliott, was conducting a workshop she developed to get people to experience firsthand what it feels like to be the victim of prejudice. The students had arrived at a campus building at 8:00 a.m. and were divided into two groups on the basis of the color of their eyes. Those with blue eyes (like Lauren) were asked to put a green felt collar around their necks and wait in a bare room with an insufficient number of chairs. Those with brown eyes waited in a different room, where there were refreshments and plenty of places to sit. Elliott told the brown-eyed students that for the next two hours they would be the privileged, powerful group that was superior to blue-eyed people. The blue-eyed students, she informed them, would be treated as inferior, unintelligent people who had no rights.

The blue-eyed students were then ushered into the room and instructed to sit in the middle, surrounded by the brown-eyed students. Some had to sit on the floor because there were not enough chairs. The exercise began with Elliott declaring, "I'm your resident bitch for today and make no mistake about it, that's exactly what this is about." For the next two hours, she belittled, insulted, and humiliated Lauren and the other blue-eyed students.

Elliott developed her exercise many years earlier, while teaching in an elementary school in a rural Iowa town. The day after Martin Luther King was assassinated, she was determined to teach her all-white students about prejudice and came up with the idea of dividing them on the basis of the color of their eyes, designating one group as inferior to the other. In 1970, ABC News produced a documentary film on Elliott's technique called *The Eye of the Storm*, and Elliott eventually left her teaching job to become a full-time diversity trainer. The exercise with college students, described above, was captured in a 2001 documentary film entitled *The Angry Eye*.[4]

Elliott is a determined woman who has dedicated her life to reducing prejudice and racism. "I'm trying to give the people who participate in this exercise the opportunity to find out how it feels to be something other than white in this society," she says in the 2001 documentary. And Elliot is convinced that it works. "I think the exercise does indeed make [the participants] more aware and I think it does indeed...allow them to have more empathy. I know it does. I think it changes the way they think about themselves and their environment. I think it changes the way they perceive others. I think it changes the way they perceive their own power." But is she right?[5]

DIVERSITY TRAINING AND MULTICULTURAL EDUCATION

Diversity training evolved in response to a variety of pressures, including the influx of women and minorities into the workforce, the internationalization of business, the integration of college campuses, and affirmative-action policies in the workplace. Dozens of nonprofit and for-profit organizations have developed training programs for businesses, schools, and other organizations that include written materials, videos, skits (like those performed by Theatre at Work), and role-playing, adding up to a $10-billion-per-year industry. Approximately 65 percent of organizations in the United States and 60 percent of organizations in the United Kingdom offer diversity training. Some focus on improving productivity in businesses that, increasingly, have multicultural workforces; some target discriminatory behavior in the workplace; others attempt to increase the hiring and promotion of women and minorities. But all such programs, directly or indirectly, are concerned with reducing prejudice and discrimination. At this point, it will probably come as little surprise that very few of these programs have been adequately tested.[6]

A few years ago, for example, administrators at the university where I teach decided that all incoming students should undergo some form of diversity training. One idea under consideration was to ask students to complete a Web-based exercise that would increase their sensitivity toward members of other groups and enlighten them about the diversity of the university community they were about to join. Who should develop the exercise? The administrators sought proposals from businesses that have sprung up to provide diversity training and invited a few finalists to make presentations about the exercises they would offer. I was able to attend a couple of these presentations and came away discouraged. Although well-meaning, the staffs of these companies appeared to know little about the literature on diversity and prejudice, and their programs were based more on common sense than on well-grounded research.

Even worse, neither they nor the university administrators planned to test how effective the Web exercise would be, other than to ask participants a few questions about their impressions of it. As I discuss in chapter 2, such questions are no substitute for an experimental design in which people are randomly assigned to a group that gets the intervention or to a control group that does not. It did not occur to the administrators, however, to ask the diversity-training companies, "How will we know if your intervention works?"

In their defense, none of the administrators was a social scientist who could be expected to know how to test interventions. And once some faculty members in the psychology department explained to the administrators the importance of testing interventions experimentally, they got it. (Because of other pressures, the diversity exercise was never implemented, but that's another story.)

My point is that we have no idea whether most diversity-training programs are having the intended beneficial effects, are a colossal waste of time, or, worse, are doing harm. This state of affairs is not limited to diversity-training programs in organizational settings like business and universities. In 1997, President Clinton formed the President's Initiative on Race, which, among other things, reviewed many of the programs in the United States that had been developed to promote racial reconciliation. In 1999, the commission published a report that identified 124 of the most promising programs, including religion-based initiatives, governmental interventions, mentoring programs, and educational interventions. However, only about 30 percent of the programs had conducted internal evaluations of their efficacy, and less than 10 percent of the programs had been evaluated rigorously by outside evaluators. And the report mentions only two programs that compared people who received interventions to control groups that did not.[7]

As I discuss in chapter 2, it is difficult, though not impossible, to test such interventions experimentally. Let's return to Jane Elliott's blue eyes/brown eyes exercise to see how it might be done. I am aware of three published studies testing the effectiveness of this exercise or versions of it. It is worth going into some detail about these studies, because they illustrate the challenge of conducting solid experimental tests of interventions.

The first study was conducted in an elementary school in North Carolina in the 1970s. One third-grade class received a version of Elliott's exercise over a two-day period, though instead of using eye color as the basis for discrimination, the class was divided into "orange" and "green" people and students wore armbands depicting the color of their group. The day after the exercise, and again two weeks later, the students completed a questionnaire measure of racial prejudice and indicated whether they would be willing to go on a picnic with children from a school attended by black students. Another third-grade class served as the control group and completed the same questionnaire, but did not participate in the exercise. As predicted, the students who participated in the exercise expressed less prejudice on the questionnaire and greater willingness to attend the picnic than students who did not, both right after the exercise and two weeks later. These results are promising, though the careful reader will note that the students were not randomly assigned to take part in the exercise or not. In studies such as this that test group exercises, it can be difficult to randomly assign individuals to the experimental condition, and it is not unusual to compare classes that get the intervention to those that do not. However, better studies include several classrooms and randomly assign classes to condition. Further, in studies such as this one, it is important to assess the students' prejudice *before* the intervention, to make sure that the students in one class are not more prejudiced to begin with. For example, we have no way of knowing whether the students in the experimental condition of the North Carolina study were less prejudiced than the control group before the exercise or whether the exercise reduced their prejudice.[8]

The second experiment was conducted in the 1980s among college students in an education course. Students in some sections of the course took part in a three-hour exercise based on Elliott's technique, in which blue-eyed people were designated as inferior to brown-eyed people. Three weeks before the exercise, and four weeks after, students in all the sections were given two questionnaires that assessed racial prejudice. One measured how comfortable people were with having African Americans occupy different social roles (e.g., physician, dance partner), whereas the other measured people's willingness to speak out in hypothetical instances of discrimination, such as overhearing a store manager refuse to hire an African American. In addition, one year later, the researchers mailed participants a request to donate money to the university's Martin Luther King, Jr., fellowship fund. The results were mixed. On one measure—people's willingness to speak out against discrimination—students who took part in the intervention scored significantly higher than students who did not (that is, they said they were more likely to speak out). However, there were no differences between the groups on the other questionnaire measure (students' comfort level with African Americans in different roles), nor were there differences in the number of students who donated to the fellowship fund.[9]

The design of this study was better than the North Carolina one, because the researchers measured prejudice before and after the intervention. However, because participants were once again not randomly assigned to condition, we need to be cautious in interpreting the results. Also, the participants in this study were almost all female members of the Church of Jesus Christ of Latter-day Saints (Mormons) and it is unclear how much the findings can be generalized to other populations.

The third study—the most scientifically rigorous—tested a workshop conducted in 2000 by Jane Elliott herself. The participants were a randomly selected group of white students at a liberal arts college who were unfamiliar with Elliott's work and who were willing to be randomly assigned either to attend an exercise on intergroup relations or to hear a presentation about intergroup relations (the control group). All participants were told that the exercise might cause stress and physical discomfort. Those randomly assigned to take part in the exercise attended a four-and-a-half-hour session conducted by Elliott like the one described at the beginning of this chapter. In addition, about half the participants attended one or more optional follow-up sessions led by college counselors in the weeks following the exercise. Finally, participants attended a follow-up discussion led by Elliot four weeks after the exercise. Those randomly assigned to the control group filled out questionnaires and attended a lecture-and-discussion section on intergroup relations. To evaluate the effects of the exercise, participants were asked to complete three well-validated questionnaire measures of prejudice four to six weeks after the exercise was completed.

The results were again mixed. On the negative side, no significant differences were found between the intervention and control groups on the Modern Racism Scale, a well-validated measure of whites' attitudes toward blacks, or in the students' willingness to form social relationships with African Americans (both groups expressed a very high level of willingness). On the positive side, white students who took part in the exercise indicated greater anger at themselves for having prejudiced thoughts and expressed a significantly greater willingness to form social relationships with Asians and Latinos/Latinas. There was, however, an important caveat to these positive results. Of the sixteen white students who took part in the exercise, only thirteen returned to complete the measures of prejudice. Two of the three students who didn't return had dropped out of the exercise because they found it too distressing. Thus it is not clear whether the modest gains were worth the cost to these two students, or, indeed, whether there would have been a net gain had the opinions of these two students been included.[10]

Jane Elliott's blue eyes/brown eyes intervention is one of the oldest and best-known diversity workshops. It is thus striking that, in the years since Elliot invented it, only three studies have been conducted to test its effectiveness, and that only one of those studies was a true experiment with random assignment to condition. After forty years, we do not have a definitive answer to the question of whether the blue eyes/brown eyes prejudice-reduction technique is more like bloodletting or penicillin.

What about less confrontational diversity-training techniques, such as the thousands of programs that businesses and schools have adopted to enlighten and educate their employees and students? As mentioned, few such programs have been tested. Of those that have, the results have been mixed. Some programs, particularly those designed for children, have proven to be ineffective. Some, designed for adults, have been shown to have positive effects on people's attitudes and behavior. These programs vary widely—they deliver lectures, assign readings, show films, engage people in small group discussions or role-playing, and increase contact with targets of prejudice—and the amount of time that people spend participating in them varies from four to eighty hours.[11]

What separates the programs that work from those that do not? One thing stands out: the effective programs increase contact between the participants and the targets of prejudice. This finding echoes a long-standing principle in social psychology, namely, that the most effective way to improve relations between groups is to bring them together—under the right conditions.

CONTACT

In 1954, Gordon Allport published a classic book, *The Nature of Prejudice*, which has informed and inspired generations of social psychologists. Allport pointed to the importance of bringing together members of hostile groups under favorable conditions, namely, when the contact is sanctioned by authorities and when the groups share common goals, have equal status, and engage in cooperative activities. Allport pointed out that there was not much research testing this hypothesis, and embraced the experimental approach, which at the time was in its infancy as a means to test changes in attitudes and social behavior. He noted that when testing the effectiveness of programs to reduce prejudice, "the need for a control group is not often realized by investigators."[12]

Social psychologists heeded Allport's advice and have subsequently conducted hundreds of studies testing the effects of contact on prejudice. Although many are correlational studies that compare people who have contact with members of a target group to those who do not, some are true experiments in which people were randomly assigned to conditions in which they do or do not interact with members of the other group. A recent review of all of these studies—more than five hundred in all—supports Allport's hypotheses. Bringing groups together under the right conditions is one of the most effective means of reducing prejudice.[13]

Most of these studies, however, have been conducted in the psychological laboratory. How might we bring people together under the right conditions in everyday life? We can't force people to hang out with individuals who are different from them, especially under the conditions necessary for prejudice to dissipate (e.g., the different groups having equal status and common goals). Maybe it would work to target an institution in which young people are likely to encounter others of different races, ethnicities, and backgrounds, namely, public schools. One reason school integration is so important is because it creates an opportunity for contact between diverse groups. But integration alone is insufficient (as we saw in the tree incident in Jena, Louisiana). Educators need to go the extra mile to ensure that Allport's conditions for contact to work are met.[14]

One of the best ways to do this is with cooperative learning techniques, in which students of different races and ethnic backgrounds work together to solve a problem. There are several versions of cooperative learning, but each tries to capture the conditions that Allport said were necessary to reduce prejudice: the contact between members of different groups is sanctioned by authorities (for example, teachers initiate and support the exercises), each member has equal status within the group, the groups share common goals (e.g., they all want to succeed academically), and to achieve those goals they must cooperate with each other. For example, in one technique, called the jigsaw classroom, the class is divided into groups of six, each consisting of students of diverse backgrounds. Each group is given an assignment, such as writing a biography of Eleanor Roosevelt, and the members of the group are each given materials relating to different parts of the assignment—such as descriptions of individual periods in Eleanor Roosevelt's life. Thus, to succeed, each member has to combine what he or she knows with the information held by each of the other group members, as though they were putting together the pieces of a puzzle. This procedure encourages cooperation between group members and increases the likelihood that they get to know one another as individuals instead of "one of those _____ [fill in the blank—blacks, whites, Hispanics, Asians, poor kids, rich kids, or whatever]."[15]

A recent review of studies that tested the effectiveness of cooperative learning techniques (such as the jigsaw classroom) found encouraging results. In sixteen of the nineteen studies reviewed, students in the cooperative learning groups were more likely to develop friendships with members of other racial or ethnic groups. The cooperative learning groups also had positive effects on academic achievement—the kids learned more than the kids in the control conditions did.[16]

Social psychologists continue to examine the exact conditions under which contact is beneficial. Some researchers suggest that the key is to get people to view the members of other groups as unique individuals, thereby breaking down stereotypes about the group. For example, once Jake learns that Mei Li is a talented athlete and that Jiangguo likes to watch *Seinfeld* reruns, it is harder for him to maintain his stereotype that Asian Americans are academic overachievers with few outside interests. Other researchers argue that it is better to get people to have positive interactions with people they view as *representative* members of another group—otherwise, it is too easy to subtype a person as an exception to the rule ("I like Mei Li and Jiangguo, but they aren't typical Asian Americans"). A third view holds that it is important to get people to redraw group boundaries so that people they previously viewed as outside the group (e.g., "She's Asian, I'm white") are now viewed as part of their in-group ("We're all students at State U"). Research on the effects of contact continues and is addressing how it can best bring about positive change.[17]

IF THEY CAN DO IT, SO CAN I

How can the story-editing approach reduce prejudice? Are there simple ways of changing people's viewpoints that can reduce barriers between members of different groups? The social psychologist Robyn Mallett and I decided to find out. Our starting point was the contact hypothesis, which, as we have already seen, suggests that the best way to reduce prejudice is to increase contact between groups under favorable conditions. But in everyday life, people are often reluctant to initiate friendships with people of different races—not necessarily because they are prejudiced, but because they are worried that it will be awkward or that their efforts will be rebuffed.

Imagine, for example, that you have accepted a position with a telecommunications company and it is your first day on the job. You spend the morning filling out forms and attending orientation sessions until it is time for a break, during which you and several of the other new employees go to the cafeteria for a snack. After paying for your coffee and muffin, you look around for a place to sit and notice that there are empty places at only two tables. At one are three white coworkers, and at the other are three black coworkers, all of whom you met earlier at the orientation session. You hesitate, unsure what to do. Should you join your white or black colleagues? Research shows that people are reluctant to cross racial lines in situations such as this one; if you are white you would likely join the white coworkers, and if you are black you would likely join the black coworkers.

The reason for your choice, however, is not necessarily that you are prejudiced. In fact, you might be interested in getting to know the black coworkers (if you are white) or the white coworkers (if you are black), but are unsure whether *they* are interested in getting to know *you*. "I'd really like to sit with Mary, Jason, and Janelle," you might think. "But it could be awkward; they probably want to be by themselves." Ironically, they might be thinking the same thing—that they wouldn't mind if you sat at their table but they aren't sure whether you really want to. One series of studies, for example, found that white and black college students were both interested in forming interracial friendships but each believed that the other group would likely spurn such overtures.[18]

You might also assume that you don't have much in common with your coworkers of a different race, when in fact you do. When the only thing we know about someone is that he or she is a member of a different race, we tend to overestimate our differences and underestimate what we have in common—such as the fact that we both like (or dislike) NASCAR racing, the Food Network, dogs, golf, or whatever. Thus, you might worry that you wouldn't have much to talk about, when in fact you would quickly find common ground ("You have a Labrador retriever? So do I!").[19]

Robyn Mallett and I found that, for these reasons, whites do, in fact, overestimate how awkward and negative an interaction with a black person will be. White college students predicted that a get-acquainted conversation with a black student would be awkward, but when they actually had the conversation, it was no more awkward than a get-acquainted conversation with a white student—in fact, it went surprisingly well. Maybe, then, whites just need a little story editing to convince them that such interactions won't be as uncomfortable as they think. That is, maybe we can redirect their narratives from "I don't have much in common with blacks and they probably won't want to get to know me" to "Maybe we do have a lot in common and they are as open to being friends with me as I am with them."

Here is how we tried to do it: we showed white University of Virginia students, at the beginning of their first semester of college, a videotaped interview of two other UVa students who had become friends. In the course of the interview, the students mentioned that they didn't think they would become friends at first, but that they discovered that they had a lot in common and enjoyed spending time with each other. Some participants saw a version of this interview in which the friends were of different races (one white, one black), whereas others (randomly assigned, of course) saw a version in which both the friends were white. We figured that white first-year students who saw the interracial friends might change their views of what it would be like to make friends with someone of another race, because, after all, it went well for the students in the video.

Hearing about one successful interracial friendship might not be a strong enough story prompt, however, because the participants could easily explain it away as a special case that doesn't apply to them. To increase the likelihood that the message would hit home, we asked some of the students to write about a time when they didn't think they would become friends with a person but were wrong. We hoped that seeing the video of the interracial friendship, and connecting it to themselves by writing about a time when they formed an unexpected friendship, would make first-year students more open to interracial friendships in their own lives.

To find out, we included several measures of participants' openness to interacting with members of other races. First, at the end of the session, we videotaped participants (with their permission) while they were interviewed by an African American research assistant. We then coded the videotapes to see how nervous participants appeared during this interview. As we expected, the students who saw the interracial video and completed the writing exercise were the least nervous, compared to those who did neither of those things or just one of them. Further, this openness generalized beyond the experimental session. The participants in the interracial-video-and-writing condition, compared to participants in the other conditions, were more likely to become friends with people of other races in the weeks after the experiment.

How do we know this? We didn't, of course, follow our participants around with clipboards, observing whom they talked with at parties or whom they sat next to in the dining hall. Instead, participants responded to an Internet survey on which they wrote down the initials of people they had met during the week after the study whom they thought were potential friends, and then indicated the race of each of these people. The participants who had seen the interracial video and completed the writing exercise wrote down a higher proportion of minorities on their lists of potential friends than did the participants in the other conditions.

It is possible, of course, that our participants were not being completely honest; maybe they exaggerated the number of their black potential friends to make themselves look open-minded. To rule out this possibility, we used a more subtle way of measuring participants' friendship patterns—we looked at their Facebook pages. We asked participants for permission to access their Facebook profiles, though we did not tell them that we would be checking on the race of their friends (nor did participants know that the study was about cross-race friendships). About two weeks after people participated in our study, we checked their Facebook profiles and counted how many friends they had who shared their university affiliation. We assumed that because students had only been enrolled in college for a few weeks, most friends with the same university affiliation would be new acquaintances. Adding a friend on Facebook automatically adds a picture of the new friend to the student's profile, and we used these pictures to categorize each new friend as white or nonwhite. As we anticipated, participants who saw the cross-race friendship videos and did the writing exercise had a higher proportion of nonwhite friends on their Facebook pages than did participants in the other conditions.[20]

Will these results generalize to non–college students? Or even to those who have settled into college life for a longer time period than our participants had? We don't know. Most people have frequent opportunities to make new friends, however, such as in the workplace, in the neighborhood, or at the dog park—and we hope that our story-editing approach can be adapted to situations such as these, thereby lowering barriers to interracial friendships.

One thing we do know is that once people form cross-group friendships, good things can happen. Researchers at Berkeley randomly assigned Latino/a and white students to friendship pairs that met for three one-hour sessions, during which they engaged in friendship-building tasks such as playing games and taking turns disclosing information about their personal backgrounds. Students who were initially prejudiced or anxious about being rejected by the other group showed signs of stress when they met their friendship partner for the first time, just as we would expect from people who are nervous about cross-group interactions. By the end of the third meeting, however, the students were much more relaxed and comfortable with their new friends. Further, those who were initially prejudiced were especially likely to initiate interactions with different members of the other group—that is, with people other than the partner they had been assigned in the study. The bottom line is that interactions with members of different ethnicities and races often go better than we think, and forming friendships with members of other groups breaks down barriers between groups.[21]

USING IT

How, you might wonder, could we "scale up" the kind of intervention Robyn Mallett and I devised, delivering it more broadly to people outside of the psychological laboratory? One possibility would be for policy makers to harness the power of the popular media. We saw in the previous chapter that the media can have negative effects: adolescents who see movie actors smoke cigarettes are more likely to begin smoking. But perhaps we could use the media to our advantage by showing positive role models. Television and radio programs have in fact been used to convey positive messages that have led to widespread behavioral changes. In the East African nation of Tanzania, for example, population growth has been a problem; the number of residents of the country more than tripled between the years 1948 and 1992. To address this problem, the ministry of health sponsored a radio drama in which popular characters engaged in family planning. The program was broadcast nationally for two years in the 1990s, except to an area of the country that served as a control group. People living in the areas in which the program was broadcast increased their use of family planning significantly more than people in the area that was blacked out. In many other countries, television and radio dramas have targeted an array of problems, including the transmission of AIDS, illiteracy, the subjugation of women, and environmental issues.

Most relevant to the topic of intergroup relations, a radio drama in Rwanda attempted to promote ethnic reconciliation ten years after the infamous 1994 Rwandan genocide, in which a staggering 75 percent of the country's Tutsi ethnic minority were killed. Considerable distrust remains in the country, as former killers, victims, and refugees try to live together and deal with their tragic past. The radio drama portrayed conflict between the majority Hutu population and the minority Tutsis in a manner that paralleled the actual events, but in the drama, members of the different groups banded together and spoke out against violence. There was an open discussion of the roots of violence and prejudice, and friendships between Hutus and Tutsis were portrayed. There was even a Romeo-and-Juliet-like romance between a pair of Hutu and Tutsi lovers, though instead of meeting a tragic end, the couple thrived and founded a youth group that promoted peace and cooperation.

Did the radio drama influence people's attitudes and behavior? To find out, a researcher randomly assigned residents of Rwandan villages to hear either the drama about reconciliation or a different radio drama about health. The villagers who heard the reconciliation drama, compared to those who heard the health drama, subsequently expressed more empathy and trust toward their fellow Rwandans and became more in favor of marriage between members of different ethnic groups.[22]

These interventions would be even more powerful if they helped viewers and listeners connect the dramas to their own experiences — as Robyn Mallett and I tried to do with our writing exercise. Some television and radio dramas have, in fact, attempted to do just this, by including epilogues in which a famous actor explains how people can apply the lessons to their everyday lives.

Of course, we can change our own behavior even if we don't listen to radio dramas. We all find ourselves in situations in which we want to start a conversation with someone who looks interesting, but hesitate because the person is of a different race or disabled or from another culture, and we aren't sure whether we'll have enough in common with the person to make the conversation go well, or whether the person is interested in talking with us. More than likely, the other person is having similar thoughts ("Surely he [or she] won't want to talk with *me*"). But if we take a chance and go over and say hello, we might discover that we have more in common than we thought, and that people we're interested in are perfectly willing to get to know us. The next time you are in such a situation, smile and say hello and see where the conversation takes you. You might make a new friend who shares your fondness for dogs, sushi, the Beatles, designer shoes, gardening, or whatever your interests happen to be.

In closing, I can't help but wonder what would have happened if the town officials in Jena, Louisiana, had tried some of the approaches outlined in this chapter. The interventions aren't magical, and would have been particularly hard to implement in the highly charged atmosphere that surrounded the racial incident at the high school. But surely it would have been better to try one of these approaches than to cut down the lone tree in the sun-baked school yard.

CHAPTER 9

It's About Me, Not My Group

Closing the Achievement Gap

Muriel Wiggins was excited when her third-grade teacher, Miss Gill, asked the students to write a poem as a homework assignment. Muriel knew a lot of poems because her father, who was college-educated, often asked Muriel and her siblings to memorize verses and recite them at the dinner table. (When Muriel was telling me this story, nearly seventy years after it happened, she recited all ten stanzas of Edward Rowland Sill's "The Fool's Prayer," a poem she had memorized for her father.) She was thus excited to try her hand at writing verses of her own, and decided to try to capture some of the religious sentiments that she, the granddaughter of a Presbyterian minister, often felt. Here is what she wrote:

> *I often dream of the star of love*
> *The star that shines so far above*
> *The star that came so long ago*
> *That men of this earth His love might know.*

Not bad for a third grader! Muriel handed in the poem the next day, proud of her work. One can only imagine the shock and humiliation she felt when, a few days later, Miss Gill reprimanded her in front of the entire class. The teacher held up Muriel's poem with two fingers, as though it were a piece of paper she had taken out of the garbage, and proceeded to tear it to shreds. "Muriel must have copied this poem because there is no way she could have written it," she said sternly, and as punishment made Muriel stand in the cloakroom for the rest of the morning.

Muriel, it so happens, was one of five African American students in a class of thirty-five kids. Miss Gill was an older white woman who had little time or affection for those five students. One time, Muriel and a black classmate ran into Miss Gill on the street after school. "Hello, Miss Gill," they said timidly.

"Don't ever speak to me outside of the classroom," the teacher snapped.

Most of the other teachers in the school (all of whom were white) turned an equally cold shoulder to the African American students. Muriel's fourth-grade teacher, Miss Rosenberger, held court on the playground for the white girls, who would cling to her dress and vie for her attention. A lucky few were allowed to hold Miss Rosenberger's hand. No black girls were allowed anywhere near this inner circle.

Fortunately, such blatant acts of racism, which occurred decades ago, are less frequent in today's schools. But they haven't disappeared. Consider what happened to a very bright Hispanic girl whom I will call Maria, the daughter of migrant workers who had recently settled in the city where I live. Maria excelled in elementary school and by the sixth grade was in the most advanced reading group. She was an enthusiastic member of both the school band and orchestra (she played the clarinet and the violin), which was highly unusual—she was one of only a handful of students to play in both musical ensembles. But when she moved up to middle school, she was inexplicably placed in a low-track English class and told that she had to choose between the band and the orchestra because she was not academically advanced enough to handle both. There is no way to know for sure, but it certainly seems like her ethnicity and social class led to this oversight. Busy school administrators probably just assumed that she did not speak English very well and could not possibly do well in middle school if she played in both the band and the orchestra. Maria protested, but to no avail. She asked her parents to talk to the principal, but they spoke limited English and did not know how to help.

This story has a happy ending, but only because of a random set of circumstances. Maria was taking violin lessons as part of a scholarship program funded by a local musician, and she mentioned to her violin teacher that she was no longer in the orchestra. The teacher happened to know my wife, who at the time was a member of the school board. My wife made a few phone calls, and Maria was soon given a reading test and found to qualify for the most advanced English class—and to be eligible to rejoin the orchestra and band. Muriel Wiggins, too, was able to overcome her teachers' racism and succeed in school, eventually graduating from college near the top of her class.

But many, many other students of color are not so fortunate and fall behind academically. Muriel reports that most of the other black kids in her school were unable to overcome the racism of the teachers. She remembers the names of the other four black kids in her class and has fond memories of playing with them on the playground and after school, but she has no memories of them in the classroom. The teachers did their best to make the black kids invisible, and to a large degree they succeeded. Even today, Hispanic and black students are more likely to drop out of school and are less likely to go to college. And, when test day arrives and standardized tests are given, Hispanics and blacks do worse, on average, than whites. Though the size of this achievement gap dropped dramatically in the 1980s, it has remained relatively stable since the 1990s and in some cases has even widened.

On a 2007 reading test, for example, white eighth graders outperformed black eighth graders by an average of 27 points and Hispanic eighth graders by an average of 25 points (on a scale of 0–500). In math, white eighth graders outperformed blacks by 32 points and Hispanics by 26 points. These differences might not seem that large, but by the age of seventeen, a black student at the fiftieth percentile is performing only as well as a white student at the twentieth percentile.[1]

Why has the achievement gap persisted so stubbornly? Is the kind of prejudice Muriel and Maria encountered responsible, or are other factors at play? Many causes have been proposed, including higher poverty rates among blacks and Hispanics; the quality of the education that blacks and Hispanics are receiving; social and cultural factors, such as different parenting styles; biases in the tests; and, most controversial of all, differences in native intelligence between racial groups. In this chapter, we will consider the evidence for each of these factors and talk about ways of reducing the achievement gap, including a promising new technique based on the story-editing approach.

DEBUNKING CLAIMS ABOUT GENETIC DIFFERENCES

We can dismiss one claim about the achievement gap outright: there is no credible evidence for innate differences in intelligence between racial groups. I will not summarize all the evidence against the hereditarian view, because Richard Nisbett has done so cogently in his book *Intelligence and How to Get It*. Here are a couple of the most telling findings: first, if there were genetic differences in intelligence between people of African and European descent, then the more ancestors a person has from Africa, the lower his or her IQ should be, on average. Several studies have tested this hypothesis by, for example, measuring people's racial heritage with blood tests and correlating that with their IQs. Overwhelmingly, these studies show no relationship between racial ancestry and intelligence. Second, the gap between blacks and whites on IQ tests and standardized tests narrowed substantially in the fifteen-year period from 1975 to 1990, which is much too rapid a change to be accounted for by changes in the gene pool. And finally, there is ample evidence that environmental factors are completely responsible for the differences between the races in IQ and standardized tests.[2]

What are these environmental factors? The conditions mentioned above probably contribute to the gap, namely, the lingering effects of racism, the quality of schooling that minorities are likely to receive, and cultural differences. As we will see, some of the efforts to address these problems have paid off. But one environmental cause of the achievement gap is not so obvious, and in fact has come to light only recently through research on story editing in social psychology. Fortunately, attempts to rectify it with small story-editing interventions have reaped big dividends. But let's first consider some of the most commonly mentioned causes of the achievement gap and the interventions designed to address them.

LOW EXPECTATIONS

As we saw in the previous chapter, racism has far from disappeared from contemporary American life. Remember the incident at the swim club, where white suburban parents objected to black and Hispanic kids using the pool? It happened in 2009 in suburban Philadelphia, a mere thirteen miles from the elementary school that Muriel Wiggins attended seventy years ago. Fortunately, blatant acts of discrimination in the schools, such as Miss Gill's treatment of Muriel, have become less common. But even so, teachers' low expectations of minority students can hurt in more insidious ways, as illustrated in one of the most famous studies in social psychology.

In the 1960s, Robert Rosenthal and Lenore Jacobson administered a test to all the students in an elementary school and gave the results to the teachers. They told the teachers that, based on the results of the test, some students were particularly likely to bloom academically in the upcoming year, whereas others were not. The catch was that, unbeknownst to the teachers, the "bloomers" were chosen by drawing names out of a hat, not by how well they actually did on the test. In fact, the test was bogus and didn't really measure anything. Instead, the researchers were interested in what would happen if they instilled expectations in the minds of the teachers and told them that some of their students were especially gifted. They sat back and waited, and by the end of the year the results were clear: the "bloomers" had scored significantly higher on an actual IQ test than the nonbloomers did!

The only way this could have happened is via a self-fulfilling prophecy in the minds of the teachers. The students themselves didn't know that they had been designated as bloomers, and neither did their parents. Only the teachers knew, and their expectations caused them to act in ways that actually made the kids smarter. But how, exactly, did this happen? Perhaps the teachers made callous, conscious decisions to treat the bloomers more favorably than their less promising class-mates. But this was not the case; the teachers did their best to treat everyone equally. Instead, despite their best efforts, the teachers acted more warmly toward the bloomers, challenged them more with diffi-cult material, and helped them with their answers when they were wrong. In short, they were better teachers toward the bloomers, with-out knowing it.

In real life, of course, psychologists do not give teachers false expectations about how well their students will do. But teachers are only human. On the first day of class, they know their students' race, gender, and social class, and maybe something about their family his-tory (for example, whether they have an older sibling who did well or poorly in school). Any one of these factors could instill expectations in the minds of the teachers and lead to self-fulfilling prophecies, just as in the Rosenthal and Jacobson study.

To the extent that teachers develop low expectations about black children, then, we have identified a contributor to the achievement gap—teachers treat black children in ways that make the teachers' expectations come true. But is there evidence that this actually happens in real classrooms? Researchers have looked for such evidence and concluded that it does exist. One study found that teachers' negative expectations are especially likely to influence students who are black or from poor socioeconomic backgrounds.[3]

Further, in everyday life, teachers' expectations can easily be transferred to the minds of their students. Muriel Wiggins reports that after a while she gave up trying very hard in school. What's the use, she thought, when Miss Gill won't even believe I'm capable of writing a four-line poem? Nor did it escape Muriel's notice that the teachers rarely called on her or the other black children, or let them perform the coveted classroom duties that are signs of status at that age, such as hall monitor. Who wouldn't give up under such circumstances?

POVERTY AND SOCIAL CLASS

In 2009, 12.3 percent of whites in the United States fell below the poverty line, according to the U.S. Census Bureau. That might not seem like a large number, but poverty levels are defined very conservatively by the United States government. For a family of two people with no children, for example, only those earning a combined income of less than $14,366 were classified as poor. For a single parent with one child, the cutoff was $14,787. Thus there are a large number of families who are struggling but are not officially designated as poor. These figures are all the starker when we consider black and Hispanic families. Even with the conservative cutoffs, 25.8 percent of blacks and 25.3 percent of Hispanics live below the poverty line.[4]

The fact that black and Hispanic children are more likely to live in poverty than white children contributes to the achievement gap in multiple ways. First, children living in poverty are more likely to experience biological deficits that influence intelligence, including prenatal exposure to drugs and alcohol, low birth weight, little or no breast-feeding, exposure to lead, and malnutrition. Second, poor children have less access to good schools, particularly those with experienced teachers and small class sizes. And they obviously have fewer of the educational advantages that money can buy, such as books, summer enrichment camps, private tutors, and SAT preparation courses. Children living in poverty are also more likely to move frequently, which can mean a disruptive change of schools in the middle of the year.

These disadvantages could be addressed by raising the income of people living in poverty. Though this is easier said than done, surely we can do better than we're doing now, given that the poverty level in the United States is higher than in many other developed nations. But there is another set of issues associated with poverty and social class that is more controversial, namely, differences in child-rearing practices between lower-class and middle-class parents. As mentioned in chapter 4, middle-class parents talk more to their children, read to them more, and are more likely to encourage them to question the world and analyze why it works the way it does, all of which likely contribute to the higher academic achievement of middle-class children.[5]

One reason that Muriel Wiggins was able to overcome the racism of her teachers and graduate from college is that she did not have these disadvantages. She came from a supportive family that expected her to do well in school. Her father was college-educated, and two of her uncles were doctors. There were lots of books in her house. The other black kids in her class, she points out, didn't have these advantages and didn't do nearly as well. One way to reduce the achievement gap, then, would be to provide enriched experiences for low-income children in preschool and beyond, essentially giving them the advantages they are not able to get at home. There have been many attempts to do this, as we will see shortly.

BIG INTERVENTIONS TO REDUCE THE ACHIEVEMENT GAP

The picture we've seen so far is bleak. A host of societal and cultural factors contribute to the achievement gap, some with deep roots. It seems like it will take major interventions to make up for the many disadvantages faced by students of color, and, indeed, this is the approach most experts and policy makers have taken. Some argue that school environments and high-quality teachers are the key and that we must throw everything we have into changing our educational system to eliminate the achievement gap. Others suggest that the gap is far too big a problem for schools to solve alone, and that we must focus on issues of poverty and class and culture outside of the classroom. We'll get to those approaches, but first let's evaluate a simpler one: giving disadvantaged students more of an incentive to do well in school.

Paying Kids

According to some experts, disadvantaged kids have little incentive for doing well in school. They have few role models showing them that education is a way out of poverty, and, in the case of students of color, academic success might reduce their popularity with their peers. Perhaps we can get kids to overcome these disincentives by giving them financial rewards. Or maybe it would work to penalize families (such as those receiving welfare) if their kids fail to meet educational goals.

There have been a number of attempts to use incentives and punishments, in the United States and elsewhere, and the results are mixed. Consider, for example, an ambitious project by the economist Roland Fryer, who helped initiate incentive programs in four American public school systems. In two, New York and Chicago, kids were rewarded for doing well on standardized tests or in their courses, that is, for their academic "outputs." In the other two, Dallas and Washington, D.C., kids were rewarded for behaviors that lead to academic success, that is, for their academic "inputs." In Dallas, for example, second graders received two dollars for every book they read. In

Washington, D.C., students were rewarded for such inputs as attending school, good conduct in the classroom, and turning in homework. All told, more than 38,000 students in 261 schools were paid a total of $6.3 million for these inputs or outputs.

To Fryer's credit, he did not just implement these incentive programs, he tested them experimentally. In each city, some schools were randomly assigned to participate in the program, whereas others were randomly assigned to a control group that did not participate. By comparing students in the two sets of schools, Fryer assessed the causal impact of the incentive programs.

The results of the programs were, for the most part, disappointing. In fact, paying kids had a statistically significant positive effect in only one city, Dallas, where kids were paid to read books. Second graders who took part in that program achieved significantly higher scores on a reading comprehension test and received better grades than did second graders in the control schools. But in the other three cities, paying kids had little or no effect on test scores or grades.

There are many reasons why paying kids did not work as well as expected. As we saw in chapter 4, there is a danger to providing kids with strong incentives: doing so can convince them that they are "doing it for the money" and undermine any intrinsic interest in school they had at the outset. On the other hand, if kids have no interest in an activity to begin with, providing them with rewards can't hurt. Unfortunately, there is no way of knowing what kids' initial level of interest in school was when they started the incentive programs, so we can't tell whether the incentives ultimately helped some kids but hurt others. The bottom line is that giving kids monetary incentives does not, as of yet, appear to be a very effective way of closing the achievement gap.[6]

Early Childhood Interventions

Given that some of the causes of the achievement gap affect children very early in life, perhaps the best approach is to intervene as early as possible. A number of interventions have attempted to do just that by offering free preschool and day care programs that include educational and enrichment activities. Head Start, the best-known program, began in 1965 and targets disadvantaged children ages three through five. In 1995, it was extended to children from birth to three years old. Both versions of Head Start provide a wide range of educational and health services to its clients. Both are expensive, costing billions of dollars each year.

Do they work? Perhaps the most shocking answer to this question is that we are only now beginning to find out. When Congress reauthorized the Head Start program in 1998, it did so with the proviso that the U.S. Department of Health and Human Services determine its impact—thirty-three years and billions of dollars after the program was implemented. The result was the Head Start Impact Study, which began in 2002. A sample of three-year-olds, who had applied to Head Start programs at 383 centers in twenty-three states, were randomly accepted into Head Start or assigned to a control group, and their progress was monitored carefully until the end of first grade.

For at least two reasons, the effects of Head Start would have to be very strong to be detected by this experiment. First, more than 40 percent of the children in the control group ended up in another preschool program, which means that the study wasn't testing whether Head Start kids did better than kids who didn't participate in any preschool program, but whether they did better than a heterogeneous control group that included kids who participated in other preschool programs (in fact, 18 percent of the kids in the control group managed to get into Head Start centers that weren't part of the study). Second, not all the kids assigned to Head Start stayed in the program when they turned four, and kids in the control condition were allowed to enroll in Head Start at age four if their parents chose to do so. The net result of this was that in year two of the program, only 63 percent of the three-year-old cohort remained in Head Start, whereas 50 percent of the kids in the control group entered Head Start at that point. The study was thus a test of whether participating in Head Start at age three has any benefits, compared to a control group of kids who (for the most part) did not participate in Head Start at age three, but many of whom did participate in other preschool programs and began Head Start at age four.

It turns out that beginning Head Start at age three did yield positive results. After the first year of the study, the Head Start children showed significant gains (relative to children in the control group) on an overall measure of academic proficiency that included tests of early writing and math skills. In addition, they exhibited fewer behavior problems than did kids in the control group, and their parents showed positive changes as well—they were more likely to read to their kids and less likely to spank them. Finally, the Head Start kids received higher scores on a measure of overall physical health and were more likely to have received dental care.

Did these positive effects persist? Some did: by the end of the first grade, there was evidence of a small advantage in oral comprehension skills in the kids who began Head Start at age three, plus these kids had better relationships with their teachers than the control kids did. Further, some of the positive parenting styles persisted: the parents of the Head Start kids reported that they had less of an authoritarian parenting style. But, perhaps not surprisingly, many of the positive effects did not persist beyond the first year of the program. Recall that, after year one, 50 percent of the children in the control group enrolled in Head Start, which may have brought some of them up to the level of the kids who began at age three. In fact, there was another group of kids who were randomly assigned to begin Head Start at age four, and they, too, showed increases in several measures of academic proficiency by the end of that year.

Other researchers have tried to estimate the long-term impact of Head Start using nonexperimental designs and have found encourag-

ing results. For example, one study compared children who participated in the program with siblings who did not, and another compared
children who lived in counties that had Head Start (because they met
poverty guidelines for the program) with children who lived in adja-
cent counties that did not (because they just missed the poverty-level
cutoffs). Both studies found that the Head Start program had long-
term benefits. In one, children who participated were more likely to
graduate from high school and attend college and less likely to commit
crimes and became teenage parents. Though these results are encouraging, we need to be cautious about them, given the built-in problems
with the research designs (e.g., the children living in neighboring
counties might have differed in lots of ways besides their participation
in Head Start).[7]

We have a better idea about the long-term effects of some other
childhood interventions because they been tested with rigorous experimental designs and the children have been followed for several years.
One of the best-known programs is the Carolina Abecedarian Project,
founded by Craig Ramey and his colleagues. Disadvantaged African
American children took part in an intensive preschool program,
beginning when they were about four months of age and continuing
until they started school. The program had just about everything one
would want—a very low teacher-to-student ratio and a multitude of
activities that targeted the children's educational, social, emotional,
and cognitive development. There was a particular focus on language
skills. The program took up the whole school day, five days a week,
twelve months a year. And this was one of the few childhood interventions that included a randomly assigned control group of children who
did not take part.

To see what effects the intervention had, the researchers followed
the children in both groups for several years. At twenty-one years of
age, those who had attended the preschool program, compared to
those who had not, had higher IQ scores; were less likely to have been

assigned to special education classes or to have repeated a grade; scored higher on tests of reading, math, and cognitive ability; were more likely to have graduated from high school and attended college; and were less likely to have become teenage parents. The magnitude of these effects was impressive—for example, at age twenty-one, the percentage of kids who were attending a four-year college was nearly three times higher in the group who had gone to the preschool (35 percent) than in the control group (13 percent).

Other early childhood intervention programs have also had positive effects, such as the Perry Preschool Project, conducted in Ypsilanti, Michigan, in the 1960s. Thus early interventions can work; and by "early," I mean soon after birth. But they must be intensive and of very high quality. And though they have lasting benefits, they do not completely eliminate the achievement gap.[8]

Redesigning Schools

A problem with early childhood interventions is that they are, well, early, and stop by the time children reach school. Although these programs can have positive long-term effects, the fact is that many children continue to live in poverty and attend poor schools. Maybe we need to develop programs for kids in elementary school and beyond.

Virtually every school district in the nation has given this a try, implementing myriad programs that target reading, math, and other subjects. Undoubtedly, some of these programs are beneficial. My beef is that we don't really know, because the programs are seldom tested sufficiently using experimental designs. Things are improving in this regard: in 2002, the United States Department of Education launched a website called the What Works Clearinghouse (WWC), which presents a set of standards for evaluating educational interventions and reviews studies that meet those standards (http://ies.ed.gov/ncee/wwc/). This is a big step, because, if nothing else, it will call attention to the need for more rigorous research.

Other educators have decided that individual programs are not enough and that we need to restructure schools from top to bottom. Hundreds of charter schools have opened throughout the country, for example, with the claim that they do a better job of educating disadvantaged children than public schools do. Again, rigorous experimental studies evaluating these schools are hard to come by, and what evidence there is suggests that most charter schools do no better than public schools at closing the achievement gap.[9]

One exception may be the Knowledge Is Power Program (KIPP), founded in 1994 by two teachers, Michael Feinberg and David Levin, who were fresh out of the Teach For America program and had innovative ideas about how to structure a school in order to help disadvantaged kids. Today there are more than sixty KIPP schools in nineteen states and the District of Columbia. The students they serve are largely from low-income families, and more than 90 percent are African American or Hispanic. One key feature of KIPP schools is that students receive about 60 percent more instructional time than do students in public schools. At a typical KIPP school, students arrive at 7:30 a.m. and stay until 5:00 p.m., attend half-day Saturday sessions twice a month, and attend a three-week summer session. KIPP schools also attempt to create an environment of high expectations, commitment, and discipline.

Although an experimental test of the effectiveness of KIPP schools is under way, for now we need to rely on nonexperimental tests that have compared KIPP students to similar, non-KIPP students. These studies have yielded promising results: KIPP students scored better on standardized tests of reading and math than did the non-Kipp students. But for now we cannot be certain that this difference is due to the schools or whether it exists because the children who attend KIPP schools are different in some way to begin with (for example, they may have parents who are especially motivated to see their children do well).[10]

We can be more confident about the success of the charter schools called Promise Academies, which are operated by the Harlem Children's Zone (HCZ). HCZ, which began in the 1970s, is an ambitious organization that attempts to mitigate the effects of poverty in the Harlem section of New York City. It targets a ninety-seven-block area of Harlem, where it has developed more than twenty programs and charter schools. As with the KIPP program, there is no experimental evaluation built into the program. But HCZ was evaluated by clever social scientists who took advantage of a key fact: by law in New York State, if a charter school receives more applications from students than it can accept, it must choose students randomly. This essentially creates an experimental design whereby the researchers can compare the academic achievement of the students who won the lottery (and thus attended the charter schools) with those who lost (and thus did not). The results? By the eighth grade, those who won and enrolled in the Promise Academies for at least two years were doing better in math and reading—by large margins—than students who lost the lottery. In fact, eighth-grade Promise Academy students, who are all minorities (about 90 percent black and 10 percent Hispanic), outperformed white students in the rest of the New York City public school system in math to a statistically significant degree. Plus, there is evidence that the schools, and not the other HCZ community programs, are responsible for these impressive gains, because kids who attended the schools, but did not take advantage of the other programs, show the same academic gains as those who did take part in the programs.[11]

It thus seems that massive attempts to redesign schools can work to close the achievement gap. We don't know for sure why the KIPP and HCZ schools have been so successful, though one key factor may be the sheer volume of instruction that the students receive. Like KIPP students, those who attend HCZ schools have an extended school day and year, and students who need additional instruction attend classes on Saturdays. Another likely factor is that the schools attract dedicated and talented teachers, and only the best of these are retained.

The impact of a good teacher cannot be overestimated. As mentioned, Muriel Wiggins had pretty much given up in elementary school after her horrific experiences with racist teachers, but then she was assigned to Miss Simons for the sixth grade. Miss Simons saw something in Muriel that the other teachers had not, and treated her with kindness. She gave Muriel coveted duties, such as cloakroom monitor (whose job it was to open the cloakroom door when it was time for the students to get their coats), and small gifts, such as a box of leftover crayons. She was also tough on Muriel when she didn't live up to her potential. One day, Muriel realized that she had forgotten to do her homework, which was to read a newspaper article and summarize it. When she went home for lunch, she grabbed the newspaper and scribbled a few words on a piece of paper. But wouldn't you know it—that afternoon, Muriel was the first person Miss Simons called on to tell the class about the article she had read. All Muriel could remember was the headline, and after reciting it she stood there in mortified silence. As punishment, Muriel lost her cloakroom-monitor job. With both encouragement and discipline, Miss Simons got Muriel back on track academically.

STEREOTYPE THREAT AND ACADEMIC ACHIEVEMENT

We've just seen that early childhood interventions and attempts to redesign schools can help reduce the achievement gap. But what about the story-editing approach, in which we try to redirect people's narratives about why they are having difficulties? Consider first the results of a study conducted by researchers at the University of Oklahoma. African American and white college students were given a standard intelligence test called the Raven's Advanced Progressive Matrices test

(Raven's APM), on which people see a series of geometric figures and have to guess which figure goes next in the sequence. The only thing the researchers varied was the instructions they gave to participants. Some were randomly assigned to receive the instructions in the manual for the test, which uses the word "test" in several places and describes it as a "measure of observation and clear thinking." Another group was randomly assigned to receive instructions that described the Raven's APM as an IQ test. "Like the SAT and ACT," these participants learned, "this test is frequently used to measure individuals' intelligence and ability." A final group was randomly assigned to receive instructions that said, "The task you will be working on is a series of puzzles." The word "puzzles" was used repeatedly, and neither the word "test" nor "intelligence" was ever used. After receiving one of these three sets of instructions, the participants spent forty minutes working on the test.

Now, keep in mind that all students took the exact same test—the only thing that varied was which set of instructions they received. It might seem like this would not influence people's performance; after all, the Raven's APM is a widely used intelligence test that has been developed and validated for decades as a "pure" measure of reasoning ability. Because it involves only geometric figures, with no verbal content, it supposedly tests basic reasoning abilities devoid of any cultural bias. Surely it doesn't matter whether the test is described as a measure of IQ or a set of puzzles. Well, it turns out it does matter, and it matters a lot, at least to one group of people: African Americans. As seen in the figure opposite, when the test was described as a measure of IQ, the standard achievement gap was evident: whites outperformed blacks, to about the same extent as is typically found on other measures of intelligence and achievement. When participants received the standard instructions, which described the test as a measure of observation and clear thinking, the achievement gap was still present, but to a lesser degree. But look what happened when the test was described as a set of puzzles: as seen in the two bars on the far right of the figure, the achievement gap completely disappeared! In fact, in this condition, African American students did slightly better than white students. What was going on here? Clearly, something about the way in which the students interpreted the test made a big difference in their performance—something that isn't supposed to happen on tests of intelligence or achievement.[12]

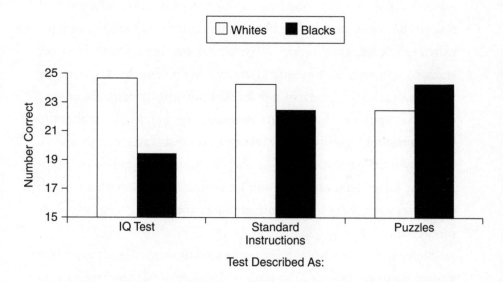

What was going on is an important phenomenon called *stereotype threat*, discovered by the social psychologist Claude Steele (and detailed in his riveting book, *Whistling Vivaldi*). Stereotype threat is a psychological state that people experience when they feel they are at risk of confirming a negative stereotype about a group to which they belong. African American students, for example, are well aware of the stereotype that blacks are less intelligent than whites. When they are given a test and told it measures their IQ, they thus might worry that they will confirm the stereotype—a concern that a white student does not have when taking the same test. This worry about confirming a negative stereotype uses up mental resources and triggers anxiety, which makes it harder to concentrate on the test. We know this from dozens of studies that have given the same tests to different groups of people with slightly different instructions about what the test measures. As seen in the study just described, when blacks are told that the test measures intelligence, they do worse than whites. But when they are not told that the test is a measure of intelligence, they do just as well as whites on the very same test.

You may have noticed in the figure that whites did best when the Raven's APM was described as an IQ test and worse when it was described a set of puzzles. Although these differences are not statistically significant, they reflect a trend that has been found in other studies—people's performance *improves* when there is a stereotype that their group does better on that task than other groups. Because of the stereotype that whites are more intelligent than blacks, whites did better when told that they were taking an IQ test than when they were told they were doing puzzles—a phenomenon that is called *stereotype lift*. Our focus here, however, will be on the conditions under which people do worse because they are at risk of confirming a negative stereotype about their group.[13]

Stereotype threat is not just experienced by minorities. It can make anyone do worse on a task, as long as doing so would confirm a negative stereotype about his or her group. Women do worse than men on math tests when gender differences in math are emphasized, for example, but do just as well when gender differences are downplayed or said not to apply on the specific math test they are taking. Women who were told that a simulated driving test was designed to investigate why men are better drivers than women were more than twice as likely to run over a pedestrian (with the simulated car) than women who took the same test with no mention of gender differences.[14]

Stereotype threat wields its insidious effects by triggering a vicious cycle of thinking, similar to the one we discussed in chapter 1. People start thinking about the stereotype and whether they will confirm it, which makes them anxious and aroused. This leads to further rumination and self-doubt, as people monitor their performance (e.g., "Oh no, I'm having trouble with this math problem; maybe the stereotype is true!"). Next, people use mental energy to try to suppress these disrupting thoughts. The problem is that all these steps—becoming anxious and aroused, monitoring one's performance for signs of stereotype confirmation, and attempting to suppress thoughts about the stereotype—use up mental resources, leaving less room to concentrate on the test. And the harder it is to concentrate, the worse people do, triggering the whole process over again. With all this stress, worry, rumination, and thought suppression going on, it is no wonder that people under stereotype threat do worse than people free to concentrate on the test without anything else to worry about.

One remarkable thing about these deficits in performance is how easily they are corrected. A simple reinterpretation of the meaning of a test can eliminate the achievement gap, as seen in the examples above. So can attempts to reduce the salience of the negative stereotype— by, for example, emphasizing positive aspects of one's group or introducing people to a positive role model from the stereotyped group (for example, a female math whiz). Teaching people about the nature of stereotype threat can also help. All these approaches can succeed in bumping people out of the vicious cycle of thinking that stereotype threat causes, allowing them to concentrate better on the task at hand.[15]

This could be taken to mean that the societal and cultural variables we discussed earlier—racism, poverty, child-rearing practices, and schooling—are not as important as we thought in creating the achievement gap. If we can eliminate the gap by removing stereotype threat from testing situations, maybe we've been barking up the wrong tree. According to this argument, the achievement gap is due largely to an uneven playing field in testing situations and not to hard-to-change societal or educational factors. Look again, for example, at the figure that showed the results of the Raven's Advanced Progressive Matrices test: when stereotype threat was removed from the testing situation, the achievement gap was completely eliminated. Black college students did just as well as white college students when the playing field was evened, psychologically speaking.

It would be a mistake, however, to conclude that the entire achievement gap is due to testing bias and that we no longer need to worry about poverty and racism. Yes, some of the difference is likely due to threats raised by the tests themselves. But we should keep in mind that most of the studies on stereotype threat have been conducted with college students, who are obviously a highly selective sample. They have already overcome numerous hurdles to get where they are, particularly if they are poor and black. Many other disadvantaged students don't make it over those hurdles. Think of Muriel Wiggins's black classmates, who didn't have the family support she had. Or the Hispanic students unfairly placed in lower reading groups who never convince school officials to retest them. In the year 2000, only 14 percent of Hispanics and 27 percent of blacks attended college, compared to 38 percent of whites. We must continue to look for ways of removing barriers for minority groups, including implementing the kinds of big interventions we discussed earlier that have shown signs of success.[16]

It is also important to note that stereotype threat can act as a barrier to early academic success, in addition to influencing how college students react in testing situations. The fear of confirming a negative stereotype can have insidious effects, not only while taking a test but in everyday life from childhood onward. The costs of such spiraling anxiety can be high, both psychologically and physically. Encountering stereotype threat, for example, has been shown to raise blood pressure among African Americans. Many of us, when constantly faced with this kind of threat, would bail out of the whole pursuit. After all, one of the best ways of coping with something that is hard to get is to devalue it, like the proverbial fox and the grapes—the grapes must be sour if we can't reach them, and school must not be very important if it is such a source of stress. Unfortunately, minorities are more likely to bail out of school than whites. In the year 2008, for example, the high school dropout rate for African Americans was double what it was for whites (9.9 percent versus 4.8 percent). And for Hispanics, it was nearly double what it was for African Americans (18.3 percent). Minority kids who stay in school generally value academics as much as nonminority kids, but the stress of stereotype threat takes its toll, lowering their performance. As Claude Steele puts it, "Disproving a stereotype is a Sisyphean task; something you have to do over and over again as long as you are in the domain where the stereotype applies."[17]

But what if we catch kids at a point where they are particularly vulnerable to stereotype threat and the downward spiral to which it can lead? Maybe a dose of story editing could redirect people's thinking in a way that reduces stereotype threat, thereby preventing the self-defeating cycle of thinking. There is reason to believe that a good time to try this is when kids start middle school. Most kids switch schools at the beginning of sixth or seventh grade and are faced with new academic pressures, and it is at this point that grades often drop and behavioral problems increase, especially for minority children. Could this be a crucial point at which stereotype threat leads to stress and poor performance? And, if so, could a story-editing intervention prevent this from happening?[18]

STORY-EDITING INTERVENTIONS TO REDUCE THE ACHIEVEMENT GAP

One of the first story-editing interventions designed to reduce the achievement gap targeted seventh graders at a rural school in Texas. About two-thirds of the students were Hispanic, 20 percent were white, and 13 percent were black, and a majority of the students (about 70 percent) qualified for a free or reduced-price lunch, which is a standard measure of poverty in schools. The researchers reasoned that this population was especially vulnerable to stereotype threat and designed two story-editing interventions to prevent this from happening. For the first intervention, the students were assigned a college-student mentor who kept in touch with them regularly throughout the school year and emphasized that many students encounter academic diffi- culties when they begin middle school, but that they typically do bet- ter when they learn how to navigate their new environments. This intervention, based on the study with college students discussed in chapter 1, was designed to prevent a self-defeating cycle of negative thinking, in which people blame themselves for poor academic perfor- mance and give up.

For the second intervention, the students were also assigned men- tors, but instead of talking to the kids about the transition to middle school, the mentors emphasized that intelligence is a skill that is learned and is not a fixed quality that people are born with. The researchers reasoned that this approach, based on Carol Dweck's research on "mindsets," is another way to prevent a self-defeating thinking cycle. As we saw in chapter 4, many kids believe that intelli- gence is a fixed quality; thus, when they encounter academic difficul- ties, they take that as a sign that they are not very smart. This can lead to giving up: why keep knocking your head against the wall if you don't have what it takes? But if kids can be convinced that intelligence is a skill that develops with practice, then they might take academic difficulties as a sign that they simply need to work harder.

Other kids were randomly assigned to a control group. These kids also received mentors, but the mentors taught them about the perils of drug use and did not discuss academics. As it turned out, both of the story-editing interventions improved academic performance. At the end of the school year, students who got either of the two interven- tions achieved significantly higher scores on a standardized reading test than kids in the control group. On a standardized math test, girls who received the interventions did substantially better than girls in the control condition, and just as well as boys. The interventions did not boost boys' performance on the math test, possibly because they were not experiencing stereotype threat in this domain as much as girls were. (The boys were, in fact, already performing at a higher level than the girls in math.) Another study that used a similar "mindset" intervention — teaching kids that intelligence is malleable instead of fixed — had similar success with minority seventh graders at a New York City school that primarily serves black and Hispanic students.[19]

Is it possible that an even simpler story-editing intervention might work just as well? Geoffrey Cohen, Julio Garcia, Valerie Purdie-Vaughns, and their colleagues decided to find out. They, too, targeted seventh graders — in this case, at a middle school in New England that was about evenly divided between African American and white students. The intervention was striking in how minimal it was, at least on the surface. At the beginning of the academic year, students completed a fifteen-minute writing exercise in one of their classes. They were given a list of things they might value, such as relationships with friends and family, religion, music, and politics, and asked to pick the two or three that were most important to them. Then they wrote about why these values were important to them. Depending on the version of the study, the students completed this writing exercise three to five times during the school year, usually at times of high stress, such as test days. Students randomly assigned to the control group either wrote about how a value that was unimportant to them might be important to others, or about a neutral topic, such as their morning routines.

That's it — there were no attempts to improve the kids' study habits or to teach them math or reading skills. The entire intervention was the writing task. Why, you might ask, did the researchers expect such a simple exercise to close the achievement gap? Because of a central principle of social psychology, namely, that people are motivated to perceive themselves as good, competent, moral people, and that when that view is threatened, they do what they can, psychologically, to repair their self-image. It is worth tracing the path that led from social psychological theory to the middle-school intervention, because it is a fascinating illustration of how theory can lead to simple yet powerful story-editing interventions—interventions that never would have occurred to people if it weren't for the prior basic research.

Literally hundreds of experiments, conducted mostly in the laboratory with college-student participants, have documented how important it is for people to maintain a positive self-image and the lengths to which they will go to accomplish this. Typically, people try to deal with threats to their self-esteem directly. For example, being a competent research psychologist is a central part of my identity, and if something threatens that view, such as receiving negative feedback on an article I have submitted to a journal, I will do my best to remove the threat. I'll rewrite the article and send it to another journal, say, or try to improve the research on which it is based. But what if that doesn't work? Human beings are excellent rationalizers, and I might well make myself feel better by finding an explanation that deflects blame away from me. The journal editors don't know what they're talking about; the expert reviewers they consulted must have been too busy to read the article carefully; my research findings are so novel and advanced that people just can't comprehend them ("Yeah, that's the ticket!" as a character on *Saturday Night Live* used to say). I don't do this consciously, of course—rationalization works best if it occurs behind the scenes, so that I don't know that I'm coming up with these ideas in order to make myself feel better. It feels like I am simply telling it like it is.

But even rationalization has its limits. I can only go so far with the "misunderstood genius" defense before it crumbles in the face of reality (further journal rejections, say). What do I do now? Throw in the towel and admit that I'm a failure in a central domain in my life? Not so fast! Claude Steele had the insight, with his *self-affirmation theory*, that there is another way out: reminding ourselves how competent we are in some other domain in our lives. "Maybe I'm not doing well as a research psychologist," I might think, "but I am a dedicated family man, which, after all, is much more important than some silly journal article." Steele and his colleagues demonstrated this process of self-affirmation in several laboratory experiments. Giving people the opportunity to affirm themselves, even with a task as simple as writing about the values that are important to them, turns out to be a powerful prophylactic against threats to their self-esteem. If music is important to us, for example, then thinking about what great musicians we are can take the sting out of doing poorly at school.[20]

What does all this have to do with closing the achievement gap in middle school? You can probably see the connection. Imagine that you are an African American seventh grader who has experienced repeated stereotype threat throughout your school career. Unlike the white kids in your class, you have a lot to worry about when taking tests or writing papers, namely, that you will confirm a negative stereotype about your group. As we've seen, stereotype threat takes a serious toll, both psychologically and physically, and lowers the performance of people who experience it. But what if we remind you that there are other parts of your life that are important to you and that you value? Areas that have nothing to do with your race and are thus "identity-safe"? Cohen and colleagues' writing exercise was designed to do just that. It allowed the students to self-affirm treasured nonacademic values, such as their love for their families or their religion. The researchers had the hunch that this would take the heat off of black students the next time they took a test or completed a difficult assignment. Academics would no longer seem like a do-or-die situation that might confirm all their worst fears about themselves as well as other people's stereotypes about them, because, after all, there are other important things in life. And to the extent that this helped students concentrate better and do well on a test, their confidence would be boosted, making it easier for them to study for the next test.

The study was a spectacular success. African American students who completed the self-affirmation writing exercises, compared to African American students randomly assigned to the control group, achieved significantly higher grades over the next two years of school. The intervention was particularly powerful among African American students who had been doing poorly academically. Among these students, those who did the writing exercise, compared to those in the control group, achieved markedly higher grades and were significantly less likely to be placed in a remediation track or to be held back a grade. The writing exercise had no effect on white students' grades, presumably because this group did not have excessive stress in school due to stereotype threat.

But why did writing about an important value a few times have such lasting effects? It did so, the researchers argue, in the same way that the small story prompts discussed in chapter 1 helped college students get better grades: by interrupting a self-defeating psychological cycle that causes students to spiral downward. African Americans in the control group were at particular risk for getting caught in a self-defeating cycle, in which poor grades signaled to them that they didn't fit into the school environment and might not have what it takes to succeed. African Americans who received the intervention, however, were more likely to avoid this cycle—if they did poorly initially, the researchers found, they were less likely to conclude that they could never make it or that they were a bad fit at the school.[21]

Similar story-editing interventions have been found to help minority college students. Black students at a predominantly white university, for example, might be particularly prone to feel that they don't fit in or belong at that university, especially if they experience an academic setback, as many students do in their first semester. If so, then an intervention designed to redirect their narratives from "I don't fit in here" to "Everyone experiences bumps in the road" might increase their sense of belonging and improve their academic performance. To find out, researchers conducted a study with black and white first-year students at a predominantly white university. In the treatment condition, the students received statistics and read interviews with upperclass students indicating that most students worry that they don't belong when they begin college, but that these worries lessen over time. To reinforce this message, the students wrote a speech illustrating how this lesson applied to them; that is, how their own worries about belonging were likely to be temporary. They delivered this speech in front a video camera, ostensibly so that it could be shown to future students at their school. Participants in the control group underwent the same procedure, except that they learned that social and political attitudes change over the course of one's college career— they heard nothing about changes in one's sense of belonging.

The entire session lasted only an hour. Yet, as with other story-editing interventions, it had dramatic long-term effects on the black students' performance and well-being. Those who got the message about belonging, relative to those in the control group, believed they fit in better at college, became more engaged in college academically (by studying more, attending more review sessions, and asking more questions in class), and achieved better grades in the rest of their college careers. Not only that, but on a questionnaire they completed right before they graduated, black students who had received the "belonging" intervention reported that they were in better health, had visited a doctor fewer times, and were happier than did black students in the control group. The "belonging" message had no effect on the white students, because most of them already felt that they fit in at their university.[22]

The researchers who conducted these story-editing studies of academic achievement emphasize that their interventions are not meant to replace other ways of closing the achievement gap, such as providing better preschool education and redesigning schools. It would be absurd to say that getting kids to write for a short time about their values is all we need to do to help minority kids do better. The intervention obviously won't teach a child who can't spell to spell. Having kids affirm themselves is likely to work best in supportive environments where children have the resources they need to learn and excel. But it would be equally absurd for schools to ignore this simple, inexpensive way of helping minority kids do better academically by avoiding stereotype threat and increasing their sense of belonging.

USING IT

Research on stereotype threat is relevant to everyone, because we all belong to groups that are the target of negative stereotypes. As we have seen, blacks do worse on achievement and intelligence tests, and women do worse on math tests, when they feel they are at risk for confirming the negative stereotypes about their groups. Some groups are less stigmatized than others, such as white males, but even this privileged group can experience stereotype threat. One study, for example, found that white men did worse on a math test when they thought their results would be compared to those of Asian men, a group thought to be superior at math. And—there is no escaping it—all of us are going to get old (if we are lucky), and old people have been found to do worse on memory tests when they think the tests are examining age differences in memory, because that triggers stereotypes about the forgetfulness of the elderly.

Given that all of us are at risk for stereotype threat at one time or another, it is important to remember the ways of preventing it. Reminding oneself that performance is more about hard work than innate talent can help. So can the kind of self-affirmation task used by Geoffrey Cohen, Julio Garcia, Valerie Purdie-Vaughns, and their colleagues, in which students write about values that are important to them. As we've seen, reminding ourselves of our treasured values can lower the heat in anxiety-provoking situations. And simply knowing about stereotype threat can help by reminding us, "Wait a minute, this memory test is about me, not my group."

We can also create a sense of belonging in those who are at risk of confirming a stereotype about their group by, for example, portraying women and minorities in photographs included in company newsletters. Although it might seem like rounding up minorities and women for a company photo shows an excessive concern with political correctness, it matters—because conveying the impression that the company has a critical mass of "people like me" is one way to reduce stereotype threat. To use Claude Steele's words, anything that makes a setting feel "identity-safe" will help, because people will then not have to dwell on their group membership.

We should not, of course, just convey the impression that minorities and women are well represented in a corporate or academic setting. We should do everything we can to make sure they actually are well represented, not only to achieve basic goals of fairness and social justice, but also because the composition of a group communicates important messages to its members. A woman who is the only female in an advanced math course, or an African American who is the only black in his graduate program, is likely to feel the spotlight of attention and be on guard about how he or she is viewed. The best way to prevent this is to increase the representation of minorities and women so that the spotlight isn't on just one or two people. Consider a study of college women who took a difficult math test along with two other students. In one condition, all three of the students were women. In another condition, two were women and one was a man. In a third condition, one was a woman and two were men. This seemingly arbitrary gender composition of the group had a dramatic effect on the women's math performance: they got 70 percent of the answers right when in an all-female group, 64 percent when one of the other group members was male, and 58 percent when two of the other group members were male. The gender composition of the group had no effect on women's performance on a verbal test, suggesting that the presence of men in the math groups triggered the stereotype that women are not as good at math.[23]

Stereotype threat is one of the most striking examples of the power of self-narratives. It is a process that occurs beneath the surface: research shows that people are not always aware that they are thinking about their group membership or that this is handicapping their performance. But with relatively simple story-editing interventions, people can be redirected out of the vicious cycle of anxiety and rumination with remarkable long-term benefits. Again, this doesn't mean we should abandon larger structural approaches to reducing the achievement gap. Early childhood interventions are important, as are ways of redesigning schools to better serve disadvantaged students. But we should also be mindful of the messages social environments send to people about who they are and how they fit in, and seek to make these environments identity-safe.

CHAPTER 10

Sustained Change
Finding Solutions

We began this book with an example of a widely used common-sense intervention designed to help people recover from traumatic events—Critical Incident Stress Debriefing (CISD). As we saw, CISD doesn't do what it is supposed to do and may even prolong people's distress. Along the way we encountered many other interventions that merit my blistering or bloodletting awards, including advice offered in many self-help books (e.g., *The Secret*), national programs to prevent child abuse (e.g., Healthy Families America), Dollar-A-Day programs to prevent repeat teen pregnancies, scared-straight programs to reduce teen delinquency, and the D.A.R.E. program to prevent drug and alcohol abuse.

But at least these programs have been rigorously tested using the experimental techniques described in chapter 2, allowing us to know that they don't work or do harm. That's more than we can say about countless other ongoing programs that have never been adequately tested, probably because their founders are certain that they work. Some of these programs undoubtedly are effective, but, as we've seen, we can't take that for granted.

I can't resist giving one more example. Recently I had the pleasure of attending a concert by Peter Yarrow of the folk group Peter, Paul & Mary. The concert was part of a remembrance of the 1960s, commemorating the fact that the 1960s have, well, turned fifty. It was heartwarming to hear Yarrow sing protest songs from that tumultuous decade and to listen to his stories, such as what it was like to perform at the 1963 March on Washington, where Martin Luther King delivered his "I Have a Dream" speech.

But the evening wasn't just about looking backward. Yarrow has never lost his commitment to social change, and he used the concert as an opportunity to energize the audience, reminding us that there are plenty of current problems that need to be addressed and imploring us to keep up the fight. Yarrow has devoted his energies to creating safe educational environments for children. In 1999, he founded a nonprofit organization called Operation Respect, which distributes videos, music, and instructional guides to schools and summer camps with the goal of preventing bullying and violence. The program is based on the song "Don't Laugh at Me," written by Steve Seskin and Allen Shamblin and recorded by Peter, Paul & Mary. According to the Operation Respect website, more than 150,000 copies of the Don't Laugh at Me curriculum have been distributed and more than 40,000 educators have attended Don't Laugh at Me workshops. In 2003, the United States Congress passed a resolution honoring Peter Yarrow and Operation Respect, and a version of the program was launched in Israel in 2009.

I hope that by now you have the same sinking feeling in your stomach as I did when I heard Yarrow talk about Operation Respect. As catchy as "Don't Laugh at Me" is, and as heartwarming as it was to hear Yarrow perform it, the cold-blooded social scientist in me couldn't help but ask, "But does it work?" Sure, it makes a certain amount of sense that it would. But the answer is that we don't know, because, like many of the interventions we have encountered in this book, it was implemented widely before being adequately tested.

The Don't Laugh at Me curriculum is based on something called the Resolving Conflict Creatively Program, which to my knowledge has never been evaluated with an experimental design in which children, classrooms, or schools were randomly assigned to participate in the program or to a control group that did not. Resolving Conflict Creatively was not considered to be an effective program, or even a promising one, by the Center for the Study and Prevention of Violence, which has vetted more than six hundred violence-prevention programs. Adding the Don't Laugh at Me component to the program makes me especially nervous, because social psychological research shows that the human mind does not process negations as well as it does affirmations. When a president says, "I am not a crook," people are more likely to think of him as a crook, because he becomes associated in their minds with that word, despite his denial. Hearing a kid sing the words "don't laugh at me" could backfire, because people might associate laughing with that kid. In short, the song might lead to a subtle reinterpretation of how kids are viewed, in precisely the opposite direction from what is intended. I sincerely hope that I am wrong about this. But the point is we don't know.[1]

"Don't be such a wet blanket," you might be thinking. "School violence and bullying are huge problems, and if we wait until you social scientists dicker around and test every program we'll never make progress. Kids are getting beat up and bullied every day." Fair enough—there are many pressing problems that need immediate attention. But recall the medical analogy from chapter 1. Even though there are numerous terrible diseases that kill children every day, we don't disseminate new cures until we are sure they work. Imagine that Peter Yarrow announced that he had concocted a new drug in his basement that he believed cured early-onset diabetes and that he was distributing the drug to children around the world. Most of us would be horrified, because Yarrow is not a physician, and even if he were, he would need to test his drug extensively and seek permission from the Food and Drug Administration before giving it to children.

But neither is Yarrow a social psychologist, and if I have accomplished nothing else in this book, I hope I have made people wary of untested interventions designed to address social and personal issues.

SOLUTIONS

This book isn't just about what doesn't work. It is about solutions—the realization that interventions can be tested to see what works, and if they don't work, refined until they do. Even better, we have powerful techniques at our disposal based on the story-editing approach. As you know by now, this is a family of techniques that share three assumptions: first, in order to change people's behavior we have to see the world through their eyes. It's not just about incentives, as it is to an economist; it's about the way in which we interpret ourselves and the social world. Second, these interpretations are not always set in stone, and in fact can be redirected with just the right approach. Third, small changes in interpretations can have self-sustaining effects, leading to long-lasting changes in behavior. We have seen myriad story-editing interventions that used these principles to address a wide range of personal and social issues.

It may have occurred to you to wonder how researchers came up with these interventions, especially the ones that seem so implausible. The researchers did not invent the interventions out of thin air, but instead based them on theory-driven psychological research, much of it conducted in the laboratory. Of course, social psychologists do not know for sure whether these interventions will work in applied settings, after they scale up a laboratory procedure to a real-world application. It's a long way from having college students write about their values to devising an intervention to close the achievement gap in middle schools. But social psychologists have a place to start and a means to find out whether their interventions work. These are huge advantages over relying on common sense alone, which, as we have seen, has led to some tragically flawed interventions that did more harm than good. With careful, theory-based research, social psychologists have discovered some remarkable solutions to long-standing problems, such as ways to reduce the achievement gap in education, lower teen violence, and reduce racial prejudice.

USING IT REDUX

The story-editing approach isn't just about solving societal problems; it can be used by you and me in our daily lives to redirect our own narratives and those of our children. True, we can't very well design experiments to test our hunches about the best way to raise our children. But we can learn from the efforts of others, and throughout this book I've pointed out ways in which the story-editing approach can be used in everyday life. I'll end by recapping some of the major points:

- Be skeptical of advice from self-help books about easy roads to riches, fame, and everlasting happiness. Instead of believing fantastic claims about the laws of the universe, try the simple writing exercises described in chapter 3, which are based on solid psychological research. They might make you happier.
- As a parent, be mindful not only of what your children do, but of the narratives they are developing about themselves, their relationships, and the world at large. You can help them develop healthy core attachment narratives by, starting at birth, being attentive and responsive to their needs and providing consistent, dependable, and prompt care.

- As your children grow older, follow the minimal sufficiency principle, whereby you use the smallest level of rewards and threats necessary to shape their behavior. The danger of going overboard with rewards and threats is that your kids will not internalize the values you are trying to impart, but will instead come to believe that they are obeying you simply to earn your love or avoid your wrath.

- When your kids reach adolescence, keep in mind that their narratives will be shaped by their peers and the media. You can't choose your kids' friends, but you can have some influence on whom they hang out with and what they see on television and at the movies. Encourage them to engage in volunteer work in areas they enjoy.

- Appreciate the power of the do good, be good principle. One of the best ways of revising our narratives is to change our behavior first. As Kurt Vonnegut said in *Mother Night*, "We are what we pretend to be, so we must be careful about what we pretend to be." This is why getting teens to engage in volunteer work can be so powerful— it fosters the narrative that they are caring people who are engaged in their communities. We can all use this principle by acting more like who we want to be.[2]

- Initiate interactions with people who are outside of your comfort zone, such as coworkers of a different race or ethnicity or social class. You might worry that such interactions will be awkward or unwelcomed, but often these fears are unfounded. Others may well have the same worries you do and will appreciate your efforts to get to know them.

- Be mindful of your own and other people's identities and how these identities can be threatened by a specific situation or context. As we saw in chapter 9, putting people in situations in which they fear they will confirm negative stereotypes about their group can be debilitating. Fortunately, there are ways to avoid this, such as by educating people about the dangers of stereotype threat and getting people to affirm their values in areas unrelated to the stereotype.

- Be a good consumer of information. As noted in chapter 9, the U.S. Department of Education created a website called the What Works Clearinghouse, which reviews the research literature and provides educators with descriptions of programs that work (http://ies.ed .gov/ncee/wwc/). The Center for the Study and Prevention of Violence at the University of Colorado evaluates the effectiveness of programs that attempt to reduce violence and drug use, and publishes their results on a website (http://www.colorado.edu/cspv/ blueprints/).

Above all, when someone proposes a way to make you happier or more tolerant of others, turn you into a better parent, or help your children avoid alcohol, cigarettes, and drugs, ask politely, "But does it work?"

Acknowledgments

Any project of this size has stops, starts, twists, and turns. My agent, Katinka Matson, and my editor at Little, Brown, Tracy Behar, were instrumental in keeping me from meandering off the path, while also encouraging me to explore alternate routes. I benefited tremendously from their insight, support, and guidance.

Several people read drafts of chapters and provided valuable feedback, including Joe Allen, Jennifer Bauerle, Daphne Bugental, Geoffrey Cohen, Ed Diener, Elizabeth Dunn, Jesse Graham, Casey Eggleston, Cheryl Hahn, Dan Lassiter, Min Ha Lee, Robyn Mallett, Dieynaba Ndiaye, Jesse Pappas, Kathleen Schmidt, Tracie Stewart, Elizabeth Wilson, and Geoffrey Wilson. Greg Walton generously read a draft of the entire book and provided a folder full of insightful comments and suggestions. Thanks to all; the book benefited tremendously from your feedback.

My longtime friend and collaborator, Daniel Gilbert, also read an entire draft. With his sharp eye, he spotted the weakest parts, and with his deft hand, he (as always) pointed me in the right direction. I have had many fine collaborators in my career, far too many to mention here. But two have had such an influence on my work that their fingerprints can be seen on everything I do, including this book — Dan Gilbert and my graduate school mentor, Richard Nisbett.

This project is the result of a long love affair with my field, social psychology, and the conviction that it has much to say about how to improve people's lives. Most of all, I thank the many colleagues whose work appears on these pages. You are the ones out there in the trenches doing the painstaking research, and I hope the book in some small way shines a light on your efforts.

Notes

CHAPTER 1: REDIRECT

1. The details of this story are taken from articles in *The Tampa Tribune* by Huntley (1998) and Tugan (2002). The quote is from Tugan, p. 1.
2. Kadet (2002).
3. The journalist who interviewed Gary Felice: Tugan (2002, p. 1). On the effectiveness of CISD: Bisson, Jenkins, Alexander, & Bannister (1997); Carlier et al. (2000); McNally et al. (2003). (McNally et al. quote is from p. 72.) Use of debriefing techniques after the Virginia Tech shootings: Horwitz (2007); "Clergy from the International Orthodox Christian Charities…" (2007).
4. Pennebaker (1997, 2004); Frattaroli (2006).
5. There are many versions of the bunny-duck figure, such as one used by Jastrow (1899). Brugger and Brugger (1993) showed a version of the figure to people on Easter Sunday or on a Sunday in October.
6. Scheier, Carver, & Bridges (2001); Taylor & Sherman (2008).
7. Cognitive behavioral therapy: Alford & Beck (1997); Greenberger & Padesky (1995). Other forms of psychotherapy also attempt to get clients to reinterpret the meaning of their feelings and behavior. In fact, family system therapists have used the term "story editing," the same term I will use to refer to the social psychological approach (e.g., Erickson, 1998).
8. Lewin (1943, 1947, 1951).
9. Wegner (1994).
10. Quote from Sontag (2008), p. 295.
11. See Wilson & Linville (1982); Wilson, Damiani, & Shelton (2002). For a similar intervention with children, see Dweck (1975).
12. Quote from Aristotle (1962), p. 34.

CHAPTER 2: TESTING, TESTING

1. Details about the St. Paul diversity training program are from Estrada (2005). The quote from Mayor Kelly is from "City Workers…" (2005); the quotes from Shoua Lee and the middle-aged man are from Estrada (2005, p. 3B).
2. For one example of indirect measures of prejudice, see https://implicit.harvard .edu/implicit/

3. The quote is from the Theatre at Work website, www.theatreatwork.com/What_we_do/Does_it_work_/does_it_work_.html (accessed July 5, 2005). The study was conducted by Houden (1998).
4. Bargh (2007); Wegner (2002); Dijksterhuis & Nordgren (2006); Wilson (2002).
5. Nisbett & Wilson (1977); Wilson (2002); Pronin, Gilovich, & Ross (2004).
6. Ross (1989).
7. Kulik et al. (2007).
8. Women's Health Initiative Steering Committee (2004).
9. Kalev et al. (2006), p. 589.
10. On the importance of random assignment: Cook (2003).
11. Ross & Nisbett (1991).
12. Pennebaker (2004); Wilson, Damiani, & Shelton (2002).

CHAPTER 3: SHAPING OUR NARRATIVES
1. On gender differences in happiness: Stevenson and Wolfers (2008); Wood, Rhodes, and Whelan (1989).
2. Article about Gus Godsey and quote: McCafferty (2003); On happiness and where we live: Schkade & Kahneman (1998).
3. "Self-Improvement Market in U.S. Worth $9.6 Billion" (2006).
4. The "eighteen-month rule": Salerno (2005).
5. Quotes from Peale (1952), p. 16.
6. Quotes from *The Secret:* Byrne (2006), p. 11; pp. 27–28; p. 130, p.135. Bob Proctor quote from *Nightline:* Retrieved November 1, 2009, from: http://www.abcnews .go.com/images/Nightline/Microsoft percent20Word percent20- percent20Proctor percent20Transcript.pdf
7. Reports of people seeking therapy after failing in the dream world of *The Secret:* Watkin (2007).
8. Oishi (2010); see also McMahon (2006).
9. Yoffe (2009).
10. Inglehart, Foa, Peterson, & Welzel (2008).
11. Becker (1973); Langer (1975); Greenberg, Solomon, & Arndt (2008).
12. Pargament (2003); Diener & Biswas-Diener (2008).
13. Sam Gross cartoon reprinted with permission. ©Sam Gross/The New Yorker Collection/www.cartoonbank.com.
14. Mikulincer et al. (2003).
15. Wiggins et al. (1992).
16. McEwan (1997), p. 141.
17. Kross (2009); Kross, Ayduk, & Mischel (2005); Kross & Ayduk (2008); Ray, Wilhelm, & Gross (2008).
18. Wilson, Centerbar, Kermer, & Gilbert (2005); Wilson & Gilbert (2008).
19. For the "George Bailey" study, and a review of the literature on gratitude journals, see Koo et al. (2008).
20. On learned helplessness theory: See Seligman (1991); Gillham et al. (2001).
21. The Life Orientation Test-Revised adapted with permission. Copyright © 1994 by the American Psychological Association. The official citation that should be

used in referencing this material is: Scheier, M. F., Carver, C. S., & Bridges, M. W. (1994). Distinguishing optimism from neuroticism (and trait anxiety, self-mastery, and self-esteem): A re-evaluation of the Life Orientation Test. *Journal of Personality and Social Psychology, 67,* 1063–1078. No further reproduction or distribution is permitted without written permission from the American Psychological Association.

22. On optimism: See Scheier, Carver, & Bridges (2001); Nes & Segerstrom (2006).
23. Riskind, Sarampote, & Mercier (1996).
24. King (2001); Harrist et al. (2007).
25. Wood, Perunovic, & Lee (2009).
26. Pham & Taylor (1999); Rivkin & Taylor (1999).
27. On optimism and dieting: See Ogińska-Bulik & Juczyński (2001); Benyamini & Raz (2007).
28. Deci & Ryan (1985).
29. Autonomy, effectiveness, and competence are key ingredients to a happy life: Niemiec, Ryan, & Deci (2009). Helping others makes people happy: Dunn, Aknin, & Norton (2008); Lyubomirsky, Sheldon, & Schkade (2005).
30. Ethan Kross, personal communication, March 24, 2010.
31. King (2001), p. 801.
32. *Peanuts* by Charles Schulz, October 11, 1964. Quoted with permission from Universal Uclick.

CHAPTER 4: SHAPING OUR KIDS' NARRATIVES
1. Harris (2009).
2. Nisbett (2009).
3. Quotes from Spock (2004), pp.1 and 2.
4. Baby Einstein website: http://www.babyeinstein.com/en/our_story/about_us/
5. DeLoache et al. (2010).
6. Shapiro (2002).
7. Pomerantz & Wang (2009); Qin, Pomerantz, & Wang (2009).
8. Roth, Assor, Niemiec, Deci, & Ryan (2009); Grolnick & Ryan (1989).
9. What grown-ups understand about child development: A national benchmark study (2000); Straus & Stewart (1999).
10. Gershoff (2002).
11. Quotes from Spock (2004), p. 418.
12. Lepper (1973).
13. Greene, Sternberg, & Lepper (1976).
14. Ross, M. (1976); Harackiewicz, Durik, & Barron (2005).
15. The study on guilt versus shame with the racing cars: Dienstbier et al. (1975). The study on littering: Miller et al. (1975).
16. Dweck (2006); Williams (2001).
17. Reprinted with permission. Sally Forth © King Features Syndicate.
18. Berlin, Cassidy, & Appleyard (2008).
19. van den Boom (1994); Cassidy et al. (2010); Berlin, Zeanah, & Lieberman (2008).

20. Iannelli (2007); Child abuse and neglect fatalities (2009).
21. U.S. Department of Health and Human Services, U.S. Advisory Board on Child Abuse and Neglect (1991); Healthy Families America: http://www.healthyfamiliesamerica.org/home/index.shtml
22. Duggan et al. (2004); Chaffin (2004).
23. Bugental et al. (1993); Larrance & Twentyman (1983).
24. Bugental et al. (2002); Bugental & Schwartz (2009); Bugental et al. (2010).

CHAPTER 5: JUST SAY ... VOLUNTEER
1. The quote from Amanda Ireland is from Kingsbury (2008). The quote from Christen Callahan is from "Teen 'pregnancy pact'..." (2008).
2. The quotes from Nancy Runton and Cynthia Quinteros are from Welsh (2008).
3. The survey results are from the Youth Risk Behavior Survey, which is conducted every two years by the Centers for Disease Control and Prevention in the United States ("Youth Online: Comprehensive Results"). Pregnancy statistics: Stein & St. George (2009); Terry-Humen, Manlove, & Moore (2005); "Teen Pregnancy" (2008).
4. Moran (2000).
5. Quotes from the Social Security Act, Section 510 (42 U.S.C. 710).
6. Quote from Kolawole (2008).
7. Stein (2010).
8. Quote from Kim & Rector (2008), p. 2.
9. 1997 meta-analysis: Franklin et al. (1997).
10. Trenholm et al. (2008).
11. Kohler et al. (2008).
12. Kirby (2007); quote from p. 115. New study on abstinence: Jemmott, Jemmott, & Fong (2010).
13. Klerman (2004). Details about Lameesha Lee from Schultz (2001).
14. Quotes from Lameesha Lee and Jean Workman: Schultz (2001), p. B1; quote about the formal evaluation of the North Carolina program: Brown et al. (1998), p. 12.
15. Study that tested the Colorado Dollar-A-Day program: Stevens-Simon et al. (1997); quote from p. 980.
16. For research on the psychological correlates of teen pregnancy, see Bonell et al. (2005); Fletcher et al. (2007); Harden et al. (2006).
17. For information about the Teen Outreach Program, and discussions of its effectiveness, see: http://wymancenter.org/teens/teen-outreach/; Allen & Philliber (2001); Allen et al. (1997).
18. O'Donnell et al. (2002).
19. Hahn et al. (1994).
20. Schirm et al. (2006).

CHAPTER 6: SCARED CROOKED
1. Crime statistics are from the U.S. Department of Justice's Office of Juvenile Justice and Delinquency Prevention; mortality statistics are from the National

Center for Injury Prevention and Control, Centers for Disease Control and Prevention.

2. The quote from Todd Walker is from Marshall (2007). The quote from Tyris Bamba is from Hill (2007).
3. Quote from Eicher (1999), p. F-05; Finckenauer & Gavin (1999).
4. Petrosino, Turpin-Petrosino, & Finckenauer (2000).
5. Wilson & Lassiter (1982).
6. Weis & Toolis (2007).
7. For descriptions of the Cambridge-Somerville Youth Study and its long-term effects, see Powers & Witmer (1972), McCord (1978, 2003), and Ross & Nisbett (1991).
8. Dishion, McCord, & Poulin (1999).
9. Tierney, Grossman, & Resch (1995); Grossman & Tierney (1998); Grossman & Rhodes (2002).
10. Olds (2006).
11. Greenberg & Kusché (2006); Domitrovich, Cortes, & Greenberg (2007).
12. Olweus (2005); Limber (2006).
13. Henggeler et al. (2009); Henggeler, Sheidow, & Lee (2007).
14. Sexton & Alexander (2002).
15. Chamberlain (2003); Leve & Chamberlain (2005).
16. Allen et al. (1997); O'Donnell et al. (1999).
17. Quotes from O'Donnell et al. (1999), p. 34.
18. Keizer, Lindenberg, & Steg (2008); Braga & Bond (2008).

CHAPTER 7: EVERYBODY'S DOING IT . . . OR ARE THEY?
1. *This American Life* episode: Koenig & Glass (2009). Drinking statistics at Penn State: http://live.psu.edu/story/23655
2. Statistics from the Centers for Disease Control and Prevention (http://www.cdc.gov/alcohol/quickstats/binge_drinking.htm) and Wechsler and Nelson (2008). Evidence that drinking is increasing on college campuses: Hingson, Wenxing, & Weitzman (2009).
3. The statistics are from the National Center for Chronic Disease Prevention and Health Promotion, Centers for Disease Control and Prevention; the CDC Teen Drivers Fact Sheet (http://www.cdc.gov/MotorVehicleSafety/Teen_Drivers/teendrivers_factsheet.html); and from the Monitoring the Future national survey of teens (Johnston et al., 2009).
4. Winerip (1998); Guest (2005); Wood (2008).
5. http://dare.com/kids/pages/dare_world/dw_about_frame.htm
6. Rosenbaum & Hanson (1998); West & O'Neal (2004); U.S. General Accounting Office (2003). A couple of studies have shown modest positive effects of D.A.R.E. participation on reported cigarette smoking or alcohol use, but neither of these studies randomly assigned students to participate in the D.A.R.E. program or not (Ahmed et al., 2002; Zagumny & Thompson, 1997). Annual costs of D.A.R.E.: Shepard (2001).
7. Quote from Rosenwald (2004).

8. Evaluation of the Take Charge of Your Life program: http://www.dare.com/home/Resources/documents/RevisedLGIwebposting2.pdf
9. Botvin & Griffin (2004); Spoth et al. (2008).
10. Sussman et al. (2002); Valente et al. (2007).
11. Chou et al. (1998); Pentz et al. (2002); MacKinnon et al. (1991).
12. Perkins (2003); Perkins et al. (2005).
13. Poster reprinted by permission, University of Virginia, Office of Health Promotion.
14. DeJong et al. (2006, 2009).
15. Doumas et al. (2009); Neighbors et al. (2004).
16. The study on electricity use: Schultz et al. (2007).
17. Study on alcohol use at Stanford: Berger & Rand (2008).
18. Chou et al. (1998); Pentz et al. (2002); MacKinnon et al. (1991); Turrisi et al. (2009).
19. Griffin et al. (2004).
20. Heatherton & Sargent (2009); Pechmann & Shih (1999); Wills et al. (2008).

CHAPTER 8: SURELY THEY WON'T LIKE ME — OR WILL THEY?

1. "African Americans at Jamestown."
2. Quotes from John-Hall (2009) and Graham (2009).
3. Turner, Ross, Galster, & Yinger (2002).
4. Golenbock (2001).
5. The quotes are from *The Angry Eye*, Golenbock (2001). Quoted by permission, Elliott and Elliott Eyes, Inc.
6. Von Bergen, Soper, & Foster (2002); Pendry, Driscoll, & Field (2007); Paluck (2006); Lynch (1997).
7. Oskamp & Jones (2000).
8. The study with the third graders was reported by Weiner & Wright (1973).
9. This study was reported by Byrnes & Kiger (1990).
10. This study was reported by Stewart et al. (2003).
11. Bigler (1999); Paluck & Green (2009); Stephan, Renfro, & Stephan (2004).
12. Allport (1979/1954), pp. 481–482.
13. Pettigrew & Tropp (2006).
14. Schofield (1995); Stephan (1978).
15. Aronson & Patnoe (1997).
16. Cooper & Slavin (2004); Roseth, Johnson, & Johnson (2008).
17. Brewer & Miller (1988); Brown & Hewstone (2005); Dixon, Tropp, Durrhiem, & Tredoux (2010); Gaertner & Dovidio (2000); Paluck & Green (2009).
18. Shelton & Richeson (2005, 2006).
19. Mallett, Wilson, & Gilbert (2008); Vorauer (2001).
20. Mallett & Wilson (2010).
21. Study on cross-group friendships: Page-Gould, Mendoza-Denton, & Tropp (2009).
22. Vaughan & Rogers (2000); Bandura (2002); Paluck (2009).

CHAPTER 9: IT'S ABOUT ME, NOT MY GROUP
1. Planty et al. (2008); Hanushek & Rivkin (2008).
2. Nisbett (2009).
3. Rosenthal & Jacobson (1968); Jussim & Harber (2005); Raudenbush (1984).
4. These statistics are from the United States Census Bureau: DeNavas-Walt, Proctor, & Smith (2010).
5. See Nisbett (2009) for a review of this evidence.
6. Fryer (2010); Dee (2010).
7. U.S. Department of Health and Human Services, Administration for Children and Families (January 2010); Ludwig & Miller (2007); Deming (2009); Pianta et al. (2010).
8. The Abecedarian Project: see Campbell et al. (2002). The Perry Preschool Program: See Schweinhart et al. (2005). For a review of these and other early childhood intervention programs, see Knudsen et al. (2006); Nisbett (2009); Pianta et al. (2010).
9. Buckley & Schneider (2007).
10. Ongoing experimental test of KIPP schools: http://www.mathematica-mpr .com/education/kipp.asp. Nonexperimental studies: Woodworth et al. (2008).
11. Dobbie & Fryer (2009).
12. Brown & Day (2006); quotes are from p. 981.
13. On stereotype lift: Walton & Cohen (2003).
14. Yeung & von Hippel (2008).
15. Aronson & McGlone (2009); Schmader, Johns, & Forbes (2008); Steele (2010).
16. College attendance figures are from the 2000 United States Census. Retrieved June 2, 2009, from: http://www.census.gov/prod/2003pubs/c2kbr-26.pdf
17. African Americans and high blood pressure: Blascovich et al. (2001). Dropout rates: U.S. Department of Education, National Center for Education Statistics (2010). Minority students who stay in school value academics: Major & Schmader (1998). Quote from Steele (2010), p. 111.
18. Adolescence as a good time to intervene: Eccles (2004).
19. On mindsets: Dweck (2006). The Texas intervention study: Good, Aronson, & Inzlicht (2003). The study in the New York school: Blackwell, Trzesniewski, & Dweck (2007).
20. On self-affirmation theory: Steele (1988); Sherman & Cohen (2006).
21. Cohen, Garcia, Purdie-Vaughns, Apfel, & Brzustoski (2009).
22. Walton & Cohen (2011).
23. Inzlicht & Ben-Zeev (2000).

CHAPTER 10: SUSTAINED CHANGE
1. Study on negations in headlines: Wegner, Wenzlaff, Kerker, & Beattie (1981).
2. Quote from Vonnegut (1975), p. v.

Bibliography

African Americans at Jamestown. National Park Service. Retrieved July 27, 2007, from http://www.nps.gov/archive/colo/Jthanout/AFRICANS.html

Ahmed, N. U., Ahmed, N. S., Bennett, C., & Hinds, J. (2002). Impact of a Drug Abuse Resistance Education (D.A.R.E.) program in preventing the initiation of cigarette smoking in fifth- and sixth-grade students. *Journal of the National Medical Association, 94,* 249–256.

Alford, B. A., & Beck, A. T. (1997). *The integrative power of cognitive therapy.* New York: Guilford.

Allen, J. P., & Philliber, S. (2001). Who benefits most from a broadly targeted prevention program? Differential efficacy across populations in the Teen Outreach program. *Journal of Community Psychology, 29,* 637–655.

Allen, J. P., Philliber, S., Herrling, S., & Kuperminc, G. P. (1997). Preventing teen pregnancy and academic failure: Experimental evaluation of a developmentally based approach. *Child Development, 64,* 729–742.

Allport, G. W. (1979/1954). *The nature of prejudice* (25th anniversary edition). Reading, MA: Addison-Wesley.

Aristotle (1962). *Nicomachean ethics* (M. Ostwald, trans.). Indianapolis, IN: Bobbs-Merrill.

Aronson, E., & Patnoe, S. (1997). *Cooperation in the classroom: The jigsaw method.* New York: Longman.

Aronson, J., & McGlone, M. S. (2009). Stereotype and social identity threat. In T. D. Nelson (Ed.), *Handbook of prejudice, stereotyping, and discrimination* (pp. 153–178). New York: Psychology Press.

Bandura, A. (2002). Going global with social cognitive theory: From prospect to paydirt. In S. I. Donaldson, D. E. Berger, & K. Pezdek (Eds.), *Applied psychology: New frontiers and rewarding careers.* Mahwah, NJ: Erlbaum.

Bargh, J. (2007). *Social psychology and the unconscious: The automaticity of higher mental processes.* New York: Psychology Press.

Becker, E. (1973). *The denial of death.* New York: Academic Press.

Benyamini, Y., & Raz, O. (2007). "I can tell you if I'll really lose all that weight": Dispositional and situated optimism as predictors of weight loss following a group intervention. *Journal of Applied Social Psychology, 37,* 844–861.

Berger, J., & Rand, L. (2008). Shifting signals to help health: Using identity signaling to reduce risky health behaviors. *Journal of Consumer Research, 35,* 509–518.

Berlin, L. J., Cassidy, J., & Appleyard, K. (2008). The influence of early attachments to other relationships. In J. Cassidy & P. R. Shaver (Eds.), *Handbook of attachment: Theory, research, and clinical applications* (2nd ed., pp. 333–347). New York: Guilford.

Berlin, L. J., Zeanah, C. H., & Lieberman, A. F. (2008). Prevention and intervention programs for supporting early attachment security. In J. Cassidy & P. R. Shaver (Eds.), *Handbook of attachment: Theory, research, and clinical applications* (2nd ed., pp. 745–761). New York: Guilford.

Bigler, R. S. (1999). The use of multicultural curricula and materials to counter racism in children. *Journal of Social Issues, 55,* 687–705.

Bisson, J. I., Jenkins, P. L., Alexander, J., & Bannister, C. (1997). Randomised controlled trial of psychological debriefing for victims of acute burn trauma. *British Journal of Psychiatry, 171,* 78–81.

Blackwell, L. S., Trzesniewski, K. H., & Dweck, C. S. (2007). Implicit theories of intelligence predict achievement across an adolescent transition: A longitudinal study and an intervention. *Child Development, 78,* 246–263.

Blascovich, J., Spencer, S. J., Quinn, D., & Steele, C. (2001). African Americans and high blood pressure: The role of stereotype threat. *Psychological Science, 12,* 225–229.

Bonell, C., Allen, E., Strange, V., Copas, A., Oakley, A., Sephenson, J., & Johnson, A. (2005). The effect of dislike of school on risk of teenage pregnancy: Testing of hypotheses using longitudinal data from a randomised trial of sex education. *Journal of Epidemiology and Community Health, 60,* 502–506.

Botvin, G. J., & Griffin, K. W. (2004). Life Skills Training: Empirical findings and future directions. *The Journal of Primary Prevention, 25,* 211–232.

Braga, A. A., & Bond, B. J. (2008). Policing crime and disorder hot spots: A randomized controlled trial. *Criminology, 46,* 577–607.

Brewer, M. B., & Miller, N. (1988). Contact and cooperation: When do they work? In P. Katz & D. A. Taylor (Eds.), *Eliminating racism: Profiles in controversy* (pp. 315–326). New York: Plenum.

Brown, H. N., Saunders, R. B., & Dick, M. J. (1998). Preventing secondary pregnancy in adolescents: A model program. *Health Care for Women International, 20,* 5–15.

Brown, R. P., & Day, E. A. (2006). The difference isn't black and white: Stereotype threat and the race gap on Raven's Advanced Progressive Matrices. *Journal of Applied Psychology, 91,* 979–985.

Brown, R., & Hewstone, M. (2005). An integrative theory of intergroup contact. In M. P. Zanna (Ed.), *Advances in experimental social psychology* (Vol. 37, pp. 255–343). San Diego, CA: Academic Press.

Brugger, P., & Brugger, S. (1993). The Easter bunny in October: Is it disguised as a duck? *Perceptual and Motor Skills, 76,* 577–578.

Buckley, J., & Schneider, M. (2007). *Charter schools: Hope or hype?* Princeton, NJ: Princeton University Press.

Bugental, D. B., Beaulieu, D. A., & Silbert-Geiger, A. (2010). Increases in parental investment and child health as a result of an early intervention. *Journal of Experimental Child Psychology, 106,* 30–40.

Bugental, D. B., Blue, J., Cortez, V., Fleck, K., Kopeikin, H., Lewis, J., & Lyon, J. (1993). Social cognitions as organizers of autonomic and affective responses to social challenge. *Journal of Personality and Social Psychology, 64,* 94–103.

Bugental, D. B., Ellerson, P. C., Lin, E. K., Rainey, B., Kokotovic, A., & O'Hara, N. (2002). A cognitive approach to child abuse prevention. *Journal of Family Psychology, 16,* 243–258.

Bugental, D. B., & Schwartz, A. (2009). A cognitive approach to child mistreatment prevention among medically at-risk infants. *Developmental Psychology, 45,* 284–288.

Byrne, R. (2006). *The Secret.* New York: Atria.

Byrnes, D. A., & Kiger, G. (1990). The effect of a prejudice-reduction simulation on attitude change. *Journal of Applied Social Psychology, 20,* 341–356.

Campbell, F. A., Ramey, C. T., Pungello, E. P., Sparling, J., & Miller-Johnson, S. (2002). Early childhood education: Young adult outcomes from the Abecedarian Project. *Applied Developmental Science, 6,* 42–57.

Carlier, I. V. E., Voerman, A. E., & Gersons, B. P. R. (2000). The influence of occupational debriefing on post-traumatic stress symptomatology in traumatized police officers. *British Journal of Medical Psychology, 73,* 87–98.

Cassidy, J., Woodhouse, S. S., Sherman, L. J., Stupica, B., & Lejuez, C. W. (2010). Enhancing infant attachment security: An examination of treatment efficacy and differential susceptibility. Under editorial review.

Chaffin, M. (2004). Is it time to rethink Healthy Start/Healthy Families? *Child Abuse and Neglect, 28,* 589–595.

Chamberlain, P. (2003). *Treating chronic juvenile offenders: Advances made through the Oregon Multidimensional Treatment Foster Care model.* Washington, D.C.: American Psychological Association.

Child abuse and neglect fatalities: Statistics and interventions (2009). Washington, D.C.: Child Welfare Information Gateway. Retrieved January 20, 2010, from http://www.childwelfare.gov/pubs/factsheets/fatality.pdf

Chou, C., Montgomery, S., Pentz, M., Rohrbach, L., Johnson, C., Flay, B., & MacKinnon, D. P. (1998). Effects of a community-based prevention program in decreasing drug use in high-risk adolescents. *American Journal of Public Health, 88,* 944–948.

City workers attend diversity seminar (June 8, 2005). *St. Paul Pioneer Press,* p. B1.

Clergy from the International Orthodox Christian Charities administered CISD procedures to students. Voices: IOCC Frontline Clergy at Virginia Tech, retrieved June 22, 2007, from http://www.iocc.org/news/5-9-07.shtml

Cohen, G. L., Garcia, J., Purdie-Vaughns, V., Apfel, N., & Brzustoski, P. (2009). Recursive processes in self-affirmation: Intervening to close the achievement gap. *Science, 324,* 400–403.

Cook, T. D. (2003). Why have educational evaluators chosen not to do randomized experiments? *The Annals of the American Academy of Political and Social Science, 589,* 114–149.

Cooper, R., & Slavin, R. E. (2004). Cooperative learning: An instructinoal strategy to improve intergroup relations. In W. G. Stephen & W. P. Vogt (Eds.), *Education programs for improving intergroup relations* (pp. 55–73). New York: Teachers College Press.

Deci, E. L., & Ryan, R. M. (1985). *Intrinsic motivation and self-determination in human behavior.* New York: Plenum.

Dee, T. S. (2010). Conditional cash penalties in education: Evidence from the learnfare experiment. NBER Working Paper No. 15126. Retrieved May 6, 2010, from http://www.swarthmore.edu/x16496.xml

DeJong, W., Schneider, S., Towvim, L., Murphy, M., Doerr, E., Simonsen, N., Mason, K., & Scribner, R. (2006). A multisite randomized trial of social norms marketing campaigns to reduce college student drinking. *Journal of Studies on Alcohol, 67,* 868–879.

DeJong, W., Schneider, S., Towvim, L., Murphy, M., Doerr, E., Simonsen, N., Mason, K., & Scribner, R. (2009). A multisite randomized trial of social norms marketing campaigns to reduce college student drinking: A replication failure. *Substance Abuse, 30,* 127–140.

DeLoache, J. S., Chiong, C., Sherman, K., Islam, N., Vanderborght, M., Troseth, G. L., Strouse, G. A., & O'Doherty, K. (2010). Do babies learn from baby media? *Psychological Science, 21,* 1570-1574.

Deming, D. (2009). Early childhood intervention and life-cycle skill development: Evidence from Head Start. *American Economic Journal: Applied Economics, 1,* 111–134.

DeNavas-Walt, C., Proctor, B. D., & Smith, J. C. (2010). *Income, poverty, and health insurance coverage in the United States: 2009.* U.S. Census Bureau, Current Population Reports, P60-238. U.S. Government Printing Office, Washington, D.C.

Diener, E., & Biswas-Diener, R. (2008). *Happiness: Unlocking the mysteries of psychological wealth.* Malden, MA: Blackwell.

Dienstbier, R. A., Hillman, D., Lehnhoff, J., Hillman, J., & Valkenaar, M. C. (1975). An emotion-attribution approach to moral behavior: Interfacing cognitive and avoidance theories of moral development. *Psychological Review, 82,* 299–315.

Dijksterhuis, A., & Nordgren, L. (2006). A theory of unconscious thought. *Perspectives on Psychological Science, 1,* 95–109.

Dishion, T. J., McCord, J., & Poulin, F. (1999). When interventions harm: Peer groups and problem behavior. *American Psychologist, 54,* 755–764.

Dixon, J., Tropp, J. R., Durrheim, K., & Tredoux, C. (2010). "Let them eat harmony": Prejudice-reduction strategies and attitudes of historically disadvantaged groups. *Current Directions in Psychological Science, 19,* 76–80.

Dobbie, W., & Fryer, R. G., Jr. (2009). Are high-quality schools enough to close the achievement gap? Evidence from a bold social experiment in Harlem. Unpublished manuscript. Retrieved May 25, 2009, from http://www.economics.harvard.edu/faculty/fryer/papers_fryer

Domitrovich, C., Cortes, R., & Greenberg, M. (2007). Improving young children's social and emotional competence: A randomized trial of the preschool 'PATHS' curriculum. *Journal of Primary Prevention, 28,* 67–91.

Doumas, D., McKinley, L., & Book, P. (2009). Evaluation of two Web-based alcohol interventions for mandated college students. *Journal of Substance Abuse Treatment, 36,* 65–74.

Duggan, A., McFarlane, E., Fuddy, L., Burrell, L., Higman, S. M., Windham, A., & Sia, C. (2004). Randomized trial of a statewide home visiting program: Impact in preventing child abuse and neglect. *Child Abuse and Neglect, 28,* 597–622.

Dunn, E. W., Aknin, L. B., & Norton, M. I. (2008). Spending money on others promotes happiness. *Science, 319,* 1687–1688.

Dweck, C. S. (1975). The role of expectations and attributions in the alleviation of learned helplessness. *Journal of Personality and Social Psychology, 31,* 674–685.

Dweck, C. S. (2006). *Mindset: The new psychology of success.* New York: Ballantine.

Eccles, J. S. (2004). Schools, academic motivation, and stage-environment fit. In R. M. Lerner & L. D. Sternberg (Eds.), *Handbook of adolescent psychology* (2nd ed., pp. 125–153). New York: Wiley.

Eicher, D. (1999, July 31). Stark prison documentary redone for MTV special. *The Denver Post,* p. F-05.

Erickson, M. H. (1998). *Life reframing in hypnosis.* Seminars, Workshops and Lectures of Milton H. Erickson, Vol. 2. London: Free Association Books.

Estrada, H. M. (2005, June 9). St. Paul raising awareness: Workers learning the act of diversity. *Star Tribune* (Minneapolis, MN), p. 3B.

Finckenauer, J. O., & Gavin, P. W. (1999). *Scared straight: The panacea phenomenon revisited.* Prospect Heights, IL: Waveland Press.

Fletcher, A., Harden, A., Brunton, G., Oakley, A., & Bonell, C. (2007). Interventions addressing the social determinants of teenage pregnancy. *Health Education, 106,* 29–39.

Franklin, C., Grant, D., Corcoran, J., Miller, P. O., & Bultman, L. (1997). Effectiveness of prevention programs for adolescent pregnancy: A meta-analysis. *Journal of Marriage and the Family, 59,* 551–567.

Frattaroli, J. (2006). Experimental disclosure and its moderators: A meta-analysis. *Psychological Bulletin, 132,* 823–865.

Fryer, R. G. (2010). Financial incentives and student achievement: Evidence from randomized trials. Retrieved April 19, 2010, from http://www.edlabs.harvard.edu/pdf/studentincentives.pdf

Gaertner, S., & Dovidio, J. (2000). *Reducing intergroup bias: The common ingroup identity model.* New York: Psychology Press.

Gershoff, E. T. (2002). Corporal punishment by parents and associated child behaviors and experiences: A meta-analytic and theoretical review. *Psychological Bulletin, 128,* 539–579.

Gillham, J. E., Shatté, A. J., Reivich, K. J., & Seligman, M. E. P. (2001). Optimism, pessimism, and explanatory style. In E. C. Chang (Ed.), *Optimism and pessimism* (pp. 53–75). Washington, D.C.: American Psychological Association.

Golenbock, S. [Producer and Director] (2001). *The Angry Eye* [Documentary Film]. Available from janeelliott.com.

Good, C., Aronson, J., & Inzlicht, M. (2003). Improving adolescents' standardized test performance: An intervention to reduce the effects of stereotype threat. *Applied Developmental Psychology, 24,* 645–662.

Graham, K. A. (2009, July 11). Campers pondering swim-club experience. *Philadelphia Inquirer.* Retrieved July 14, 2009, from http://www.philly.com/philly/news/local/50528097.html

Greenberg, J., Solomon, S., & Arndt, J. (2008). A basic but uniquely human motivation: Terror management. In J. Y. Shah & W. L. Gardiner (Eds.), *Handbook of motivation science* (pp. 114–134). New York: Guilford.

Greenberg, M., & Kusché, C. (2006). Building social and emotional competence: The PATHS curriculum. In S. R. Jimerson & M. Furlong (Eds.), *Handbook of school violence and school safety: From research to practice* (pp. 395–412). Mahwah, NJ: Erlbaum.

Greenberger, D., & Padesky, C. A. (1995). *Mind over mood: Change how you feel by changing the way you think.* New York: Guilford.

Greene, D., Sternberg, B., & Lepper, M. R. (1976). Overjustification in a token economy. *Journal of Personality and Social Psychology, 34,* 1219–1234.

Griffin, K., Botvin, G., Nichols, T., & Scheier, L. (2004). Low perceived chances for success in life and binge drinking among inner-city minority youth. *Journal of Adolescent Health, 34,* 501–507.

Grolnick, W. S., & Ryan, R. M. (1989). Parent styles associated with children's self-regulation and competence in school. *Journal of Educational Psychology, 81,* 143–154.

Grossman, J. B., & Rhodes, J. E. (2002). The test of time: Predictors and effects of duration in youth mentoring relationships. *American Journal of Community Psychology, 30,* 199–219.

Grossman, J. B., & Tierney, J. P. (1998). Does mentoring work? An impact study of the Big Brothers Big Sisters Program. *Evaluation Research, 22,* 403–426.

Guest, J. (2005, December 1). High spirits: Wahoos tackle fourth-year fifth. *The Hook.* Retrieved August 5, 2009, from http://www.readthehook.com/Stories/2005/12/01/coverHighSpiritsWahoosTack.html

Hahn, A., Leavitt, T., & Aaron, P. (1994). Evaluation of the Quantum Opportunities Program (QOP): Did the program work? Waltham, MA: Heller Graduate School, Brandeis University.

Hanushek, E. A., & Rivkin, S. G. (2008). Harming the best: How schools affect the black-white achievement gap (National Bureau of Economic Research working paper 14211). Retrieved April 30, 2009, from http://www.nber.org/papers/w14211

Harackiewicz, J. M., Durik, A. M., & Barron, K. E. (Eds.) (2005). *Multiple goals, optimal motivation, and the development of interest.* New York: Cambridge University Press.

Harden, A., Brunton, G., Fletcher, A., Oakley, A., Burchett, H., & Backhans, M. (2006). Young people, pregnancy and social exclusion: A systematic synthesis of research evidence to identify effective, appropriate and promising approaches for prevention and support. London: EPPI-Centre, Social Science Research Unit, Institute of Education, University of London.

Harris, J. R. (2009). *The nurture assumption: Why children turn out the way they do* (rev. ed.). New York: Free Press.

Harrist, S., Carlozzi, B. L., McGovern, A. R., & Harrist, A. W. (2007). Benefits of expressive writing and expressive talking about life goals. *Journal of Research in Personality, 41,* 923–930.

Heatherton, T. F., & Sargent, J. D. (2009). Does watching smoking in movies promote teenage smoking? *Current Directions in Psychological Science, 18,* 63–67.

Henggeler, S. W., Letourneau, E. J., Borduin, C. M., Schewe, P. A., & McCart, M. R. (2009). Mediators of change for Multisystemic Therapy with juvenile sexual offenders. *Journal of Consulting and Clinical Psychology, 77,* 451–462.

Henggeler, S. W., Sheidow, A. J., & Lee, T. (2007). Multisystemic treatment (MST) of serious clinical problems in youths and their families. In D. W. Springer & A. R. Roberts (Eds.), *Handbook of forensic mental health with victims and offenders: Assessment, treatment, and research* (pp. 315–345). New York: Springer.

Hill, A. (2007, February 5). Mentor uses unique tactic to scare kids straight. *Oakland Tribune.* Retrieved June 25, 2009, from http://www.insidebayarea.com/search/ci_5160476?IADID=Search-www.insidebayarea.com-www.insidebayarea.com

Hingson, R. W., Wenxing, Z., & Weitzman, E. R. (2009). Magnitude of and trends in alcohol-related mortality and morbidity among U.S. college students ages 18–24, 1998–2005. *Journal of Studies on Alcohol and Drugs,* Supplement No. 16, 12–20.

Horwitz, S. (2007, June 22). 8 minutes after 911 call, a rescue from madness. *Washington Post,* pp. A01, A10–A11.

Houden, L. L. (1998). Co-creating sacred space: The use of theatre in the transformation of conflict. *Dissertation Abstracts International, 58 (9-A),* 3366.

Huntley, S. (1998, January 6), Firefighters warn of burglar bars peril. *The Tampa Tribune,* Florida/Metro section p. 1.

Iannelli, V. (2007). Child abuse statistics. Retrieved January 24, 2010, from http://pediatrics.about.com/od/childabuse/a/05_abuse_stats.htm

Inglehart, R., Foa, R., Peterson, C., & Welzel, C. (2008). Development, freedom, and rising happiness: A global perspective (1981–2007). *Perspectives on Psychological Science, 3,* 264–285.

Inzlicht, M., & Ben-Zeev, T. (2000). A threatening intellectual environment: Why females are susceptible to experiencing problem-solving deficits in the presence of males. *Psychological Science, 11,* 365–371.

Jastrow, J. (1899). The mind's eye. *Popular Science Monthly, 54,* 299–312.

Jemmott, J. B. III, Jemmott, L. S., & Fong, G. T. (2010). Efficacy of a theory-based abstinence-only intervention over 24 months: A randomized controlled trial with young adolescents. *Archives of Pediatric Adolescent Medicine, 164,* 152–159.

John-Hall, A. (2009, July 10). Ugliness in the water at Valley Club. *Philadelphia Inquirer.* Retrieved July 10, 2009, from http://www.philly.com/philly/news/local/20090710_Annette_John-Hall_Ugliness_in_the_water_at_Valley_Club.html

Johnston, L. D., O'Malley, P. M., Bachman, J. G., & Schulenberg, J. E. (2009). *Monitoring the Future: National results on adolescent drug use: Overview of key findings 2008* (NIH Publication No. 09-7401). Retrieved August 3, 2009, from http://www.monitoringthefuture.org/pubs/monographs/overview2008.pdf

Jussim, L., & Harber, K. D. (2005). Teacher expectations and self-fulfilling prophecies: Knowns and unknowns, resolved and unresolved controversies. *Personality and Social Psychology Review, 9,* 131–155.

Kadet, A. (2002, June). Good grief! *Smart Money, 11,* 109–114.

Kalev, A., Dobbin, F., & Kelly, E. (2006). Best practices or best guesses? Assessing the efficacy of corporate affirmative action and diversity policies. *American Sociological Review, 71,* 589–617.

Keizer, K., Lindenberg, S., & Steg, L. (2008). The spreading of disorder. *Science, 322,* 1681–1685.

Kim, C. C., & Rector, R. (2008). Abstinence education: Assessing the evidence. Washington, D.C.: The Heritage Foundation. Retrieved July 3, 2008, from http://www.heritage.org/Research/Welfare/bg2126.cfm

King, L. (2001). The health benefits of writing about life goals. *Personality and Social Psychology Bulletin, 27,* 798–807.

Kingsbury, K. (2008, June 18). Pregnancy boom at Gloucester High. *Time.* Retrieved July 1, 2008, from http://www.time.com/time/printout/0,8816,1815845,00.html

Kirby, D. (2007). *Emerging answers 2007: Summary.* The National Campaign to Prevent Teen and Unplanned Pregnancy. Retrieved July 2, 2008, from http://www.thenationalcampaign.org/EA2007/default.aspx

Klerman, L. V. (2004). Another chance: Preventing additional births to teen mothers. The National Campaign to Prevent Teen and Unplanned Pregnancy. Retrieved October 14, 2008, from http://www.thenationalcampaign.org/default.aspx

Knudsen, E. I., Heckman, J. J., Cameron, J. L., & Shonkoff, J. P. (2006). Economic, neurobiological, and behavioral perspectives on building America's future workforce. *Proceedings of the National Academy of Sciences of the United States of America, 103,* 10155–10162.

Koenig, S., & Glass, I. [Producers] (2009, December 18). *This American Life: #1 Party School* [Radio broadcast]. Chicago: Chicago Public Radio. Podcast retrieved from http://www.thisamericanlife.org/Radio_Episode.aspx?sched=1330

Kohler, P. K., Manhart, L. E., & Lafferty, W. E. (2008). Abstinence-only and comprehensive sex education and the initiation of sexual activity and teen pregnancy. *Journal of Adolescent Health, 42,* 344–351.

Kolawole, E. (2008, September 10). Off base on sex ed: A McCain campaign ad claims Obama's "one accomplishment" was a bill to teach sex ed to kindergarten kids. Don't believe it. Retrieved November 14, 2008, from http://www.newsweek.com/id/158314

Koo, M., Algoe, S. B., Wilson, T. D., & Gilbert, D. T. (2008). It's a wonderful life: Mentally subtracting positive events improves people's affective states, contrary to their affective forecasts. *Journal of Personality and Social Psychology, 95,* 1217–1224.

Kross, E. (2009). When the self becomes other: Toward an integrative understanding of the processes distinguishing adaptive self-reflection from rumination. *New York Academy of Sciences, 1167,* 35–40.

Kross, E., & Ayduk, O. (2008). Facilitating adaptive emotional analysis: Distinguishing distanced-analysis of depressive experiences from immersed-analysis and distraction. *Personality and Social Psychology Bulletin, 34,* 924–938.

Kross, E., Ayduk, O., & Mischel, W. (2005). When asking "why" does not hurt: Distinguishing rumination from reflective processing of negative emotions. *Psychological Science, 16,* 709–715.

Kulik, C. T., Pepper, M. B., Roberson, L., & Parker, S. K. (2007). The rich get richer: Predicting participation in voluntary diversity training. *Journal of Organizational Behavior, 28,* 753–769.

Langer, S. K. (1975). *Mind: An essay on human feeling* (Vol. 1). Baltimore: Johns Hopkins University Press.

Larrance, D. T., & Twentyman, C. T. (1983). Maternal attributions and child abuse. *Journal of Abnormal Psychology, 92,* 449–457.

Lepper, M. R. (1973). Dissonance, self-perception, and honesty in children. *Journal of Personality and Social Psychology, 25,* 65–74.

Leve, L. D., & Chamberlain, P. (2005). Association with delinquent peers: Intervention effects for youth in the juvenile justice condition. *Journal of Abnormal Child Psychology, 33,* 339–347.

Lewin, K. (1943). Defining the "field at a given time." *Psychological Review, 50,* 292–310.

Lewin, K. (1947). Group discussion and social change. In Newcomb, T. M., & E. L. Hartley (Eds.), *Readings in social psychology* (pp. 330–341). New York: Henry Holt.

Lewin, K. (1951). *Field theory in social science: selected theoretical papers* (Ed. by D. Cartwright). New York: Harper & Row.

Limber, S. (2006). The Olweus Bullying Prevention Program: An overview of its implementation and research basis. In R. Jimerson & M. Furlong (Eds.), *Handbook of school violence and school safety: From research to practice* (pp. 293–307). Mahwah, NJ: Erlbaum.

Ludwig, J., & Miller, D. L. (2007). Does Head Start improve children's life chances? Evidence from a regression discontinuity design. *Quarterly Journal of Economics, 122,* 159–208.

Lynch, F. R. (1997). The diversity machine. New York: The Free Press.

Lyubomirsky, S., Sheldon, K. M., & Schkade, D. (2005). Pursuing happiness: The architecture of sustainable change. *Review of General Psychology, 9,* 111–131.

MacKinnon, D. P., Johnson, C. A., Pentz, M. A., Dwyer, J. H., Hansen, W. B., Flay, B. R., & Wany, E. Y. (1991). Mediating mechanisms in a school-based drug prevention program: First-year effects of the Midwestern Prevention Project. *Health Psychology, 10,* 164–172.

Major, B., & Schmader, T. (1998). Coping with stigma through psychological disengagement. In J. Swim & C. Stangor (Eds.), *Prejudice: The target's perspective* (pp. 219–241). New York: Academic Press.

Mallett, R. K., & Wilson, T. D. (2010). Increasing positive intergroup contact. *Journal of Experimental Social Psychology, 46,* 382–387.

Mallett, R. K., Wilson, T. D., & Gilbert, D. T. (2008). Expect the unexpected: Failure to anticipate similarities when predicting the quality of an intergroup interaction. *Journal of Personality and Social Psychology, 94*, 265–277.

Marshall, C. (2007, July 26). Coach's toughest drill is a grim lesson on life. *The New York Times.* Retrieved June 25, 2009, from http://query.nytimes.com/gst/fullpage .html?res=940CE5D91E3FF935A15754C0A9619C8B63

McCafferty, D. (2003, March 9). The happiest guy. *USA Weekend.* Retrieved January 24, 2010, from http://www.usaweekend.com/03_issues/030309/030309 happiestman.html

McCord, J. (1978). A thirty-year follow-up of treatment effects. *American Psychologist, 33*, 284–289.

McCord, J. (2003). Cures that harm: Unanticipated outcomes of crime prevention programs. *Annals of the American Academy of Political and Social Science, 587*, 16–30.

McEwan, I. (1997). *Enduring love.* London: Jonathan Cape.

McMahon, D. (2006). *Happiness: A history.* New York: Atlantic Monthly Press.

McNally, R. J., Bryant, R. A., & Ehlers, A. (2003). Does early psychological intervention promote recovery from posttraumatic stress? *Psychological Science in the Public Interest, 4*, 45–79.

Mikulincer, M., Florian, V., & Hirschberger, G. (2003). The existential function of close relationships: Introducing death into the science of love. *Personality and Social Psychology Review, 7*, 20–40.

Miller, R. L., Brickman, P., & Bolen, D. (1975). Attribution versus persuasion as a means for modifying behavior. *Journal of Personality and Social Psychology, 31*, 430–441.

Moran, J. P. (2000). *Teaching sex: The shaping of adolescence in the 20th century.* Cambridge, MA: Harvard University Press.

National Center for Chronic Disease Prevention and Health Promotion, Centers for Disease Control and Prevention. 2007 Youth Risk Behavior Surveillance System. Retrieved June 27, 2009, from http://www.cdc.gov/HealthyYouth/yrbs/index .htm

National Center for Injury Prevention and Control, Centers for Disease Control and Prevention. WISQARS leading causes of death reports, 1999–2006. Retrieved June 27, 2009, from http://webappa.cdc.gov/sasweb/ncipc/leadcaus10.html

Neighbors, C., Larimer, M., & Lewis, M. (2004). Targeting misperceptions of descriptive drinking norms: Efficacy of a computer-delivered personalized normative feedback intervention. *Journal of Consulting and Clinical Psychology, 72*, 434–447.

Nes, L. S., & Segerstrom, S. C. (2006). Dispositional optimism and coping: A meta-analytic review. *Personality and Social Psychology Review, 3*, 235–251.

Niemiec, C. P., Ryan, R. M., & Deci, E. L. (2009). The path taken: Consequences of attaining intrinsic and extrinsic aspirations in post-college life. *Journal of Research in Personality, 43*, 291–306.

Nisbett, R. E. (2009). *Intelligence and how to get it.* New York: W. W. Norton.

Nisbett, R. E., & Wilson, T. D. (1977). Telling more than we can know: Verbal reports on mental processes. *Psychological Review, 84*, 231–259.

O'Donnell, L., Stueve, A., Doval, A. S., Duran, R., Atnafou, R., Haber, D., Johnson, N., Murray, H., Grant, U., Juhn, G., Tang, J., Bass, J., & Piessens, P. (1999). Violence prevention and young adolescents' participation in community services. *Journal of Adolescent Health, 24*, 28–37.

O'Donnell, L., Stueve, A., O'Donnell, C., Duran, R., Doval, A. S., Wilson, R. F., Haber, D., Perry, E., & Pleck, J. H. (2002). Long-term reductions in sexual initiation and sexual activity among urban middle schoolers in the Reach for Health Service Learning Program. *Journal of Adolescent Health, 31*, 93–100.

Ogińska-Bulik, N., & Juczyński, Z. (2001). Coping with stress as a determinant of reducing overweight in women. *Studia Psychologica, 43*, 23–31.

Oishi, S. (2010). Culture and well-being: Conceptual and methodological issues. In E. Diener, D. Kahneman, & J. F. Helliwell (Eds.), *International differences in well-being* (pp. 34–69). New York: Oxford University Press.

Olds, D. L. (2006). The nurse-family partnership: An evidence-based preventive intervention. *Infant Mental Health Journal, 27*, 5–25.

Olweus, D. (2005). A useful evaluation design, and effects of the Olweus Bullying Prevention Program. *Psychology, Crime & Law, 11*, 389–402.

Oskamp, S., & Jones, J. M. (2000). Pathways to one America in the 21st century: Promising practices for racial reconciliation. The President's Initiative on Race (1999, January). In S. Oskamp (Ed.), *Reducing prejudice and discrimination* (pp. 319–334). Mahwah, NJ: Erlbaum.

Page-Gould, E., Mendoza-Denton, R., & Tropp, L. (2009). With a little help from my cross-group friend: Reducing anxiety in intergroup contexts through cross-group friendship. *Journal of Personality and Social Psychology, 95*, 1080–1094.

Paluck, E. L. (2006). Diversity training and intergroup contact: A call to action research. *Journal of Social Issues, 62*, 577–595.

Paluck, E. L. (2009). Reducing intergroup prejudice and conflict using the media: A field experiment in Rwanda. *Journal of Personality and Social Psychology, 96*, 574–587.

Paluck, E. L., & Green, D. P. (2009). Prejudice reduction: What works? A critical look at evidence from the field and the laboratory. *Annual Review of Psychology, 60*, 339–367.

Pargament, K. I. (2003). The bitter and the sweet: An evaluation of the costs and benefits of religiousness. *Psychological Inquiry, 13*, 168–181.

Peale, N. V. (1952). *The power of positive thinking.* Englewood Cliffs, NJ: Prentice-Hall.

Pechmann, C., & Shih, C. F. (1999). Smoking scenes in movies and antismoking advertisements before movies: Effects on youth. *Journal of Marketing, 63*, 1–13.

Pendry, L. F., Driscoll, D. M., & Field, S. C. T. (2007). Diversity training: Putting theory into practice. *Journal of Occupational and Organizational Psychology, 80*, 27–50.

Pennebaker, J. W. (1997). *Opening up: The healing power of expressing emotions* (rev. ed.). New York: Guilford.

Pennebaker, J. W. (2004). *Writing to heal: A guided journal for recovering from trauma & emotional upheaval.* Oakland, CA: New Harbinger Publications.

Pentz, M. A., Mihalic, S. F., & Grotpeter, J. K. (2002). *Blueprints for violence prevention: The Midwestern Prevention Project.* Boulder, CO: Institute of Behavioral Research.

Perkins, H. W. (2003). The emergence and evolution of the social norms approach to substance abuse prevention. In H. W. Perkins (Ed.), *The social norms approach to preventing school and college age substance abuse: A handbook for educators, counselors, and clinicians* (pp. 3–17). San Francisco: Jossey-Bass.

Perkins, H., Haines, M., & Rice, R. (2005). Misperceiving the college drinking norm and related problems: A nationwide study of exposure to prevention information, perceived norms and student alcohol misuse. *Journal of Studies on Alcohol, 66,* 470–478.

Petrosino, A., Turpin-Petrosino, C., & Finckenauer, J. O. (2000). Well-meaning programs can have harmful effects! Lessons from experiments of programs such as scared straight. *Crime and Delinquency, 46,* 354–379.

Pettigrew, T. F., & Tropp, L. R. (2006). A meta-analytic test of intergroup contact theory. *Journal of Personality and Social Psychology, 90,* 751–783.

Pham, L., & Taylor, S. (1999). From thought to action: Effects of process- versus outcome-based mental simulations on performance. *Personality and Social Psychology Bulletin, 25,* 250–260.

Pianta, R. C., Barnett, W. S., Burchinal, M., & Thronburg, K. R. (2010). The effects of preschool education: What we know, how public policy is or is not aligned with the evidence base, and what we need to know. *Psychological Science in the Public Interest, 10,* 49–88.

Planty, M., Hussar, W., Snyder, T., Provasnik, S., Kena, G., Dinkes, R., KewalRamani, A., & Kemp, J. (2008). The conditions of education 2008 (NCES 2008-031). National Center for Education Statistics, Institute of Education Sciences, U.S. Department of Education, Washington, D.C. Retrieved May 1, 2009, from http://www.eric.ed.gov/ERICWebPortal/custom/portlets/recordDetails/detailmini.jsp?_nfpb=true&_&ERICExtSearch_SearchValue_0=ED501487&ERICExtSearch_SearchType_0=no&accno=ED501487

Pomerantz, E. M., & Wang, Q. (2009). The role of parental control in children's development in Western and East Asian countries. *Current Directions in Psychological Science, 18,* 285–289.

Powers, E., & Witmer, H. (1972). *An experiment in the prevention of delinquency.* Montclair, NJ: Patterson Smith.

Pronin, E., Gilovich, T., & Ross, L. (2004). Objectivity in the eye of the beholder: Divergent perceptions of bias in self versus others. *Psychological Review, 111,* 781–799.

Qin, L., Pomerantz, E. M., & Wang, Q. (2009). Are gains in decision-making autonomy during early adolescence beneficial for emotional functioning? The case of the United States and China. *Child Development, 80,* 1705–1721.

Raudenbush, S. (1984). Magnitude of teacher expectancy effects on pupil IQ as a function of the credibility of expectancy induction: A synthesis of findings from 18 experiments. *Journal of Educational Psychology, 76,* 85–97.

Ray, R., Wilhelm, F., & Gross, J. (2008). All in the mind's eye? Anger rumination and reappraisal. *Journal of Personality and Social Psychology, 94,* 133–145.

Riskind, J. H., Sarampote, C. S., & Mercier, M. A. (1996). For every malady a sovereign cure: Optimism training. *Journal of Cognitive Psychotherapy: An International Quarterly, 101,* 105–117.

Rivkin, I., & Taylor, S. (1999). The effects of mental simulation on coping with controllable stressful events. *Personality and Social Psychology Bulletin, 25,* 1451–1462.

Rosenbaum, D. P., & Hanson, G. S. (1998). Assessing the effectiveness of school-based drug education: A six-year multilevel analysis of Project D.A.R.E. *Journal of Research in Crime and Delinquency, 35,* 381–412.

Rosenthal, R., & Jacobson, L. (1968). *Pygmalion in the classroom: Teacher expectations and student intellectual development.* New York: Holt, Rinehart & Winston.

Rosenwald, M. S. (2004, April 20). Face off for critics: Healy takes message to DARE officials. *The Boston Globe,* p. B1.

Roseth, C., Johnson, D., & Johnson, R. (2008). Promoting early adolescents' achievement and peer relationships: The effects of cooperative, competitive, and individualistic goal structures. *Psychological Bulletin, 134,* 223–246.

Ross, L., & Nisbett, R. (1991). *The person and the situation: Perspectives of social psychology.* New York: McGraw-Hill.

Ross, M. (1976). Salience of reward and intrinsic motivation. *Journal of Personality and Social Psychology, 32,* 245–254.

Ross, M. (1989). Relation of implicit theories to the construction of personal histories. *Psychological Review, 96,* 341–357.

Roth, G., Assor, A., Niemiec, C., Deci, E., & Ryan, R. (2009). The emotional and academic consequences of parental conditional regard: Comparing conditional positive regard, conditional negative regard, and autonomy support as parenting practices. *Developmental Psychology, 45,* 1119–1142.

Salerno, S. (2005). *Sham: How the self-help movement made America helpless.* New York: Crown.

Scheier, M. F., Carver, C. S., & Bridges, M. W. (1994). Distinguishing optimism from neuroticism (and trait anxiety, self-mastery, and self-esteem): A re-evaluation of the Life Orientation Test. *Journal of Personality and Social Psychology, 67,* 1063–1078.

Scheier, M. F., Carver, C. S., & Bridges, M. W. (2001). Optimism, pessimism, and psychological well-being. In E. C. Chang (Ed.), *Optimism and pessimism* (pp. 189–216). Washington, D.C.: American Psychological Association.

Schirm, A., Stuart, E., & McKie, A. (2006). *The Quantum Opportunity Program demonstration: Final impacts.* Washington, D.C.: Mathematica Policy Research, Inc.

Schkade, D. A., & Kahneman, D. (1998). Would you be happy if you lived in California? A focusing illusion in judgments of well-being. *Psychological Science, 9,* 340–346.

Schmader, T., Johns, M., & Forbes, C. (2008). An integrated process model of stereotype threat effects on performance. *Psychological Review, 115,* 336–356.

Schofield, J. W. (1995). School desegregation and intergroup relations: A review of the literature. In G. Grant (Ed.), *Review of research in education* (Vol. 17, pp. 335–409). Washington, D.C.: American Educational Research Association.

Schultz, P. W., Nolan, J. M., Cialdini, R. B., Goldstein, N. J., & Griskevicius, V. (2007). The constructive, destructive, and reconstructive power of social norms. *Psychological Science, 18,* 429–434.

Schultz, S. (2001, March 25). Teen moms find support, a little cash: A Guilford County program doles out dollars and guidance to prevent repeat pregnancies in teens. *Greensboro News & Record,* p. B1.

Schweinhart, L. J., Montie, J., Xiang, Z., Barnett, W. S., Belfield, C. R., & Nores, M. (2005). *Lifetime effects: The High/Scope Perry Preschool Study through age 40.* Ypsilanti, MI: High/Scope Foundation.

Self-improvement market in U.S. worth $9.6 billion (2006, September 21). PRWeb Press Release Newswire. Retrieved October 29, 2009, from http://www .prwebdirect.com/releases/2006/9/prweb440011.htm

Seligman, M. E. P. (1991). *Learned optimism.* New York: Knopf.

Sexton, T., & Alexander, J. (2002). Family-based empirically supported interventions. *Counseling Psychologist, 30,* 238–261.

Shapiro, J. (2002, August 22). Keeping parents off campus. *The New York Times,* p. A23. Retrieved February 24, 2010, from http://www.nytimes.com/2002/08/22/ opinion/keeping-parents-off-campus.html?scp=3&sq=judith+shapiro&st=nyt

Shelton, J., & Richeson, J. (2005). Intergroup contact and pluralistic ignorance. *Journal of Personality and Social Psychology, 88,* 91–107.

Shelton, J., & Richeson, J. (2006). Interracial interactions: A relational approach. In M. P. Zanna (Ed.), *Advances in Experimental Social Psychology* (Vol. 38, pp. 121–181). San Diego, CA: Elsevier Academic Press.

Shepard, E. M. III (2001). The economic costs of D.A.R.E. Institute of Industrial Relations Research Paper Number 22. Retrieved May 1, 2010, from http://www .reconsider.org/issues/education/economic_costs_of_d.htm

Sherman, D. K., & Cohen, G. L. (2006). The psychology of self-defense: Self-affirmation theory. In M. P. Zanna (Ed.), *Advances in Experimental Social Psychology* (Vol. 38, pp. 183–242). San Diego, CA: Elsevier Academic Press.

Social Security Act, Section 510 (42 U.S.C. 710). Retrieved July 3, 2008, from http:// www.ssa.gov/OP_Home/ssact/title05/0510.htm#fn019

Sontag, S. (2008). *Reborn: Journals and notebooks 1947–1963.* New York: Farrar, Straus & Giroux.

Spock, B. (2004). *Dr. Spock's baby and child care.* Updated and revised by Robert Needlman, M.D. New York: Pocket Books.

Spoth, R. L., Randall, G. K., Trudeau, L., Shin, C., & Redmond, C. (2008). Substance use outcomes 5½ years past baseline for partnership-based, family-school preventive interventions. *Drug and Alcohol Dependence, 96,* 57–68.

Steele, C. M. (1988). The psychology of self-affirmation: Sustaining the integrity of the self. In L. Berkowitz (Ed.), *Advances in experimental social psychology* (Vol. 21, pp. 261–302). San Diego, CA: Academic Press.

Steele, C. M. (2010). *Whistling Vivaldi: and other clues to how stereotypes affect us.* New York: W. W. Norton.

Stein, R. (2010, March 27). Abstinence programs gain federal reprieve. *Washington Post,* p. A2.

Stein, R., & St. George, D. (2009, March 19). Teenage birth rate increases for second consecutive year. *Washington Post*, pp. A1, A4.

Stephan, C. W., Renfro, L., & Stephan, W. G. (2004). The evaluation of multicultural education programs: Techniques and a meta-analysis. In W. G. Stephan & W. P. Vogt (Eds.), *Education programs for improving intergroup relations* (pp. 227–242). New York: Teachers College Press.

Stephan, W. G. (1978). School desegregation: An evaluation of predictions made in *Brown v. Board of Education*. *Psychological Bulletin, 85*, 217–238.

Stevens-Simon, C., Dolgan, J. I., Kelly, L., & Singer, D. (1997). The effect of monetary incentives and peer support groups on repeat adolescent pregnancies. *Journal of the American Medical Association, 277*, 977–982.

Stevenson, B., & Wolfers, J. (2008). Happiness inequality in the United States. *Journal of Legal Studies, 37*, 533–579.

Stewart, T. L., LaDuke, J. R., Bracht, C., Sweet, B. A. M., & Gamarel, K. E. (2003). Do the "eyes" have it? A program evaluation of Jane Elliott's "Blue-Eyes/Brown Eyes" diversity training exercise. *Journal of Applied Social Psychology, 33*, 1898–1921.

Straus, M. A., & Stewart, J. H. (1999). Corporal punishment by American parents: National data on prevalence, chronicity, severity, and duration, in relation to child and family characteristics. *Clinical Child and Family Psychology Review, 2*, 55–70.

Sussman, S., Dent, C., & Stacy, A. (2002). Project Towards No Drug Abuse: A review of the findings and future directions. *American Journal of Health Behavior, 26*, 354–364.

Taylor, S., & Sherman, D. (2008). Self-enhancement and self-affirmation: The consequences of positive self-thoughts for motivation and health. In J. Y. Shah & W. L. Gardner (Eds.), *Handbook of motivation science* (pp. 57–70). New York: Guilford.

Teen "pregnancy pact" has 17 girls expecting (2008, June 20). MSNBC News Services. Retrieved July 1, 2008, from http://www.msnbc.msn.com/id/25272678/

Teen Pregnancy (2008). Centers for Disease Control and Prevention. Retrieved July 3, 2008, from http://www.cdc.gov/reproductivehealth/AdolescentReproHealth/

Terry-Humen, E., Manlove, J., & Moore, K. A. (2005). Playing catch-up: How children born to teen mothers fare. National Campaign to Prevent Teen Pregnancy. Retrieved July 2, 2008, from http://www.teenpregnancy.org/works/pdf/PlayingCatchUp.pdf

Theatre at Work. Retrieved July 5, 2005, from http://www.theatreatwork.com

Tierney, J. P., Grossman, J. B., & Resch, N. L. (1995). *Making a difference: An impact study of Big Brothers Big Sisters*. Philadelphia, PA: Public/Private Ventures.

Trenholm, C., Devaney, B., Fortson, K., Clark, M., Quay, L., & Wheeler, J. (2008). Impacts of abstinence education on teen sexual activity, risk of pregnancy, and risk of sexually transmitted diseases. *Journal of Policy Analysis and Management, 27*, 255–276.

Tugan, B. (2002, May 5). Team's job eases heavy hearts. *The Tampa Tribune*, Florida/Metro section p. 1.

Turner, M. A., Ross, S. L., Galster, G. C., & Yinger, J. (2002). Discrimination in metropolitan housing markets: National results from phase I HDS 2000. Washington, D.C.: The Urban Institute Metropolitan Housing and Communities Policy Center. Retrieved May 20, 2009, from http://www.huduser.org/Publications/pdf/Phase1_Report.pdf

Turrisi, R., Larimer, M., Mallett, K., Kilmer, J., Ray, A., Mastroleo, N., Geisner, I., Grossbard, J., Tollison, S., Lostlutter, T., & Montoya, H. (2009). A randomized clinical trial evaluating a combined alcohol intervention for high-risk college students. *Journal of Studies on Alcohol and Drugs, 70*, 555–567.

U.S. Department of Education, National Center for Education Statistics (2010). The condition of education 2010 (NCES 2010-028). Retrieved December 7, 2010, from http://nces.ed.gov/fastfacts/display.asp?id=16

U.S. Department of Health and Human Services, U.S. Advisory Board on Child Abuse and Neglect (1991). Creating caring communities: Blueprint for an effective federal policy on child abuse and neglect (Rep. No. 9-1991). Washington, D.C.: U.S. Government Printing Office.

U.S. Department of Health and Human Services, Administration for Children and Families, Office of Planning, Research, and Evaluation (2010, January). Head Start impact study: Final report. Retrieved May 5, 2010, from http://www.acf.hhs.gov/programs/opre/hs/impact_study/

U.S. Department of Justice, Office of Juvenile Justice and Delinquency Prevention. Statistical briefing book. Retrieved June 25, 2009, from http://ojjdp.ncjrs.gov/ojstatbb/crime/JAR_Display.asp?ID=qa05200

U.S. General Accounting Office (2003). Youth illicit drug use prevention: DARE long-term evaluations and federal efforts to identify effective programs (Report GAO-03-172R). Washington, D.C.: U.S. Government Printing Office.

Valente, T., Ritt-Olson, A., Stacy, A., Unger, J., Okamoto, J., & Sussman, S. (2007). Peer acceleration: Effects of a social network tailored substance abuse prevention program among high-risk adolescents. *Addiction, 102*, 1804–1815.

van den Boom, D. (1994). The influence of temperament and mothering on attachment and exploration: An experimental manipulation of sensitive responsiveness among lower-class mothers with irritable infants. *Child Development, 65*, 1457–1477.

Vaughan, P., & Rogers, E. (2000). A staged model of communication effects: Evidence from an entertainment-education radio soap opera in Tanzania. *Journal of Health Communication, 5*, 203–227.

Von Bergen, C. W., Soper, B., & Foster, T. (2002). Unintended negative effects of diversity management. *Public Personnel Management, 31*, 239–251.

Vonnegut, K. (1975). *Mother night*. New York: Dell.

Vorauer, J. D. (2001). The other side of the story: Transparency estimation in social interactions. In G. Moskowitz (Ed.), *Cognitive social psychology: The Princeton Symposium on the Legacy and Future of Social Cognition* (pp. 261–276). Mahwah, NJ: Erlbaum.

Walton, G. M., & Cohen, G. L. (2003). Stereotype lift. *Journal of Experimental Social Psychology, 39*, 456–467.

Walton, G. M., & Cohen, G. L. (2011). A brief social-belonging intervention improves academic and health outcomes of minority students. *Science, 331,* 1447–1451.

Watkin, T. (2007, April 8). Self-help's slimy "Secret." *Washington Post,* p. B1. Retrieved November 6, 2009, from http://www.washingtonpost.com/wp-dyn/content/article/2007/04/06/AR2007040601819.html

Wechsler, H., & Nelson, T. (2008). What we have learned from the Harvard School of Public Health College Alcohol Study: Focusing attention on college student alcohol consumption and the environmental conditions that promote it. *Journal of Studies on Alcohol and Drugs, 69,* 481–490.

Wegner, D. M. (1994). Ironic processes of mental control. *Psychological Review, 101,* 34–52.

Wegner, D. M. (2002). *The illusion of conscious will.* Cambridge, MA: MIT Press.

Wegner, D. M., Wenzlaff, R., Kerker, R. M., & Beattie, A. E. (1981). Incrimination through innuendo: Can media questions become public answers? *Journal of Personality and Social Psychology, 40,* 822–832.

Weiner, M. J., & Wright, F. E. (1973). Effects of undergoing arbitrary discrimination upon subsequent attitudes toward a minority group. *Journal of Applied Social Psychology, 3,* 94–102.

Weis, R., & Toolis, E. E. (2007). Military style residential treatment for disruptive adolescents: A critical review and look to the future. In T. C. Rhodes (Ed.), *Focus on adolescent behavior research* (pp. 75–118). New York: Nova Science.

Welsh, P. (2008, December 14). They're having babies. Are we helping? *Washington Post,* p. B1, B4.

West, S. L., & O'Neal, K. K. (2004). Project D.A.R.E. outcome effectiveness revisited. *American Journal of Public Health, 94,* 1027–1029.

What grown-ups understand about child development: A national benchmark study (2000). Washington, D.C.: Zero to Three, National Center for Infants, Toddlers, and Families. Retrieved Jan. 21, 2010, from http://www.eric.ed.gov/ERICDocs/data/ericdocs2sql/content_storage_01/0000019b/80/16/c6/5c.pdf

Wiggins, S., Whyte, P., Higgins, M., Adam, S., Theilmann, J., Bloch, M., Sheps, S. B., Schechter, M. T., & Hayden, M. R. (1992). The psychological consequences of predictive testing for Huntington's disease. *New England Journal of Medicine, 327,* 1401–1405.

Williams, P. (2001). *How to be like Mike: Life lessons about basketball's best.* Deerfield Beach, FL: Health Communications.

Wills, T., Sargent, J., Stoolmiller, M., Gibbons, F., & Gerrard, M. (2008). Movie smoking exposure and smoking onset: A longitudinal study of mediation processes in a representative sample of U.S. adolescents. *Psychology of Addictive Behaviors, 22,* 269–277.

Wilson, T. D. (2002). *Strangers to ourselves: Discovering the adaptive unconscious.* Cambridge, MA: Harvard University Press.

Wilson, T. D., Centerbar, D. B., Kermer, D. A., & Gilbert, D. T. (2005). The pleasures of uncertainty: Prolonging positive moods in ways people do not anticipate. *Journal of Personality and Social Psychology, 88,* 5–21.

Wilson, T. D., Damiani, M., & Shelton, N. (2002). Improving the academic performance of college students with brief attributional interventions. In J. Aronson (Ed.), *Improving academic achievement: Impact of psychological factors on education* (pp. 88–108). San Diego, CA: Academic Press.

Wilson, T. D., & Gilbert, D. T. (2008). Explaining away: A model of affective adaptation. *Perspectives on Psychological Science, 3*, 370–386.

Wilson, T. D., & Lassiter, G. D. (1982). Increasing intrinsic interest with superfluous extrinsic constraints. *Journal of Personality and Social Psychology, 42*, 811–819.

Wilson, T. D., & Linville, P. W. (1982). Improving the academic performance of college freshmen: Attribution therapy revisited. *Journal of Personality and Social Psychology, 42*, 367–376.

Winerip, M. (1998, January 4). Binge nights: The emergency on campus. *The New York Times*, Section 4A, p. 29. Retrieved August 5, 2009, from http://www .nytimes.com/1998/01/04/education/binge-nights-the-emergency-on-campus. html

Women's Health Initiative Steering Committee (2004). Effects of conjugated equine estrogen in postmenopausal women with hysterectomy: The Women's Health Initiative randomized controlled trial. *Journal of the American Medical Association, 291*, 1701–1712.

Wood, I. (2008, November 24). From fifth to first: The fourth year 5K must expand to meets its vital goal. *The Cavalier Daily*. Retrieved August 5, 2009, from http:// www.cavalierdaily.com/news/2008/nov/24/from-fifth-to-first/

Wood, J. V., Perunovic, E., & Lee, J. W. (2009). Positive self-statements: Power for some, peril for others. *Psychological Science, 20*, 860–866.

Wood, W., Rhodes, N., & Whelan, M. (1989). Sex differences in positive well-being: A consideration of emotional style and marital status. *Psychological Bulletin, 106*, 249–264.

Woodworth, K. R., David, J. L., Guha, R., Wang, H., & Lopez-Torkos, A. (2008). San Francisco Bay Area KIPP schools: A study of early implementation and achievement (final report). Menlo Park, CA: SRI International.

Yeung, N., & von Hippel, C. (2008). Stereotype threat increases the likelihood that female drivers in a simulator run over jaywalkers. *Accident Analysis and Prevention, 40*, 667–674.

Yoffe, E. (2009, November 18). Artful Prague: Post-communist relics. Slate.com. Retrieved November 19, 2009, from http://www.slate.com/id/2235642/entry/ 2235780/

Youth Online: Comprehensive Results. National Center for Chronic Disease Prevention and Health Promotion, Centers for Disease Control and Prevention. Retrieved June 29, 2009, from http://apps.nccd.cdc.gov/yrbss/CategoryQuestions. asp?Cat=4&desc=Sexual percent20Behaviors

Zagumny, M. J., & Thompson, M. K. (1997). Does D.A.R.E. work? An evaluation in rural Tennessee. *Journal of Alcohol and Drug Education, 42*, 32–41.

Index

Index

prejudice, 20, 21, 25, 181–202, 206, 239
  against African Americans, 181–183, 204, 205, 206
  diversity-training programs to reduce, 186–192
  effects of contact on reducing, 193–195
  exercise to raise awareness about racism and, 183–187, 189–192
  experiments on interracial friendship, 195–200
  against Hispanics/Latinos, 182–183, 191, 199–200, 204–206
  housing bias, 183–184
  use of media for reducing, 200–201
  See also achievement gap
pre-post design, in research, 29–31
President's Initiative on Race, 188
President's Leadership Group Award, 158
Prevent Child Abuse America (PCA America), 106–107
Princeton Review, 155
Proctor, Bob, 46
Project Towards No Drug Abuse (Project TND), 163–165
Promise Academies, 218
Promoting Alternative Thinking Strategies (PATHS), 146–147
psychotherapy, 10, 13, 57, 104, 141, 147–150, 245n7. *See also* cognitive-behavioral therapy (CBT)
Purdie-Vaughns, Valerie, 227, 232
purpose, 50, 51, 52, 69–71, 72, 73–74, 80–85, 110, 111
Purvis, Kenneth, 182

Quantum Opportunities Program (QOP), 129–131
Quinteros, Cynthis, 115, 131

racism, 182, 185, 186, 191, 204, 205, 207, 210, 223, 224. *See also* prejudice
Rahway State Prison (New Jersey), 136–137, 138, 140
Ramey, Craig, 215
random assignment to condition, 30–32, 34–35, 36, 37
rationalization, 228
Raven's Advanced Progressive Matrices test (Raven's APM), 219–225
Reach for Health Community Youth Service (RFH), 128–129, 131, 149–150
Reality Bites (movie), 179

religion, 52, 53, 56, 57, 74
research. *See* scientific studies
Resolving Conflict Creatively Program, 237
Restoring Inner City Peace (R.I.P.) program, 135–136, 152–153
rewarding children, 91–97, 211–212
RHF program. *See* Reach for Health Community Youth Service (RFH)
Robbins, Tony, 41
Robert Wood Johnson Foundation, 161
Rosenthal, Robert, 207–208
Rudolph, Maya, 45
Runton, Nancy, 114–115
Russell Sage College (New York State), 117
Rwanda, 200–201
Ryder, Winona, 179

Salerno, Steve, 42
Saturday Night Live, 45–46, 50, 67
scared straight programs, 136–138, 143, 235
Scared Straight! 20 Years Later (TV documentary), 137
Schuppel, Tommy, 3, 4, 5
scientific studies, 23–38
  on conducting, 19–21, 236–239, 241
  diversity-training programs and, 24, 29–36
  on hormone replacement therapy, 32–33
  pre-post design in, 29–31
  self-help industry and, 42–45, 47
  small-scale, 35–36
  statistics and, 32–33
  story-editing and, 36–37, 38
  theory-driven psychological research, 238–239
  See also correlation does not equal causation problem in research; random assignment to condition
Secret, The (Byrne), 41, 42–44, 45–47, 66, 68–69, 235
self-affirmation theory, 228–230
self-defeating/self-enhancing cycle of thinking, 14–17, 19, 37, 177, 225, 226, 230
self-efficacy, 146
self-esteem, 15, 68, 146, 228, 229
self-help industry, 41–47, 66, 68–69, 77, 235, 239
self-image, 228
self-narratives, 17, 91, 234
  See also narratives

About the Author

TIMOTHY D. WILSON is the Sherrell J. Aston Professor of Psychology at the University of Virginia, where he has received the All University Outstanding Teaching Award and the Distinguished Scientist Award. He is the author of *Strangers to Ourselves*, which was named by the *New York Times Magazine* as conveying one of the most influential ideas of 2002, and is the coauthor of the bestselling social psychology textbook *Social Psychology*, now in its seventh edition. Wilson has also published articles in *Science* and the *New York Times*, among other publications and journals. His research has been funded by the National Science Foundation, the National Institute of Mental Health, and the Russell Sage Foundation, and in 2009, he was elected to the American Academy of Arts and Sciences. He lives in Charlottesville, Virginia.